D1121606

Geopolitics Reframed

New Visions in Security

Series Editor: Richard Ned Lebow

Geopolitics Reframed

Security and Identity in
Europe's Eastern Enlargement

Merje Kuus

GEOPOLITICS REFRAMED

First published in 2007 by
PALGRAVE MACMILLAN™
175 Fifth Avenue, New York, N.Y. 10010 and
Houndmills, Basingstoke, Hampshire, England RG21 6XS.
Companies and representatives throughout the world.

PALGRAVE MACMILLAN is the global academic imprint of the Palgrave
Macmillan division of St. Martin's Press, LLC and of Palgrave Macmillan Ltd.
Macmillan® is a registered trademark in the United States, United Kingdom and
other countries. Palgrave is a registered trademark in the European Union and
other countries.

ISBN-13: 978-1-4039-7029-9
ISBN-10: 1-4039-7029-7

Library of Congress Cataloging-in-Publication Data is available from the
Library of Congress.

A catalogue record of the book is available from the British Library.

Design by Scribe Inc.

First edition: August 2007

10 9 8 7 6 5 4 3 2 1

Printed in the United States of America.

To my parents

Contents

List of Figures

Preface

This book is rooted in my fascination with the political force and substantive ambiguity of security claims in Europe. As I followed political debates in my home country of Estonia throughout the 1990s, I noticed that the ubiquitous references to security and geopolitics were simultaneously conspicuous and vague. They were contained within a circular narrative in which security was explained by citing identity and geopolitics; identity was defined in terms of security and geopolitics; and geopolitics was conjured up as a matter of identity and security. Despite the ever-present evocation of security threats, it remained unclear what specifically was being threatened, by whom, and from where, and how European Union (EU) and North Atlantic Treaty Organisation (NATO) accessions were supposed to protect Estonians from these threats. Estonian politics had become a monomania in which all politics was reduced to security issues and all security issues were reduced to membership in the EU and NATO. This monomania did not invoke an external threat as the ultimate motive for foreign and security policy, but rather culture and identity.

A similarly malleable and cryptic discourse that confuses security, identity, and geography was and is operational across Central Europe—an entity defined here as the new member states of the EU and NATO. There is hardly a political statement about or a scholarly analysis of these states that gets by without references to security and identity. Throughout the region, EU and NATO accessions were promoted not only for economic reasons but equally and sometimes primarily as security measures. Statements about security—"our security concerns"—both start and end arguments about issues ranging from foreign and defense policy to citizenship, immigration, and education. Intimations of direct foreign threats were gradually removed from official political rhetoric over the 1990s, but references to "sensitive geopolitical locations," "gray zones," "historical legacies," or "unpredictable neighbors" remained central to public debate. Central Europe was incorporated into the world's most powerful military alliance in the name of securing it, yet most commentators across Europe agreed that the region was under no military threat.

This book argues that such bundling of security and identity is a central dynamic in Europe's eastern enlargement and in the external relations of the EU. I treat enlargement as a multilayered sociopolitical process that expands the EU's and NATO's normative space—that is, the area in which the rules of these two institutions have constitutive effects on political processes. Defined in this way, Europe's eastern enlargement started considerably before 2004 and continues today, even if it does not result in the addition of any new member states. Enlargement is a geopolitical practice, but not in the sense of expressing natural borders and geographic realities. It is geopolitical in the sense of infusing political practice with assertions and assumptions about the location of borders and the essence of places. It places and demarcates security and insecurity, Europe and non-Europe, Us and Them. Vaclav Havel's reflections on the meaning of "the West" illuminate this dynamic. The West, Havel says, is first "a geographically delimited territory that can be described as the Euro-Atlantic or Euro-American region." It is also, he continues, an entity defined to an "equal if not greater" degree by its values, culture, and a "common set of spiritual sources." Yet Havel then returns to a geographical definition. "While many other countries now also profess these values," he posits, "they belong to other geographical areas and therefore—if only for this purely external reason—cannot be considered part of the West."[1] Havel tellingly invokes the West as both a nongeographical and also an irreducibly geographical unit. His thoughts may seem inconsistent at first but they are richly illustrative of the ways in which political debate is presently entangled with geographical claims and assumptions. This line of reasoning shifts security from the political to the cultural realm and encases debates about identity within the framework of existential threats. Issues of security and geopolitics are thereby reframed in cultural terms. They become simultaneously geographical, cultural, and strategic concepts, and they diffuse into ever more spheres of political life.

Yet this trend is not the traditional geopolitics of territorial aggrandizement. Geopolitical language serves to cast security as a matter of identity, culture, and values. What are to be secured are not just state interests but also national and European identities. The enlargements of the EU and NATO are often rhetorically folded into one as "the eastern enlargement of Europe" because both processes are conceived as matters of security and identity. Security claims are politically effective precisely because they combine "soft," "subjective" issues like culture and identity with "hard," "objective" categories like threat into a seemingly natural geographical framework. Just as the source and character of the threat is opaque, however, so is the geographic demarcation of the identity to be secured by Europe's eastern enlargement. The trope of Europe, as in "European identity" or "European values," is omnipresent, yet the borders of Europe are notoriously vague—"most crucial, but blurred," as Jan Zielonka puts it.[2] Central Europe, the very region that was to be stabilized by the double enlargement, is a prime example of this blurriness. Whereas Central Europe in the early 1990s usually denoted the three Visegrad states of Poland, Hungary, and Czechoslovakia,[3] the common usage of the term expanded over the course of the decade to include all former satellite states of the Soviet Union. As of 2007, Central Europe connotes the East-Central European states that acceded into either the EU or NATO in 2004. In a context in which political groups, whole countries, and even groups of countries vie for the most pro-European credentials, and in which security is defined in terms of Europe, such a shift in the borders of Europe is consequential. We cannot understand the enlargement of the EU and NATO without unraveling the geographical imaginaries that anchor these processes.

Such a plastic definition and demarcation of security and identity highlight the agency of the intellectuals of statecraft—government officials, academics, journalists, and pundits—who do the defining and the demarcating. The 1990s were an enchanted era for these people. As my professional life took me back and forth across the Atlantic Ocean and the Baltic Sea, I witnessed the agency of these individuals from the peculiar position of a not-quite-Westerner and a not-quite-Central European—or more precisely Eastern European, as Estonians were usually then regarded. Central Europe was still new to Western experts because it was not yet what Westerners considered the "normal boring" West. The Western experts who were shuttling between Western and Central European capitals needed local interpreters—literally and figuratively—to help them navigate the "rediscovered" postsocialist world. Their new colleagues showed them around, told them about the strange realities of socialist and postsocialist life, and stressed their countries' desire to return to the West. The Westerners were eager to teach, the locals were eager to please, and the beer was cheap. It gradually became clear to me that the conventional way of thinking about security and geopolitics—a model in which Central Europeans learn from the West— was inadequate and misleading. It neglected the strategic use of particular Western concepts by Central European intellectuals of statecraft. The geopolitical claims that passed as authentic Central European views were often skillfully crafted intellectual products made specifically for export to Western audiences. Geopolitics was being conducted through the mutual citation and lending of legitimacy between Western and Central

European intellectuals of statecraft. Their interaction, or their "collision and collusion," as Janine Wedel calls it, was not a footnote but rather a central part of the making of geopolitics in Europe.[4]

This book takes the simultaneous malleability and political force of security claims as a starting point. It investigates the ways in which security and identity are bound up with geographical definition. It uses the latest round of EU and NATO enlargement in 2004 to examine the constitution of security threats through demarcating "our" space and "theirs," and conversely, the definition of identity through evoking existential threats to "our" space from "theirs." My objects of analysis are not threats or identities as directly observable phenomena. Rather, I take representations of threats as my objects of analysis and examine how they work. Instead of asking about the source of threats and their gravity, I ask about the production of insecurity. My concern is not with the essence of geopolitics but with the practice of its implementation. I treat security and identity as discourses in which the threatened Self and the threatening Other come into being through statements made and policies conducted in their name. It is only through these discourses, I argue, that identities and threats are defined as such. To study these discourses then is not to explore perceptions of or ideas about security—a kind of icing on the cake. It is to examine how security and identity are constituted.

By investigating how security discourses work, the book denaturalizes the geographical imaginaries that anchor security debates in Central Europe—formulations like "geopolitical location," "historical insecurity," or "civilizational clash." The work disperses the air of inevitability that surrounds popular and academic accounts of security and geopolitics, and opens up venues for analysis and debate less encumbered by the weight of unexamined geographical assumptions. In particular, the book accentuates and unravels the geographical imaginaries that are all too often used without much reflection. Although my analysis concentrates empirically on the round of EU and NATO enlargement in 2004, I highlight dynamics and tendencies that go far beyond Central Europe of the 1990s. Debates about New and Old Europe, the EU's and NATO's future enlargements, transatlantic relations, and the "war on terror" all involve security as their central concern. As EU and NATO further expand their influence in areas cast as "not yet" or "not fully" European, the fusion of security and identity will continue to underpin European geopolitics. Understanding the multiple scales and strategies by which the categories of security and insecurity, order and disorder, Self and Other are located and demarcated therefore remains an urgent task.

Acknowledgments

This book is the product of eight years of research carried out in three countries on both sides of the Atlantic. Its intellectual project traverses the fields of geography and international relations. The book would not have materialized without the generous help of many individuals from both disciplines who have graciously commented on individual chapters as well as on the various papers that preceded the book manuscript, and who have lent their support throughout my career. Within the discipline of geography, I would like to thank especially Robert Kaiser, Simon Dalby, and John Agnew for their invaluable support. Klaus Dodds, Jennifer Hyndman, Sallie Marston, and James Sidaway likewise offered perceptive feedback at various stages of the project. At the Department of Geography, the University of British Columbia, I have benefited from an open and supportive intellectual climate. A particular note of gratitude goes to Geraldine Pratt for her generous engagement with my work. I am also indebted to Trevor Barnes, Derek Gregory, Daniel Hiebert, David Ley, and Graeme Wynn for their feedback and collegiality. Within the discipline of international relations, special thanks go to Pertti Joenniemi for his intellectual curiosity and professionalism. I am also grateful to Stefano Guzzini, Edward Rhodes, Iver Neumann, and Alison Bayles for comments and encouragement. Research for the book in Estonia would not have been possible without Raivo Vetik, Mati Heidmets, Alexander Astrov, and Erik Terk, all of whom kindly extended their contacts, experience, and expertise. Although the book does not draw on my doctoral work, it would not have been realized without John Mercer and Donald Mitchell, whose early support was crucial. Gregory Feldman commented on the earlier versions of all chapters and read the whole manuscript with great care. Thank you! I am glad that we have managed to analyze each other's work and stay married too! My greatest debt, however, is to my parents, Leida and Aksel Kuus. The book is dedicated to them.

In addition to numerous conferences and workshops, the book has benefited from feedback from interdisciplinary audiences. Earlier versions of chapter 6 were presented at the Center for Russia, East Europe, and Central Asia (CREECA) at the University of Wisconsin–Madison, as well as the Swedish Institute of International Affairs (SIIA) in Stockholm. An early draft of chapter 2 was presented at the Department of Geography of the University of Toronto. Furthermore, parts of the argument that later evolved into chapter 2 were published as "Europe's Eastern Enlargement and the Re-Inscription of Otherness in East-Central Europe" in *Progress in Human Geography* 18 (2004): 472–89. These sections are used here with permission from Sage Publications. Similarly, chapter 6 developed out of an argument that appeared as "'Those Goody-Goody Estonians': Toward Rethinking Security in the European Union Applicant States," *Environment and Planning D: Society and Space* 22 (2004): 191–207. This material is used with permission from Pion Limited. An earlier and more limited version of the argument in chapter 5 appeared as "Intellectuals and Geopolitics: The 'Cultural Politicians' of Central Europe," *Geoforum* 37 (2007): 241–51; it is used with permission from Elsevier Limited. Research for the book was funded in part by grants from the United States Institute of Peace (USIP), the John D. and Catherine T. MacArthur Foundation, and the Social Sciences and Humanities Research Council of Canada. The book benefits greatly from the skillful research assistance of Christopher Drake, Bjoern Surborg, and William Magruder. All findings are mine and do not necessarily reflect the views of the above-named individuals or funding institutions.

I

The Plasticity of Geopolitics

Notions of national security, most notoriously, have invoked realities and necessities that everyone is supposed to acknowledge, but also vague generalities about everything and nothing. Much of the rhetorical force and political legitimation expressed through modern discourses of security rests ultimately on this simultaneous appeal to the hard and the vacuous, the precise and the imprecise, the exaction of blood and sacrifice in the name of the grand generalization.

Robert B. J. Walker, 1997[1]

"Love, Peace, and NATO"

From November 20 to November 22, 2002, 46 heads of state, 2,800 delegates, and 3,000 accredited journalists converged on Prague for the summit meeting of the North Atlantic Treaty Organisation (NATO).[2] The alliance invited seven new members: Estonia, Latvia, Lithuania, Slovakia, Romania, Bulgaria, and Slovenia. It was a spectacular affair, involving not only the official summit meeting but also a range of supporting events organized by nongovernmental organizations (NGOs) and private companies. Mingling with defense specialists were Central European leaders of civil society; former dissidents like Adam Michnik were drinking beer with prominent pro-NATO lobbyists.[3] The tight security, provided by 16,500 Czech policemen and military personnel, 250 U. S. Marines, and sophisticated technology like 15 U. S. Air Force jets for the total cost of 620 million koruny (approximately $20 million U.S.), did not dampen the festive spirit.[4] "Love, Peace and NATO" is the title that Timothy Garton Ash chose for his eyewitness account of the summit.

"NATO has become a European peace movement," Garton Ash writes, "Imagine, that Europe is a place where wars don't start. As John Lennon sang: 'Imagine.'"[5]

Peace was indeed a key theme of the meeting. The celebratory speeches made little mention of military defense but revolved instead around the issues of common European identity and values. Vaclav Havel, the president of the host country, referred to the meeting as a kind of peace conference that finally ended World War II.[6] Bruce Jackson, the director of the US Committee on NATO, a pro-expansion lobby group, said: "The year 1989 represented a moral revolution, not a political one, and this we must bear in mind. Today, all countries in the east cling to Europe more than ever: Democracy has a unique opportunity to control them from the North to the whole circumference of the Black Sea."[7] The president of Latvia, Vaira Vike-Freiberga, emphasized that NATO would bring its new members "the full sunshine of the liberties and rights that NATO has been defending so long." The summit, she said, had been a "sign of hope" for any nation "that has expressed the desire to join those nations that hold the same values."[8] The atmosphere was exultant and emotional. The Estonian ambassador to NATO, Sulev Kannike, had tears in his eyes when Lord George Robertson officially issued the membership invitation.[9] Reactions across Central Europe celebrated invitations to membership as the ultimate recognition and codification of the Western identity of the Central European states. *Lietuvos Aidas*, a Lithuanian daily, called the invitation a "transition from one world to another." *Lietuvos Rytas*, that country's main daily, proclaimed that "The clock of history in Lithuania has started showing real Western civilization time."[10]

The side events were likewise saturated with the imagery of European identity and values. For example, 180 university students from 35 countries were gathered at an army base 40 kilometers from the Czech capital for the Prague Atlantic Student Summit (PASS), which was a simulation exercise "conceived to help students understand the value of the NATO alliance and its future challenges." The delegates represented the member and the accession states as well as such states as Macedonia, Georgia, and Azerbaijan, which were hoping for invitations in the future. The delegates discussed topics like enlargement, terrorism, biological and nuclear weapons, and the possibility of war in Iraq. "We think that it is important that a new generation gets acquainted with the means and procedures of international life," said Antonio Borges de Carvalho, the secretary general of the Atlantic Treaty Association (ATA), an NGO that had organized the event. "It is even more important now when people are on the street protesting against our values and our way of life." "I believe it is a great experience for every student here," echoed Lazar Elenovski, a senior member of the Macedonian delegation at a reception in the Radio Free Europe building. "They will learn about the ideology of NATO; they will learn about democratic values and about human rights and freedom. They will learn that we will be one in this alliance."[11]

The performing arts and a general showcasing of culture were central to the summit's symbolic apparatus. President Havel invited outstanding Czech artists to contribute to the program. As a prologue to the formal concluding dinner in the Prague Castle on November 21, the dignitaries were entertained to an avant-garde ballet titled "Birth-Day," in which dancers in eighteenth-century costumes performed an allegorical ballet of life and love. Prerecorded scenes projected on to a large screen included one in which male and female dancers in foppish underwear mimed the act of love on an enormous double bed.[12] For the dinner itself, which was attended by 700 guests, Havel had commissioned a musical medley of John Lennon's "Power to the People," Bedrich Smetana's *My Country*, Beethoven's *Ode to Joy*, the American spiritual "Oh, Freedom," and "La Marseillaise." The *International Herald Tribune* commented, "If anybody had forgotten, NATO had the music—the theatrical power—for its message."[13] Outside the castle, a giant neon red heart was installed to blink above the castle, ostensibly to commemorate the thirteenth anniversary of the 1989 revolution.[14] Garton Ash exuberantly linked the celebratory atmosphere to anti-Soviet resistance during the Cold War. "I could see exactly what this meant to Havel—the spirit of '68, Czech style, memories of the 'velvet underground' in the long years of oppression . . ."[15]

The Comeback of Geopolitics

The Prague summit was the culminating spectacle of a process that shifted security and geopolitics away from the spheres of politics and the military toward the realm of culture. By 2002, a tendency to speak of security in cultural terms by invoking cultural identity and "European values" rather than state interests and power politics had become hegemonic in Europe. This narrative underpins both EU and NATO enlargements, which are often linked together as the eastern enlargement of Europe.

The two enlargements seem to have little to do with geopolitics, understood traditionally as the "geographic factors that lie behind political decisions."[16] On the contrary, the cultural narrative appears as a liberation from interstate geopolitics of territory and resources. Europe is no longer about the crude geopolitics of material interests; it is about cultural identities and universal values. In the accession states, membership in the EU and NATO was promoted through positive terms like "European identity" and "shared civilizational values" rather than through negative categories like "foreign threat." In the words of the Polish foreign minister, Adam Rotfeld, "The impact of geography, space or borders on political processes has been eminently reduced." None of the EU documents, Rotfeld stresses, delineates the borders of the new expanding Europe. The dimensions of that Europe are determined not by geography, but rather by "common history, tradition, culture and [a] set of values supported by economic, political and military integration."[17]

And yet the enlargements of the EU and NATO are profoundly geopolitical processes. Making Europe "whole and free," as the double enlargement is often described, invokes and inscribes the borders of Europe and Europeanness, of the West and Western values. As the EU exercises constitutive influence on social processes far beyond its borders, it is increasingly treated as a coherent geopolitical entity. Even as the union is declared to be a community of values rather than a geographical unit, there is an intense concern with its borders and its sphere of influence.[18] Spatial concepts like "neo-medieval spatialities" and "new regionalism," as well as the more familiar binaries of inside/outside, center/periphery, and core/margin, pervade the debate about power relations within the EU and between the EU and its exterior. For example, debates on the European Neighbourhood Policy (ENP) pivot on questions about the cultural frontiers of Europe.[19] European security continues to be articulated in terms of boundaries and dividing lines.[20] Thomas Diez observes that geographical and cultural othering is on the increase, marking the return of geopolitics in European identity construction.[21] There is indeed an intensified concern with whether the new enlarged Europe demands a new geopolitics.[22] Europe functions as both a geographical and a cultural entity. It is said to transcend geography, yet it is also defined in terms of geography. In the words of Vaclav Havel:

> Europe has always been and remains one indivisible political entity, diverse, intricately structured. This is not just a result of geography, a concentration of many more or less related peoples. Thousands of years of common history, lived in different multinational empires, molded Europe into a single spiritual area interconnected by so many political links that severing any one risks disintegration.[23]

Such use of geographical claims in political rhetoric is part and parcel of the remarkable resurgence of geopolitics as an analytical and popular concern. After decades of being shunned for its association with social Darwinism and Nazi ideology, geopolitics has become newly fashionable since the end of the Cold War. The end of the bipolar superpower rivalry, which had been the containing territorial structure of political thought for over forty years, fueled interest in and anxiety about the spatial organization of power. Renewed fascination with geopolitics is one effect of that anxiety and vertigo. In academic research, there is a renewed interest in the spatial configuration of global power beyond states, as testified by the burgeoning work on empires, cores, and world regions. There is also renewed interest in geopolitical thinkers like Halford Mackinder and Rudolf Kjellen.[24] In writing directed to policy practitioners and the general public, such explicitly geopolitical treatises on resources or identity as Robert Kaplan's The *Coming Anarchy* or Samuel Huntington's *The Clash of Civilizations and the Remaking of the World Order* have become bestsellers [25] To speak of geopolitics is no longer backward; it is an accepted and even celebrated part of political analysis.

Geographical knowledge plays a complicated role in this renaissance of geopolitics. Much of the mainstream writing on security and geopolitics treats geography as "natural not historical, passive not dynamic," as a stable and solid ground of politics.[26] In the influential formulation written by Nicholas Spykman seventy years ago, "geography does not speak, it just is." Geography, Spykman continues, is "the most fundamental conditioning factor in the formulation of national policy because it is the most permanent. Ministers come and go, even dictators die, but mountain ranges stand unperturbed."[27] Although the tradition of classical geopolitics from which Spykman speaks has been discredited by its connection to the Nazi regime, the everyday use of the term geopolitics still treats geography as a stable given. To speak of geopolitics is still to speak of geographical realities. Security debates, for example, are based on assumptions about "natural" borders, whether physical or cultural ones. The rhetorical power of security claims stems in significant part from their link to supposedly natural geographical realities. While the classical geopolitics of the first half of the twentieth century is castigated as a pseudoscience—"the domain of the puppets of expansionary power"— geography is by the same stroke of the pen naturalized as a "good honest science."[28] Geopolitics is rendered political, but geography is by the same stroke defined as natural.

This comeback of geopolitics is clearly visible in the countries of Central Europe. Throughout the region, the use of geographical and geopolitical arguments to explain political decisions is ubiquitous. Central Europe is the region that concerned writers like Friedrich Ratzel or Halford Mackinder. Classical geopolitical theory might have read quite differently without the particular context of Central Europe.[29] In the post-Cold War era, Central Europe likewise functions as the test case for various geopolitical scenarios, particularly of power relations within Europe and between East and West. Visions of Central Europe often read like a textbook of classical geopolitics, replete with references to buffer zones, shatterbelts, and balance of power, as well as to historical animosities and essential identities.[30] Across Central Europe, the struggle over one's place on geopolitical maps, specifically over who will be accepted as part of the West and under what circumstances, is central to daily politics. Public debates rely heavily on geographical and geopolitical claims about the geopolitical location of the region as a whole and each country within it near the border of Europe.[31] In the words of Adam Michnik, "The issue is not whether one is left or right of center, but West of center."[32] Security claims are central to this struggle. Although mainstream political rhetoric does not necessarily identify a direct foreign threat, it commonly evokes a more diffuse cultural insecurity that results from Central Europe's location in a "geotectonically active" region. "Security problems" are everywhere, from interstate relations to such issues of civil society as minority rights and immigration, and these problems are often traced to "geopolitical factors." When all else fails, there is always "geopolitical location." Academic debates tend to echo political rhetoric and pundits' commentaries. While realist assumptions are increasingly criticized in Western international relations (IR) theory, realism is highly influential in Central Europe. Authors like Samuel Huntington are controversial within the Western academy but are often hailed as cutting-edge thinkers in Central Europe.[33] Although several other common clichés about East-Central Europe, most notably "transition," have received sophisticated critiques since the mid-1990s, most discussions of security in Central Europe still assume that the region is geopolitically insecure.[34] Central Europe's geopolitical insecurity today functions as a truism. We are left with a highly predictable narrative of "historical legacies," "existential insecurities," and the necessity of urgent action for which there is no alternative. This narrative presents generic reiterations of "security threats" or "geopolitical memory" with little explication of how these terms function in political practice. This narrative gives an appearance of a causal chain or logic in which each event inevitably leads to a predetermined conclusion. Events seem to unfold naturally.[35] The narrative thus naturalizes the foreign policy of Central European states as the only possible option in the face of geopolitical uncertainty. Precisely when the end of the Cold War seemed to give a final blow to traditional geopolitics, Central Europe appears to exemplify its return—from Marx to Mackinder, as Stefano Guzzini fittingly puts it.[36]

Critical Geopolitics

As a counterpoint to such uncritical use of geopolitical language in large parts of popular and academic analyses of Central Europe, this book investigates geopolitics as a contested political process. It borrows from a substantial body of work that scrutinizes rather than merely asserts geopolitical claims. This approach, which is often labeled critical geopolitics, starts from the assumption that geographical knowledge is not innocent and objective. It treats geography as a technology of power that does not simply describe but also produces political space.[37] Geographical claims are necessarily geopolitical, because they inscribe places as particular types of places to be dealt with in a particular manner. Conversely, all politics is also geopolitics, because it necessarily involves geographical assumptions about territories and borders. These assumptions are not abstract images floating above political interests but rather form an integral part of the ways in which interests and identities come into being. Every global consideration of human affairs involves geographical imaginaries whether acknowledged or not.[38] Considerations of security, for example, necessarily involve bounding the threat as well as the threatened object, and defining them as particular kinds of places. Security issues draw on and construct what Hugh Gusterson calls "securityscapes"—the distributions of military force and the military-scientific resources among and within nation-states as well as the imaginaries of identity, power, and vulnerability that accompany them.[39] They locate inside and outside, center and margin, core and periphery. Even claims about "escaping" geography and geopolitics are geopolitical insofar as they assume a particular geographical configuration of power that is to be eluded.

Geopolitical writing, then, is not a neutral consideration of "geographical" facts but a deeply ideological form of analysis. It is "a discursive practice by which intellectuals of statecraft 'spatialize' international politics and represent it as a 'world' characterized by particular types of places, peoples and dramas."[40] Its theoretical and practical significance lies in its productive capacity—namely, the ways in which geopolitical analysis naturalizes and normalizes particular political claims and practices as "geographical" and hence given. Ironically, such analysis does not engage geographic complexities; it rather disengages from these complexities in favor of simplistic demarcations of inside and outside, Us and

Them. Critical geopolitics takes as its task the disruption of geopolitical discourses: to study not the geography of politics within pre-given or commonsense places, but rather to foreground "the politics of the geographical specification of politics."[41] It intersects with constructivist and poststructuralist strands in IR theory, but it also retains a distinct focus on the geographical assumptions that anchor international politics.

Close attention to these assumptions is especially urgent in Central Europe because the geographical specification of politics has received less attention in that region than in Western Europe and North America. During the Cold War, East European studies was a deeply ideological field, closely linked to Western governmental agendas and insulated from theoretical debates in the social sciences.[42]Although there were exceptions to this rule, much of the research on Central Europe represented "mere footnotes to Sovietology."[43] In international relations, as Richard Ned Lebow and Thomas Risse-Kappen pointed out, research on East-Central Europe was plagued by "widely shared and deeply ingrained" theoretical and methodological assumptions about the primacy of theory-building over empirical context. This unwillingness to treat empirical situations in the Eastern bloc as worthy objects of analysis, they argued, played a pivotal part in the failure of IR theory not only to anticipate the end of the Cold War but also to even "recognize that possibility that such changes could take place."[44] As I will argue in chapter 2, such neglect of developments on the ground has persisted. Central Europe continues to be subjected to sweeping generalizations about "markets," "democracy," or "Europeanization." The region also continues to be a troublesome place for these generalizations. It is not on a linear trajectory of catching up with the West, as the optimists had originally presumed. On the other hand, neither has it descended into a vicious circle of Communist resurgence and violent nationalisms, as the pessimists had implied. It has stumped Sovietologists, transitologists, and EU bureaucrats alike, as all have seen their most elaborate theoretical frameworks undermined by inconvenient developments on the ground.

Neither has Central Europe received much attention in critical geopolitics. Although this field of scholarship stresses geographical diversity and contextual messiness on the theoretical level, it tends to focus only on power centers on the empirical level. By neglecting the role of specific actors in the daily operation of geopolitical discourses, it tends to reinforce a one-way conception of power from the center to the margin. Yet hegemonic geopolitical discourses are influential in part because they are produced in *both* the power centers and the power margins. We must therefore examine their production on such margins of power as the countries of Central Europe. As Andrew Sayer reminds us, where relations between things are contingent, their form must always be an empirical question to be examined through empirical cases.[45] To pay close attention to local complexities is not to endorse the empiricist belief that facts speak for themselves, neither is it to posit some authentic Central European position or to single out specific Central European traits. It is rather to provide balance to the current focus on Western discourses; to recognize that the production of geopolitics happens in specific places and can be adequately studied only in the context of these places.[46] It is to link the most localized details with the most global structures in order to bring them into simultaneous view.[47]

Discursive analyses of geopolitics and security, such as this one, involve four interlinked methodological nuances, which often remain implicit yet are crucial for understanding the operation and impact of such analyses. The first of these concerns truth. The primary concern of discursive analyses is not to reveal deep hidden meanings of political practice—what individual decision-makers "truly" think or what beliefs are shared among the population. Their concern is rather with the persistent assumptions, themes, and tropes that both enable and constrain political debate and political practice. These assumptions often remain unnoticed, not because they are hidden but because they are taken for granted. They lie "so artlessly before our eyes that they are almost impossible to see."[48] In and of themselves, discourses are neither true nor false. Their significance lies in producing certain claims as meaningful and true. They constitute particular political claims as natural and normal and thereby remove them from political debate. Security discourses then represent neither an objective reality nor a subjective fear. They are practices in which the meaning of security is constructed through statements made in its name. To study these practices is not to unearth secret Machiavellian maneuvers but rather to expose and examine the parameters of public debate.[49] Such study does not imply that security is an intangible matter of the mind but rather that it cannot be discussed outside the practices used to define security threats as such. Analyzing the construction of Russia as a security threat then says nothing about whether the Russian threat is real or unreal. It shows that the Russian threat functions as real and has tangible political effects on public debate and policy-making.

The second methodological nuance pertains to speech and language. The core concern of discursive analyses is not the specific content of what is said or written about geopolitics. The concern of such analyses is rather with the structures and rules that make particular political practices legible and legitimate while making other practices illogical, unfeasible, or illegitimate. Put differently, discursive analyses do not focus on speech but on practice. They expose the conditions of possibility for particular political practices. Discourses are discernible not in terms of their core substance but in terms of their effects. They are not a property of the speaker but of the particular political arena. Politicians do not put forth discourses but operate within discourses. I therefore do not attempt a comprehensive review of geopolitical claims in Central Europe (namely, what is said about geopolitics) or to unearth the roots of these claims; I rather elucidate the geographical and territorial assumptions that enable these claims.[50]

The third nuance relates to causality. Discourses do not "cause" particular policy responses. Rather, they frame political debate in such a way as to make certain policies appear reasonable and feasible while marginalizing other policy options as unreasonable and unfeasible. Put differently, discourses define geopolitical problems as such, and they develop the conditions in which possible responses can be given.[51] Discourses are ultimately open-ended processes. The relationship between their enabling capacity and the specific effects is contingent on a particular social context.[52] To study discourses is not to trace causes in the sense of predicting specific events but rather to lay bare the conditions of possibility for the phenomenon in question[53]. It is to illuminate the societal context in which particular decisions emerge logically.

The fourth methodological nuance concerns disagreement. Discourses do not enforce complete agreement or a unified methodology. They operate through fractured, flexible, and contingent practices that nonetheless form a certain regulation. They channel disagreement into a framework within which the act of disagreement obscures the actors' shared allegiance to categories that contain their disagreements.[54] To speak of security discourses, then, is not to deny debate but to foreground the arguments and modes of analysis that encase the debate.[55] Security discourses are not contained within state institutions or projected from these institutions. They are produced in many spheres of the civil society, including the fields of education, entertainment, and the media.[56] Their power lies in their dispersed and routine ordinariness.[57] A study of security discourses thus involves examining not just government practices but the wider sphere of public debate.

Security/Identity

Identity and culture have been keywords in the study of geopolitics and international relations since the end of the Cold War. It is now widely accepted that insecurity is culturally produced because it is intertwined with the cultural concepts of community and identity. Nevertheless, the precise relationship between identity and security is a matter of considerable theoretical debate.[58] Numerous scholars have pointed out that the invocation of identity in political analysis has not necessarily been accompanied by a corresponding move away from categorical, essentialist, and unitary understandings of that concept.[59] Identity still tends to be treated simply as that which is not material, as an ideational variable to be stirred into structural analyses. The premise underlying this approach is that identity influences the "interplay of deep-rooted cultural and fast-changing material factors in deciding how national interests—and so international behavior—are determined."[60] This premise channels analysis toward identifying the most relevant features of state or national identity as a causal factor in state action. Each state, according to this line of reasoning, protects its putative internal identity against external threats. By rendering social practices intelligible as variables, this approach reifies a complex and contested process into an object or a substance.[61] It converts differences, discontinuities, and conflicts within the state into an absolute difference between a domain of domestic society and a domain of external anarchy. It does not adequately consider the ongoing struggles over what constitutes group identity and who constitutes the group or the subject of that identity. Ironically, cultural identity emerged as a key concern in security studies precisely when other disciplines in the social sciences became increasingly wary of using the term culture, at least as a noun.[62]

The treatment of culture and identity as causal variables is much in evidence in Central Europe. At least since Milan Kundera's evocative definition of Central Europe as a place that is not a location but "a culture or a fate," identity and geopolitics have been tightly linked in the region.[63] National identity is widely regarded as the key underlying dynamic of post-Communist transformations. "At the most fundamental level," says Claus Offe, "a decision must be made as to who 'we' are, that is, a decision of identity, citizenship, and the territorial as well as social and cultural boundaries of the nation state."[64] Although the literature on identity and security in Central Europe is not monolithic, it tends to presume that there are core identities, albeit historically constructed, which one must unearth to understand the actors' actions. Only after we understand their identities, the argument goes, can we understand the foreign and security policies of Central European states.[65] The many studies of identity and security thus enumerate such various features of identity as nationalism, multiculturalism, or Europeanness, and assess their impact on perceptions of security. They do not, however, examine how this identity is produced within and through discourses of security. Identity emerges as a chaotic catchall to explain virtually everything as well as a reified and ultimately static thing.

Yet, as this book shows, security threats are not simply external to the community to which they allegedly pose a threat. They are also necessary components of maintaining and consolidating that community's identity. Identity resides in the nexus between the Self and the Other. In William Connolly's succinct formulation, "Identity requires difference in order to be, and it converts difference into otherness in order to secure its own self-certainty."[66] Although difference is not necessarily converted into otherness, security discourses display a strong tendency to escalate and reify differences into otherness and threat. These discourses depend upon rigid separation between those peoples "inside," who pursue "universal" values, and those "outside," who allegedly practice different values. As Simon Dalby puts it, "The essential moment of geopolitical discourse is the division of space into 'our' place and 'their' place."[67] Even if threats are domestic, among "ourselves," they are still conceived as foreign in origin, and it is their outside quality that makes them suspect or dangerous. Foreign and security policies then emerge as boundary-producing practices that constitute the moral Self in the form of the state and assign evil to various outside Others.[68] They illuminate not only what is identified as foreign and threatening on the outside but also what is constituted as normal inside the state. Danger from the "outside" is thus not a threat to but a precondition for national identity within the state's borders. Insecurity can thereby become the principal mechanism of legitimation for the state.[69] An analysis of insecurity must thus start from denaturalizing the identity that is being secured. In Central Europe, then, the question is not how Polish or Estonian identity affects the foreign and security policies of these states; the question rather is how categories like Polish or Estonian identity are constructed through such practices as foreign and security policies that name and locate threats to these putative identities.

Oracles of Security

Security and geopolitics function in a dualistic manner. On the one hand, diplomacy and foreign policy are commonly conceived as highbrow issues shrouded in secrecy. These are matters for experts, set apart from the hurly-burly of domestic politics, too important and too specialized for the layperson. An aura of dignity sets off the statesman from the politician.[70] The power to define security threats is highly structured: only a limited number of individuals in specific positions in the state structure have the legitimacy to do this.[71] These individuals—the security intellectuals—claim superior knowledge of the international sphere as well as access to classified material to implement and legitimize foreign and security policy. Their authority rests on their command of the specialized language of international relations and military technology. Their epistemology is deeply positivist and their vocabulary is influenced heavily by economics and the natural sciences, especially physics. The international system is full of "forces," "pressures," and "vacuums"; alliances are "bargains"; and military attacks have "payoff matrices." This analytical toolbox frames security in terms of natural laws and geographical certainties. It limits the discussion of security to those inside the security establishment and regards critical voices as incompetent as well as irrational.[72] Hugh Gusterson traces the security intellectuals' spectacular failure to foresee the collapse of the Soviet Union in part to just such intellectual arrogance and limited analytical repertoire.[73]

On the other hand, and in parallel with this reliance on specialized language, discourses of security and geopolitics draw heavily on commonsense narratives about places and identities.[74] Even though policy-making relies on the expert knowledge of security intellectuals, the categories of Us and Them, community and identity, are formed on the popular level. Most geopolitical reasoning is not formal but practical. It draws on common sense rather than esoteric academic and technical arguments. Writers like Samuel Huntington or Robert Kaplan are influential precisely because of their skillful use of popular assumptions about places like the tropics, the Balkans, the Orient, or the West. High-ranking politicians use sports analogies and themes from popular culture to make their points, and the popular media play an important role in explaining geopolitics and international affairs to the electorate. Issues of security and geopolitics excite popular fascination and play on popular beliefs, while the authority to speak on them is limited to relatively small, elite circles. This duality is a necessary part of security discourses. To be effective, these discourses need both sides. They need the claims of science and statecraft as well as the seemingly unproblematic references to geography.

The dual legitimation of security claims is a central feature of Central European politics. On the one hand, as geopolitics and security are understood as matters of life and death, there is a perceived need for concerted professional action by committed experts. As EU and NATO accessions are framed as security measures, they are shifted into a realm above political debate. Furthermore, in the highly securitized climate of political debate, in which almost anything can be a matter of security, debate is suppressed and the clout of "experts" is very high. Yet on the other hand, as EU and NATO memberships are viewed as preconditions for becoming internationally recognized Western subjects, support for accession is also defined as an integral part of citizenship. Put differently, these memberships are framed as matters on which every responsible citizen should have an opinion. As security is bundled together with identity, both are supposed to be self-evident to everyone and felt by everyone on a personal level. Security and geopolitics thus function not just as highbrow scholarly topics but also as matters of folk knowledge. Furthermore, as I will explain in chapter 5, membership in the cadre of security intellectuals has been in greater flux in Central Europe than in the West. In the Baltic states as well as in Slovenia, this group was built up only in the 1990s, after these states (re)established their sovereignty. Membership in it was determined not only by formal education but also by one's access to and ability to emulate the vocabulary of Western security studies. At the same time, because of institutional flux, many Central European security experts entered the field from other walks of life, including the arts and the humanities, and they command these other vocabularies as well. Partly as a result of these idiosyncracies, geopolitics in Central Europe is represented as both self-evident and mysterious, a topic for everyman as well as experts.[75] Voters are encouraged to both have an opinion about geopolitics and leave the actual decisions to professionals.

To capture the dualistic character of geopolitical discourses, Gearoid O'Tuathail and John Agnew have coined the term intellectuals of statecraft to refer to politicians, intellectuals, and pundits who regularly comment on, participate in, and influence the activities of statecraft.[76] This phrase is a broader term than security intellectuals, as it includes celebrity journalists and various public intellectuals whose influence is based on their mastery of everyday language rather than on technical aspects of military strategy. Intellectuals of statecraft can combine "scientific" claims and references to scholarly works with seemingly self-evident observations. They create the conditions in which other segments of the population use geopolitical reasoning.[77] Their practices are not homogenous, nor are they necessarily accepted by the population at large. They do, however, establish the parameters of expertise and debate. They are the gatekeepers of the lofty realm of security and geopolitics. To concentrate on intellectuals of statecraft is not to assign superior or authentic knowledge to them or to deny contestation and debate within and beyond their circles. Rather, it is to analyze the intellectual machinery that legitimizes political power: the practices that qualify a person as an informed expert and a legitimate participant in public political debate.[78] It is also to offer a more "peopled" account of geopolitics. It is to clarify the agency of specific actors and the role of specific cultural resources in the operation of security discourses.

Central European intellectuals of statecraft are a peculiar breed. As noted above, the circle of individuals that can legitimately comment on security extends far beyond government, academia, and think tanks. It includes intellectuals with humanistic and artistic backgrounds who would not command the air of geopolitical expertise in the more specialized circles of experts in large Western countries. Especially in the early 1990s, Central Europe's political elites included many prominent intellectuals who had been trained in the humanities. Literary abilities, imaginative use of language, profound knowledge of their respective countries' high culture, and in many cases advanced academic degrees were key components of these "cultural politicians'" popular appeal.[79] To this day, the cultural elites of Central Europe are considered experts on security, and security is constructed not so much through the technical vocabulary of strategy as through poetic reflections about identity, homeland, history, and traditions. It is often their legitimacy in speaking about identity and values that lends Central European intellectuals of statecraft the authority to speak on security.

Furthermore, in the heady days of the 1990s—that golden era when the East was still exciting and many Western transitologists still had little direct experience in dealing with the erstwhile enemy—Central European intellectuals of statecraft were pivotal in carving out a place for Central Europe on Western mental maps. More so than their Western counterparts, they translated their countries to the outside world and vice versa. Statements that function as authentic views from Central Europe are often carefully crafted and marketed products tailor-made for Western consumption. Conversely, claims and narratives, like that of "civilizational clash," which are presented as state-of-the-art Western theories in Central Europe, enjoy favorable publicity in part because they are promoted by local intellectuals of statecraft. The received wisdom, according to which EU and NATO enlargement involves Central European intellectuals of statecraft who are simply learning and internalizing Western norms, is therefore misleading. A closer examination, which I offer in chapter 6, reveals that these intellectuals have an important role in the making of geopolitics. This book highlights that role. It sheds light on the extensive consultation between Western and Central European elites. It thereby illuminates the daily production of geopolitics—not how it is supposed to happen but how it actually takes place.

Where Is Central Europe?

I use the term Central Europe as shorthand for the countries that acceded into the EU or NATO or both in 2004. To group together these ten countries—Estonia, Latvia, Lithuania, Poland, the Czech Republic, Slovakia, Hungary, Bulgaria, Romania, and Slovenia—is not to imply an essential similarity among them or to attempt a comprehensive account of geopolitical discourses in all of them. It is rather to recognize that the discursive bundle of geopolitics and culture in these countries bears two family resemblances.

The first of these family resemblances is that these ten countries are framed as Central European in the discourse of Europe's eastern enlargement. They are a part of the Europe that is enlarging; they are also a part of Eastern Europe that is joining Western Europe. The geographical content of Central Europe is highly malleable and politically consequential. In the early 1990s, Central Europe generally denoted the three Visegrad states of Poland, Hungary, and Czechoslovakia; however, over the course of the decade, common usage of the term gradually expanded to include all former satellite states of the Soviet Union.[80] This enlargement of Central Europe happened in significant measure through the efforts of the accession countries to rebrand themselves as fundamentally Western and to thereby shift the negative connotations of "Eastern Europe" further eastward. The erstwhile Eastern Europe—the swath of land east of the former Iron Curtain—was thereby split into Eastern and Central Europe. In the early 2000s, few would characterize the member states of the EU and NATO as Eastern European; that term is now reserved for Russia, Ukraine, and Belarus. Central Europe is thus best thought of not as a place or a region but rather as a political and intellectual project. It is a successful venture of "making place out of space," of ascribing Europeanness to places and thereby changing these places' locations on Western mental maps.[81] To this day Central Europe connotes a place that lies geographically within Europe but culturally and politically is still learning to be fully European. Central Europe remains a waiting room between Eastern Europe and Europe proper. To examine Central Europe then is to examine the places that are relegated to a liminal position midway between Europe and the East.[82]

The second family resemblance among Central European states concerns the high political profile of security in these states. The notion that Central Europe is uniquely insecure due to its marginal position in Europe is a pillar of national identity construction throughout the region. Central Europe, says Milan Kundera, knows existential threats intimately because the very existence of its nations has been put into question throughout history.[83] Such proclamations were the mantras of debates about EU and NATO accession; they are extraordinarily consistent across Central Europe. Whereas the specific geopolitical claims vary within the region, these claims are filtered through the widely shared territorial imaginaries of Europe and threat.

My focus then is not on the specific features of security debates in every Central European country, but on the processes by which security and identity are bound up with geographical definition; on the dynamics of geopolitical discourses in the context of the double enlargement. I examine these dynamics in particular places, but my argument is not about these places *per se*. I in fact consciously seek to avoid yet another commonsensical story of "how quickly [country X] can return to Europe." I follow Caroline Humphrey's reminder that "It's not much good describing two different situations and then totting up, 'There is X here, but not there; there's Y here, but not there,' and so on." We should investigate broadly while we are in the process of trying to understand any one situation. "Comparison should inform description, not the other way around."[84] The task is not to link specific instances to other specific instances, which would divert attention from the broader discursive field in which these instances exist. The task rather is to link particular instances to broader dynamics, a sheep raid to a revolution, as Clifford Geertz put it in another context.[85] It is not to generalize across cases but to generalize within them. Although Central European countries are quite different on the level of concrete events, insofar as my analysis illuminates the *context* of political practices, that analysis is applicable across and indeed beyond these countries.[86] In other words, even though examples from Poland or Estonia are not replicated elsewhere, they can nonetheless illuminate developments elsewhere. Context is not a background—an exploration of how the context is structured and how different actors fit into it is central for explanation.[87]

To bring the broader dynamics to eye level, chapters 3 through 6 include close-up looks at one country—Estonia. That country illuminates the nexus of security and identity because it is widely regarded as both a test case and a success story of the post-Cold War transformations of these categories. Estonia is commonly treated as a Huntingtonian border state by both Western and local intellectuals of statecraft. Huntington himself uses the Baltic states as an important illustration of his argument.[88] In many instances, it is because of this presumed borderline location that Estonia enters the orbit of Western politicians and researchers. Yet along with its image as a tiny country in a precarious geopolitical location, Estonia is at the same time regarded as one of the most successful postsocialist countries in terms of proving its European and Western credentials. For most of the 1990s, Estonia was the darling of the West. Although minority rights and tense relations with Russia did concern the West, Estonia successfully cultivated the image of "the little country that could."[89] Its neoliberal economic reforms endeared Estonia to the Western transitology establishment. It was the first of the former Soviet republics to be invited to accession negotiations with the EU. The *Economist* has described Estonia as "goody-goody," a "feisty midget" with a "shiny reputation."[90] Estonia's favorable image is all the more significant when we consider that the depth of postsocialist transformations in terms of building up the institutions of a sovereign state was greater there than in the states traditionally considered Central European.

Because of its darling image, Estonia offers especially telling examples of the agency of local intellectuals of statecraft in the making of geopolitics. For that image did not emerge miraculously out of the damp Baltic air—it came about in the context of Western intellectuals of statecraft learning about this "new" country and their Estonian counterparts explaining it to them. The image was cultivated by specific individuals in specific locations: not only in the foreign ministries of the West but also in the charming restaurants of Tallinn's medieval Old Town. As I started my research in security and geopolitics in the 1990s, I had the good fortune to glimpse the process at work. It was fascinating to be "from" Estonia in the West—"from" in quotation marks because my primary professional affiliation has been at various North American universities since 1992. The West needed token representatives from a token country. There was still a faint surprise that Estonia was not a fiction but a real place. Many Westerners still did not expect expertise beyond local anecdotes from an exotic former Soviet republic. They were still eager to teach. But I could also reap the benefits of Estonia's "hip" image. Many Westerners had encountered token Estonians before and had felt comfortable with them. Estonians dressed and conversed in Western ways. Estonian women had dropped the "atrocious pink lipstick" that had been a sure marker of postsocialist Eastern Europe, and Estonian men had adopted Western styles of eyewear. From the "other" side—Estonian, that is—I observed the mill of conferences and workshops and book chapters that provided Estonian intellectuals of statecraft with extra income, opportunities for foreign travel, and prestige. Being a token Estonian was a lucrative business. There was already a cadre of people who had learned the vocabulary, had extensive Western experience, and knew the code words of security studies. As I listened to Westerners explaining Estonia to me—explanations that they had learned in many cases from their Estonian counterparts over a glass of beer—I could not help noticing the creative agency of Estonian intellectuals of statecraft. Although the Westerners were certainly learning to "read" the locals, their Estonian colleagues—whose stakes were higher and power positions weaker—were often learning faster. Looking back from the mid-2000s, one can now tell the story of this mutual learning of geopolitics, as primary accounts of these hectic years become available in academic research, political memoirs, and interviews in the media. That story, however, is not an account of what Estonians (or other Central Europeans) "really" think or used to think, and it is certainly not a story of monolithic Western or Estonian approaches. It is a more complex story of the mutual citation and lending of legitimacy between Western and Estonian intellectuals of statecraft.

The dynamics involved in Estonia's quest for membership in the EU and NATO therefore bring into focus much larger questions about the operation of security discourses within and beyond the EU and NATO. My close-up accounts of Estonia then do not attempt a representative snapshot of all accession countries.[91] They rather give rich empirical content to the trends identified on the regional level. They move beyond generic accounts of "identity" and "interest" and the equally generic discussions of "discourses" as such and help to illuminate the messiness and contingency of geopolitics.

***

The rest of the book offers a close reading of the key facets and mechanisms of the bundling of geopolitics and culture. The following three chapters dissect three central tropes that bundle: "Europe," "civilization," and "national sovereignty." Chapter 2 examines the binary of Europe and the East. It highlights the pivotal position of that binary in Central European security discourses and shows how it has been transformed from a clear dichotomy to an East-West slope of Europeanness and Eastness. Chapter 3 dissects the civilizational narrative that frames Central Europe as a part of the West juxtaposed against and threatened by a fundamentally different Orthodox civilization. The chapter foregrounds the ways in which such cultural framing of security makes threats more diffuse and more flexibly defined. Chapter 4 examines the mutual constitution of national security and state sovereignty. It highlights the manner in which security discourses are informed by an imaginary in which each state protects its own culturally and territorially defined nation. That imaginary, I argue, fuels the securitization of national sovereignty and serves to depict any foreign influence, including that of the West, as a security threat. The subsequent two chapters focus on the role of Central European intellectuals of statecraft in the production of security. Chapter 5 examines the uses made by these intellectuals of their cultural and moral capital, especially the kind derived from their artistic and humanistic background, to produce a particular "cultural" conception of security. The chapter shows that their authority to speak about culture is an important condition of possibility for the cultural conception of security in Central Europe. Chapter 6 investigates the "ritual of listening to foreigners"[92]—the practice whereby Central European elites deftly flatter their Western counterparts while discreetly guiding these Westerners' interpretations of Central Europe. By highlighting this practice, the chapter illuminates the role of Central Europeans in the production of geopolitical arguments about Central Europe. The seventh and concluding chapter uses the insights explained in the previous sections to return to theoretical concerns about the territorial specification of politics. It emphasizes that the cultural reframing of geopolitics will play a constitutive role in the future rounds of enlargement as well as EU's and NATO's relations with their exterior. The full significance of the Prague spectacle that opened this chapter, then, lies less in the specific events that took place than in the normalization of a particular cultural conception of security.

2

Inscribing Europeanness, Erasing Eastness

With the disintegration of the Soviet Union and the decline in US domination, Europe has [been] . . . cut loose for resignification. With no immanent invader, no New World, no occupiers against whom it can take shape, the "mirror of man" has been turned back on itself. It can and it must now define itself. Among the most alluring alterity with which it flirts is that ancient phantasm, the Orient . . .

John Borneman and Nick Fowler, 1997[1]

The concept of Europe is central to post-Cold War geopolitics in Europe. The double enlargement of the European Union and NATO was intended to erase at last the long-standing division of Europe between West and East and reunite the continent as a cultural whole. In the new member states, *Europe* is a rhetorical pillar of foreign and security policy. The "we" in whose name these policies are conducted is not just the nation; it is also Europe. These are not just state interests but also the nation's European identity that are to be secured.[2] Despite the rhetorical emphasis on unity, however, the concept of Europe functions to maintain and reproduce the division between East and West. Although the Cold War demarcations of Europe and Eastern Europe are fading, insecurity emanating from the East still pervades security discourses in Central Europe. The figure of "Eastern Europe" as the East of Europe is still an integral part of the Europe that EU and NATO enlargements have supposedly secured. The important question then is not whether or when Europe will be "whole and free," or the precise location of the border between Europe and the East. The question rather is how claims and assumptions about Europe and the East function in political debates and policy-making.[3] We cannot understand security discourses in Central Europe without dissecting the metageography of Europe and the East.

The present chapter probes this metageography by examining the new demarcation of Europeanness and Eastness in the process of Europe's eastern enlargement. I maintain that Europe is bound up with a narrative in which Eastern Europe in its various demarcations is both insecure because of external pressures and also a source of insecurity to Europe as a whole. At the same time, the East-West binary has been reconfigured into a more flexible constellation, an East-West slope of Eastness and Europeanness respectively. The enlargement processes have undermined the Cold War-era division of Europe into two parts while simultaneously fuelling a tripartite division of the continent into the European core; Central Europe, which is not yet fully European but in tune with the European project; and the eastern peripheries of Europe, effectively excluded from membership.[4] This division is not simply imposed by the West; it is also used by Central Europeans themselves to stress Central Europe's insecurity and to shift it to Europe proper by inscribing Eastness further east. The double enlargement is not undermining but working in tandem with the notion of a multitiered Europe in which Europeanness declines as one moves east.

Still "Not Properly Brought Up": The Problem of the East

The East has been Europe's constitutive Other since the inception of the European idea. The concept of Eastern Europe as a variant of the East was invented in the eighteenth century, when Eastern Europe was demarcated as being a part of Europe by geography but still in process of becoming fully European in the political and cultural sense. The region's difference from Western Europe became conceptualized as distance from an idealized Europe. Eastern Europe was included in the geographical entity called Europe but simultaneously excluded from it as a political or cultural entity.It is crucial to remember, however, that Eastern Europe did not emerge as an irredeemably alien outsider, and this makes it different from the Orient.[5] Eastern Europe rather became a repository of negative connotations within Europe. Conceptually, it became a halfway house between Europe and Asia—not simply backward, but a learner, an experiment, and a testing ground, "a gigantic specimen to which the most advanced legal and administrative ideas could be applied with a completeness impossible in western Europe."[6]

This figure of Eastern Europe has undergone a number of transformations since its inception, but its premise of otherness has persisted. The

Cold War was particularly important in maintaining and reifying the concept. During the Cold War geopolitical discourse, the Soviet Union, and by extension its satellite states, were not simply antagonistic or backward; they were also partly Asiatic. Konrad Adenauer's famous 1946 dictum that "Asia stands on the Elbe," and George Kennan's 1947 references to "the Russian or oriental mind" may serve as examples.[7] The totalitarianism of the Soviet Union was linked in part to traditional Oriental despotism, which in turn was considered an essential attribute of the Russian mentality.[8]

East European studies as a field was instrumental in maintaining the concept of Eastern Europe. Similarly to other strands of area studies, the discipline tended to exoticize and reify differences as an essential core identity.[9] As the British and French colonial empires collapsed in the decades following World War II, the field experienced a considerable flow of professionals from colonial administration to the conduct of the Cold War.[10] The Cold War became the containing structure within which area specialists learned to constitute East-Central Europe as an object of study.[11] Philip Roeder remarks that "The years prior to 1989 were the glory days for area specialists. The Cold War gave our special knowledge unique value: we knew the enemy and it was 'ours.'"[12] Though there were significant exceptions to this attitude, many Western experts worked on Eastern Europe either because of their virulent anticommunism or because of their leftist sympathies. Consequently, their interests did not lie as much in the region as in the task of showing the inferiority or the appeal of the socialist system.[13] All too often Central and Eastern Europe was treated as a uniform bloc, and little distinction was made between Russia, the Soviet republics, and the satellite states. This disengagement from geographic complexities was particularly pronounced in security studies. That field was especially tightly linked to the governmental-intelligence and military-industrial complexes. Its concern was not with East-Central Europe but with superpower rivalry. The post-Cold War critiques of Sovietology and international relations theory identify this disregard for social complexities in favor of simplistic "scientific" assumptions as the key reason behind these fields' failure to predict the end of the Cold War. In the words of John Lewis Gaddis, "One might as well have relied upon stargazers, readers of entrails, and other 'pre-scientific' methods for all the good [the] 'scientific' methods did."[14]

Transitology—the strand of Sovietology concerned with the transition of the postsocialist countries to democracy, Europe, and the free market—was central to the post-Cold War geopolitical scripting of Central Europe.[15] Transitology was conceptually indebted to modernization theory, which claims that progress and development follow a single course toward a market economy and democracy. Modernization theory had "always lurked not far below the surface of Sovietology as a repressed wish fulfillment," and its post-Cold War renaissance was entirely logical within the assumption of a not-yet-fully-European East-Central Europe.[16] As East-Central Europe became the object of the Western-led transition effort, the region was in a sense downgraded on the scale of Europeanness. Whereas the Soviet Union and its satellite states had been viewed as capable of industrial, scientific, and technological development, postsocialist East-Central Europe was construed primarily as a space under Western tutelage.[17] It remained an exotic place or, as Alain Finkielkraut put it, a place of "yelling and unpronounceable nations, each with its singular historical memory, its weird coat of arms and its brand new old flag." "Today," Finkielkraut continued, "we are still stumbling in the phonetical pitfall which unexpectedly replaced the unfortunate, homogenous and so convenient area we used to call Eastern Europe."[18] East-Central Europe both appeared on the doorstep of Europe and was kept conceptually separate from it. Like its predecessor field of Sovietology, transitology was at once geopolitical and antigeographic, because it was concerned with the universal course of development rather than local specificities. In transitology-speak, such buzzwords as transition, democratization, or civil society developed a set of meanings linked more to other rhetorical proclamations than to developments on the ground.[19] Institutionally, transitology was tied to many of the same political and intelligence organizations that had managed the Cold War. György Csepeli, Antal Örkény, and Kim Lane Scheppele have captured its institutional and epistemological continuities:

> Someone who studied weapons procurement might switch to studying ethnic conflict. Someone who used to work on mutually assured destruction could study privatization . . . The categories and concepts to be used in the brave new world of grant proposals were created not by experts, but instead by surprised Western journalists writing in the daily press. [20]

Once again, professionals relocated from managing the "non-West" to "helping" Eastern Europe. Within the Western aid community, East-Central Europe was where the action was, and aid agencies routinely diverted personnel from the so-called Third World to the Second World.[21] Janine Wedel observes that the East-Central Europe of the early 1990s had a kind of frontier ambiance, as Western consultants—dubbed the "Marriott Brigade" in Poland after their favorite hotel—flew in to give crash courses in economics and politics.[22] East Europeans themselves were assigned the role of furnishing empirical data, usually statistics and some anecdotal evidence. Their role was to bear witness to Westerners analyzing their situation.[23] In theory, Western aid experts recognized the distinctiveness of East-Central Europe, but their working assumptions were often the same ones they had used in the Third World. Their policy model was a mix of neoliberal policies "tried and found wanting in the West" and traditional developmentalism transplanted from the Third World.[24] The aid agreements drawn up by the United States for the Visegrad states, for example, were boilerplate documents originally developed for the Third World. These documents stipulated that U.S. aid officials were to be exempted from income taxes as well as duties on alcohol and tobacco, and given diplomatic immunity. The implications of these terms were not lost on the locals. A Hungarian law professor compared the waves of American constitutional lawyers to "missionaries trying to convert savages."[25] A Czech official remarked wryly, "We have flatly refused [the request for diplomatic immunity]. It is the product in our eyes of some bureaucrats who have difficulty distinguishing the Czech Republic from Shangri-La."[26] The situation was worst with respect to the former Soviet states, which had not even appeared on the Cold War political maps. An Estonian foreign minister, Toomas Hendrik Ilves, has said that prior to the EU's decision in 1997 to invite Estonia to membership talks, Estonia was treated as just another former Soviet republic, "sort of Tomska-Tomsk, Minsk-Pinsk, Tallinn-Stalin. It was all the same."[27]

Although the kind of antigeographic assumptions critiqued above were not entirely dominant even during the Cold War, they set the tone of inquiry. Against that background, the post-Cold War field of East European studies has experienced considerable internal debate as well as closer engagement with other subdisciplines in the social sciences.[28] The results have been revitalizing: the field now includes important critiques of transitology and its simplistic conceptions of democracy and privatization. At the same time, as leftist scholarship was discredited by its connection to Marxism, it was often the more conservative and epistemologically positivist scholarship that made the greatest impact in Central Europe. As the fortunes of traditional area studies declined, the impact of quantitative studies that involve little area knowledge indeed increased at times. The study of security has been particularly resistant to change because it has remained sheltered at the center of political rhetoric and funding priorities.

Of course, there has never been one monolithic "Western" approach. The influence of aid agencies, the International Monetary Fund (IMF), and the World Bank waned over the 1990s as the EU became the main source of advice. Although the EU model differs markedly from that of neoliberal shock therapy or transitology. However, it too assumes a less European Central Europe that still needs to pull itself up to European levels.[29] French President Jacques Chirac's remark that EU accession countries displayed a "not well brought up behavior" when their foreign policies differed from those of France is just one example of this assumption.[30] The moniker of postcommunism lingers on, over fifteen years since the fall of Communist regimes.[31] Central Europeans are still not in a position to argue as equals. As the Polish writer Adam Krzeminski noted in 2003, "In the dispute with the great minds of the West, the East-Central Europeans nowadays mostly arm themselves with sarcasm. . . . Or with irony . . . When they wish to argue on the basis of principles, they put on the toga of American neoconservatives and earn catcalls."[32] Andrzej Stasiuk, another Polish writer, has an ironic vision of Europe that offers a pithy example of just such sarcasm as Krzeminski has in mind:

> The plan for the coming decades looks more or less like this: the Sinti will arrive with their wagons and will set up camp in the middle of Champs-Elysees; Bulgarian bears will perform their tricks on Berlin's Kudamm; half-wild Ukrainians will encamp their misogynistic Cossack troops on the plain of Po before the gates of Milan; drunken Poles raps in prayer will ravage the vineyards of the Rhine and Mosel and will plant bushes that bear fruit of pure denatured alcohol and then move on; they will sing their litanies and will not stop until they reach the edge of the continent in the arch-Catholic Santiago de Compostela, famous for its miracles. It is difficult to say what the Romanians will do with their millions of sheep. They are people known especially for their sheep breeding, but also for their unpredictability. Serbs, Croatians, and Bosnians will cross the English Channel in Dalmatian dugout canoes and Balkanize Britain, which will finally be divided, as God commanded it, into Scotland, England and Wales.[33]

Return to Europe/Return of the East

Yet much has changed since the end of the Cold War. First and foremost, the concept of Europe has moved to center stage in scholarly and journalistic writing about central Europe. During the Cold War, the concept of Europe was peripheral to East European studies because East-Central Europe was not necessarily considered a part of Europe. Furthermore, debates about Europe were relatively subdued at the time. The parameters of inquiry and politics were given by the rivalry between the superpowers; consequently, the borders and meaning of Europe remained relatively marginal in political debate.[34] In the 1990s, however, as EU enlargement became conceptualized as "making Europe whole and free," the concept of Europe was opened up to debate. That concept indeed became central to political debate as complex societal changes were reconceived in terms of the essence of Europe and Europeanness. An analysis from the *Economist* in 2002 offers a glimpse into this geographical framework. Discussing various countries' pursuits of EU membership, *The Economist* argues that:

> . . . despite fitful attempts to progress, Bulgaria and Romania remain, like Ukraine, firmly in the East. By contrast, Slovenia looks little different from rich neighbour Austria, and is essentially western. The Baltics are tiny; besides, Estonia is practically Nordic in all but income. That leaves a Central Europe of Poland, the Czech Republic, Hungary and Slovakia, which now make up the first tranche of Europe's eastward enlargement.[35]

The foregoing examples make it clear that East-Central Europe was not incorporated into the imagined community of a united Europe. It was instead assigned a special place in Europe's waiting room .

Yet the framework of Europe and the East does not force uniformity; rather, it provides the parameters that contain the debate. Within it, there are two seemingly opposite types of accounts of East-Central Europe, one of linear transition to the West, and the other of older patterns of geopolitics. Neither version is particularly new. Anatol Lieven points out that Western journalists have been swinging between these two stereotypes of East European nations for about a century. The first stereotype is that of "gallant little freedom-loving peoples fighting against wicked empires for the sake of independence and liberal democracy." The second is "horrid little anti-semitic peasants, trying to involve us in their vicious tribal squabbles."[36] Lieven's characterization, dating from the early 1990s, is perhaps too harsh for the early 2000s, but it foregrounds some themes insidiously present even today. Both types of accounts conceive of Europe's eastern enlargement in terms of Central Europe either following Western Europe or failing to do so. In both arguments, what is European is good and whatever is good is European.[37] Both essentialize identity and security, and both pervade not only Western but also local accounts of East-Central Europe. I will next outline these two patterns of representation—here labeled as "Return to Europe" and "Return of the East" respectively—in order to specify the inscriptions of otherness/insecurity that underlie them.

Return to Europe

In the "transition" or "return to Europe" accounts, Central Europe is in a period of transition to the West while being coached by the West. These accounts treat accession to the EU and NATO as a result of and a reward for likeness to Europe. Milan Kundera articulates this position well in his dramatic and celebrated essay "The Tragedy of Central Europe." For Central Europeans, he says, "Europe does not represent a phenomenon of geography, but a spiritual notion synonymous with the west." "The moment Hungary is no longer European—that is, no longer western," Kundera continues, "it is driven from its own destiny, beyond its own history; it loses the essence of its identity."[38]

This narrative is most clearly discernible in accounts that accentuate dynamism and rapid change in Central Europe. Such accounts depict Central Europe as a place of great potential, albeit still helpless and insecure; they are at once both celebratory and patronizing. The opening section of the *Economist*'s survey of EU enlargement from 2001 serves as an example. The survey takes the reader to a muddy football field in Bulgaria, where hundreds of locals have gathered to witness the arrival of Günter Verhuegen, the EU's enlargement commissioner. After Verhuegen, "soft-spoken and cashmere-coated," descends from the helicopter, locals relay their grim story of economic decline, and plead with him that the EU "is the last hope for us."[39] Scholarly accounts are usually not as graphic but are not necessarily less patronizing. They commonly discuss political changes in East-Central Europe as a learning process in which the locals come into contact with Western norms and thereby learn to behave in a more European manner. Within this process, accession countries "are taught the community values and norms and must prove their willingness and ability to internalize them."[40] Only in the context of *black* scenarios is it mentioned that East-Central Europe may yet have to "devise its own fate."[41] The comparison between Eastern Europe and the West thus tends to turn into a comparison of the former with the latter, clearly ascribing normality to one side only, against which the other has to measure itself.[42] The West is conceived as a model that the EU accession countries—framed as blank sheets with no (proper) institutions and laws—ought to follow.[43] The East is energetic and dynamic, to be sure, but also naïve and raw. Europeanization is conceived as a kind of graduation from Eastern Europe to Europe proper, a process in which the accession countries must prove that they are "willing and able" to internalize Western norms.[44] Studies of privatization, marketization, and democratization plot postsocialism on a scale of transition from (traditional and irrational) Eastern Europe to (modern and rational) Europe/West.[45] The celebratory language of "nation-building" and "the restarting of history" that pervades the "return to Europe" type of narrative indirectly reinforces rather than undermines the inferiorization of

East European countries. Iver Neumann's description captures well such persistent othering in the case of Russia. Russia, Neumann says:

> stands out for its five hundred-year history of always *just* having been tamed, civil, civilized; just having begun to participate in European politics; just having become a part of Europe. Since the Enlightenment it has, furthermore, been seen as a pupil and a learner, whether a successful one (the dominant version of the Enlightenment), a misguided one (the alternative version of the Enlightenment), a laggard who should learn but refuses to do so (the dominant version of the nineteenth century), a truant (the twentieth-century version), or a gifted but somewhat pigheaded one (the present version).[46]

Although representations of Central Europe are generally much more positive than those of Russia, the core point of Neumann's observation is applicable to East-Central Europe as a whole. Ole Wæver observes that such a gradation of the East has been very effective in "disciplining" East-Central Europe because it keeps the door of Europe cracked partly open rather than closed. "With the possibility of drawing on the classical uncertainty about the eastern boundary of Europe," Wæver argues, "the EU manages to place nobody as non-European but everybody as more or less European, more or less close to the center (of Europe and of Europeanness)".[47] Membership is not denied but rather deferred until a particular state becomes fully European. For Wæver, Europe thereby becomes a temporal as opposed to a spatial category—everyone can be European at some later stage of development. This later stage is crucial, as becoming European always happens at a "later stage." It is always "not yet," "still not" or "not quite."[48] It is a kind of a "released prisoner on probation."[49] After detaching itself from the "West of European East," it has become the "East of the European West."[50] To criticize this narrative is not to deny the need to harmonize the applicant states' policies with those of the EU and NATO. It is rather to problematize the hierarchy of places that is implicit in the narrative. This hierarchy views difference in terms of essential core features of places rather than in terms of specific historical circumstances.

Return of the East

Seemingly opposite to the generally triumphalist "return to Europe" narrative is the emphasis on ethnic nationalism and traditional geopolitics, or what Rogers Brubaker calls the "seething cauldron" or "return of the repressed" stereotype.[51] This narrative frames East-Central Europe first and foremost not in terms of its idealized European future but in terms of its equally reified "geopolitical" past. I call it the "return of the East" narrative here because it frames politics in terms of the presence or absence of Eastness as an identity or a trait.

The inscription of Eastness is strongly bound up with an analytical accent on the "presence" of history; it is almost obligatory in accounts of East-Central Europe. Even in the first decade of the twenty-first century, contemporary events are still habitually explained as a natural unfolding of historical tendencies.[52] Such oppositions as reason and passion, modern tolerance and ancient hatreds, civic nationhood and ethnic nationalism are still commonplace.[53] To the peoples of Central Europe, this line of thought goes, "the past is never dead: It is not even past."[54] Central Europeans themselves sometimes corroborate this view, emphasizing that historical events "may have relevance to the present in the feelings of Central Europeans (and also Eastern Europeans) in a way that Westerners rarely feel."[55] Whereas the Western part of Europe strives to "reattach" itself to the Eastern part, the argument continues, "The East explodes in ethnic conflicts which seem almost medieval."[56] In this framework, East-Central Europe is still in the grip of entrenched animosities that could resurface unless Europe offers its stabilizing influence. Joschka Fischer, the foreign minister of Germany, remarked in his programmatic speech on the future of Europe in 1999 that there was a "real danger" of Eastern Europe's lapsing back into "the old system of balance of power with the permanent danger of nationalist ideologies."[57] A similar assumption regarding the teaching and learning of European norms is involved in NATO accession. It is a received wisdom now that one of NATO's most important contributions to security has been that it serves as an incentive to Westernize.[58]

This narrative casts security in terms of deeply rooted historical animosities, presenting nationalist violence as an omnipresent possibility.[59] In particular, it assumes that Central Europeans, because of their deep-seated identities, naturally and almost instinctively mistrust Russia and the Russians. In the Baltic context, for example, it is common to assert that: "Due to historical reasons, the Baltics *cannot but* 'securitize' their relations with Russia, from which it follows that . . . their relations with the West are also understood in security terms."[60] Ironically, East-Central Europe tends to attract most Western attention when it is perceived as conflict-prone.[61] The East is most interesting when it behaves like the East.

Explicitly geopolitical language is central to the "return of the East" narrative. The following analysis of the Clinton administration's policies toward Central Europe illustrates this line of reasoning:

> After a half century of relative obscurity due to the clear domination of the Soviet Union in the region, the geopolitical strategists once again have the chance to consider "Mitteleuropa" in all its regional dimensions. Rather than accepting or even debating the proposition that the area between the Oder and the Dnieper has always been a "shatterbelt" or "crush zone," western leaders, such as Madeleine Albright, claim that NATO expansion into this region returns it to Europe, in effect releasing the *occident kidnappe*, in Milan Kundera's phrase. The near total avoidance of geopolitical language and concepts is both clever and short-sighted; historical geopolitical memories in the region could eventually undermine the strategic decision to expand NATO or at least, the challenges sown by the geopolitical fragments that continue to resonate in the region could tie NATO down in more Kosovo-like conflicts.[62]

This argument exemplifies the uncritical use of categories like "geopolitical memories," "shatterbelt," or "buffer zone," as well as the unspoken assumption that the region shares essential immutable characteristics ("has always been"). Instead of a naïve celebration of Europe, this approach displays an equally unreflective assumption of nationalist geopolitics as a core trait of Central European societies. This assumption is especially visible in analyses of minority rights and citizenship legislation. This legislation has been amended in a number of Central European countries as a result of Western pressure from the EU, the Organization for Security and Co-operation in Europe (OSCE), and even NATO.[63] A large part of the voluminous research on the topic discusses these changes in terms of pragmatic, although sometimes reluctant, compliance with European norms. Post-Cold War identity politics, this line of reasoning goes, does not have free rein "but is crucially constrained and increasingly suppressed by the spatial practices of expanding European governance."[64] Even studies that stress shifts in identity politics tacitly assume that the "original" or "authentic" identity is a nationalistic one, albeit modified by European norms. The references to "external norms," the "internal logic" of state behavior, or a "disjuncture" between the two all bolster the conception of East-Central European countries as still in process of acquiring layers of Europeanness.[65] To foreground such a conception of political and social change is neither to deny that Central European countries amended their citizenship legislations as a result of

EU pressure, nor to criticize such amendments. It is to highlight and problematize a particular inscription of causation: the assumption that it is *because* of the West that we (no longer) hear of widespread human rights abuses or ethnic strife in Central Europe.[66]

The Reinscription of Otherness

The framework of Europe and the East operates not through a clear-cut geographical demarcation of Europe and the East but through a more complex gradation of Europeaness and Eastness, maturity and immaturity. This gradation breaks the East into Central Europe, which is more secure and more European, and Eastern Europe, which possesses less security and Europeanness.[67] We can think of this process as a sliding scale of Europeanness that not only maintains the overall framework of Europe and the East but also makes it more flexible.

Such a sliding scale of merit is not new either in Central Europe or in the West. In virtually all the Central (and Eastern) European states, narratives of national identity frame the eastern border of that particular state as the eastern border of Europe.[68] In the West, the idea of European nations as aid recipients indeed upset the worldview of the development community in the early 1990s because that community could not easily characterize the region as either developed or underdeveloped. To resolve the ambiguity as to whether East-Central Europe is developed or still developing, the more "developed" Visegrad countries were categorized as needing only to catch up, while the rest of East-Central Europe was relegated to underdeveloped status.[69] In the 1990s, the slope of Europeanness was firmly integrated into foreign affairs and political life more broadly.[70] It became the discursive basis of Central Europe's integration with the West.

The concept of Central Europe offers an illuminating example of the demarcation and redemarcation of Europeanness and Eastness on the East-West slope. The concept emerged in the mid-1980s as a Cold War appeal to the West issued by Czech, Hungarian, and Polish dissidents. In Milan Kundera's famous formulation from 1984, Central Europe is "the part of Europe situated geographically in the center—culturally in the West and politically in the East." The anti-Soviet struggle in Prague and Warsaw "was not a drama of Eastern Europe," Kundera continues, "it was a drama of the West, a West that, kidnapped, displaced, brainwashed, nevertheless insisted on defending its identity."[71] Kundera differentiates Central from Eastern Europe in terms of the moral superiority of the more European Central Europe over the less European Eastern Europe, especially Russia. He explicitly cites the organization of space as a factor that fundamentally distinguishes Central Europe from Russia. In Europe, Kundera claims, the organizing principle of nation building is "the greatest variety within the smallest space." "How could Central Europe not be horrified," he continues, "facing a Russia founded on the opposite principle: the smallest variety within the greatest space?"[72]

This depiction of Central Europe was a powerful message that resonated with nationalist myths in Central Europe and also fit snugly into Western conceptions of Europe and Russia. In the post-Cold War era, it became an effective nation- and region-building tool, as first the three Visegrad states (Poland, Hungary, and Czechoslovakia before its division) and then the other postsocialist countries jumped on the bandwagon of the "formerly kidnapped" West. As early as 1994, the U.S. Department of State started applying the term "Central Europe" to what had previously been "Eastern Europe."[73] United States Secretary of State Madeleine Albright tellingly remarked about the Baltic states in the late 1990s that one does not have to be located in Central Europe to have Central Europe in one's heart.[74] By the early 2000s, such demarcation had been mainstreamed. "Today's Central Europe," to quote the Polish foreign minister, Adam Rotfeld, "covers all post-communist countries located—in general terms—between the CIS [Commonwealth of Independent States] and Western Europe."[75]

The concept of Central Europe is premised on the binary of Europe and Eastern Europe. Its chief political function was and is to be set apart from Eastern Europe. Milica Bakic-Hayden defines this layering of Europe and the East as nesting Orientalism, a pattern of representation that reproduces the dichotomy of Europe and the East but introduces a gradation between these two poles.[76] Within this pattern, Central Europe is closer to an idealized Europe than to Eastern Europe, and Eastern Europe is closer than Russia. Central Europe is thus the most European and least Eastern of Europe's internal Easts, while Russia and Yugoslavia are the most Eastern or Oriental. The nests of otherness are enforced as much by Central Europeans as by the West. Joining Europe then becomes a way of establishing maximum distance from the East or Eastness. Central and East European politics involved a discernible tendency to monitor one's neighbors' weaknesses, in particular those that could prove a lesser degree of cultivation and Europeanness in the neighbor so as to prove one's own superior command of Europeanness.[77] Everyone tries to find "Eastern" actors or practices that can be scapegoated for any failure to move upward toward the West with the desired speed.[78] In the former Yugoslavia, for example, there were not only

Western but also Slovene and Croat intellectuals who represented Serbia in Orientalist terms.[79] Likewise in the Baltic states, Russian otherness has been "of utmost importance" in their post-Cold War nation-building projects.[80] Estonian and Latvian intellectuals have been among the most adamant in casting Russia as inherently un-European.[81]

Security is central to this reinscription of otherness. Difference from an idealized Europe is framed not only as inherently backward but also as threatening.[82] "Contemporary security relations on our continent," said the Polish foreign minister, Krzysztof Skubiszewski, in 1992, "have lost their simplicity and may be geographically described as concentric circles progressing from the stable nucleus of the countries of the European Communities, the Western European Union and the North Atlantic Alliance, to the most unstable peripheries."[83] National histories in Central Europe are told in terms of a centuries-long struggle against Russian domination or the threat of it. The following (presumably ironic) summary of Polish history from 1996 captures this attitude nicely:

> 966 beginning, 1772 Russians [in a derogatory form, "Ruscy"] entered, 1793 Russians entered, 1795 Russians entered, 1831 Russians left but they entered again, 1863 Russians left but they have entered again, 1918 Russians have left, 1920 Russians entered but left soon, 1930 Russians entered, 1944 Russians entered, 1981 allegedly Russians were about to enter, 1992 Russians say that they will leave in a moment, 1993 Russians have left, 1994 Russians say that they will come again, 1995 Russians say that it [is] too early for NATO, 1996 Russians have invented the corridor to have a way to enter[84]

A similar geography of multiple Easts informs popular attitudes. "Where is it written," one Czech official asks rhetorically "that something won't infiltrate through Slovakia?" The official continues, "It does not have to be an open infiltration. It could be, for example, the invasion of these Ukrainian Mafias to such an extent that they undermine us completely."[85] "As far as we are concerned here in Europe," another official argues, "we do not have any real natural barriers that would protect us in case of an invasion of the Genghis Khan hordes. It is evident that if masses of Islam or Chinese invade, this will be a tragedy for us. It doesn't have to be direct, it can filter through unhappy Russia."[86] EU and NATO memberships are necessary, according to that logic, not only for Central Europe's but also the rest of Europe's security. Central Europe is, ironically, still the buffer between Europe and the East. Importantly, the Eastern threat is linked not so much to the actions of the Russian state as to a vaguer and more flexible notion of Eastness or likeness to the East.

The concept of Central Europe is certainly not monolithic or uncontested. In the West, Timothy Garton Ash among others argues that Central Europe is characterized as much by differences as by similarities. All attempts to distill some common "essence" from the history of Central Europe, he maintains, are "absurdly reductionist, or pointlessly vague."[87] In Central Europe, Kundera's essentialist account has received considerable criticism. Kundera indeed later disavowed his original "kidnapped West" argument on the grounds that it had been tailor-made for Western consumption.[88] Because of its perfect fit with the cultural definitions of Europe, however, the concept of Central Europe has become a successful intellectual product for export in the accession states' relations with the West. It provides a platform from which they can issue pleas for Western acceptance and assistance. It is especially prominent in texts addressed to Western audiences. Evoking Central Europe has become, to quote Iver Neumann, "a way of making place out of space: a way of forging a certain collective self, and charging that political self with political power."[89] The power of the concept lies in its political expediency.[90] The function of Central Europe in the framework is to recycle the East and to pass it further to the east. It is not only a project to exclude others but also "a means for a people worried about their own European credentials to retrieve a place at the heart of European politics and culture."[91] Far from being separate from Eastern Europe, Central Europe owes much of its political success to being compatible with Europe-wide representations of Eastern Europe. Russia is not a threat to Central Europe; rather, it is Central Europe's condition of possibility.[92] Utterances about Central Europe's superior Europeanness with respect to the East can be understood only within the unequal power relationships between the Central European countries and the West.[93] It is these power relationships that make it attractive and possible to inferiorize places further east. At the same time, demarcating a place as Central European still frames it as marginal, a bridgehead, in a precarious borderland location.[94] It locates the place in a liminal space, neither developed nor underdeveloped, neither learned nor wholly ignorant, in the process of becoming European though not yet there. It both reaffirms a country's Europeanness and simultaneously places it on the margin of Europe. It is premised on insecurity. We thus have the conundrum of a space that proclaims itself a center and a border at the same time.[95] Milica Bakic-Hayden points out that the profuse use of the terms Europe and European orientation in East-Central Europe reveals considerable insecurity as to whether "Europe" really considers East-Central Europe a part of Europe.[96] "Tell me your Central Europe," Garton Ash muses, "and I tell you who you are."[97] The

Hungarian writer Péter Esterházy captures the ironies of Central Europe's shifting position from the lower end of the East-West slope:

> Once, I was an Eastern European; then I was promoted to the rank of Central European .... Then a few months ago, I became a New European. But before I had the chance to get used to this status—even before I could have refused it—I have now become a non-core European .... In our time, this is how we become cosmopolitans.[98]

Something Old, Something New

To foreground the metageography of Europeanness and Eastness is not to deny significant transformations of and flexibility in the discourse of Europe's eastern enlargement. It is rather to highlight some key geographical underpinnings of "Europe whole and free." These underpinnings do not force uniformity, but they do channel debate and disagreement in particular ways. They do not tell us what Europe and the East are or where they are; they tell us how to look for Europe and the East, and where to look. On the one hand, the framework of Europe and the East remains entrenched in accounts of the EU's enlargement. It is not simply a waning legacy of an earlier era but also a tacit premise of EU and NATO enlargement. It forms the basis for conceptualizing Europe and Europeanness in terms of concentric rights or zones. On the other hand, that framework has become more malleable since the early 1990s. It functions as a set of various internal Europes and Easts that fit into and reinforce the discourse of Eastern Europe. In the words of Hayden White, Europe "is less a concept than a figure the function of which is to hold a place in a metadiscourse where other figures can be collected, endowed with 'Europeanicity,' and used to produce a meaning-effect."[99] Europe and the East are best understood not as locations but rather as characteristics or tendencies attributed to places differently in different circumstances. They operate as floating signifiers activated and operationalized in particular circumstances for particular goals. They form a metageography in which various places and issues, such as security, are endowed with varying degrees of Europeanness and Eastness.[100]

The common thread in such reconfigurations of Europe and the East is that just as places are endowed with Europeanness, they are also endowed with Eastness. Thus, although the levels of Eastness and Europeanness in particular places or practices are a matter of debate, the notion that some places in Europe—usually those in the western part of the continent—are more European than others—usually located in the eastern part of Europe—is still the commonsense container of the EU and NATO enlargement discourse. Inasmuch as enlargement is construed as a learning process in which the eastern peripheries learn European norms, that discourse indeed requires these insecure peripheries. From a discourse of competing modernizations (Sovietology) we now have an era in which quantitative progress reports are accompanied by a marked emphasis on qualitative cultural and regional differences. The Other is differentiated not in terms of being not-European, insecure, or nondemocratic, but in terms of being not "fully" or "truly" or "not yet" European.[101] The issue is not with the borders of Europe or Eastern Europe but rather with the context-specific, often mundane and banal, ways in which varying degrees or shades of Europeanness and Eastness are attributed to places.

Civilizational Geopolitics

In class and ideological conflicts, the key question was "Which side are you on?" and people could and did choose sides and change sides. In conflicts between civilizations, the question is "What are you?" That is a given that cannot be changed.

Samuel Huntington, 1993[1]

To evoke a "civilization" is to call up a foundational identity, a mystical and mythical transcendental presence that is vague yet absolutely fundamental. . . . It is to impose closure upon events, situations, and peoples.

Gearoid O'Tuathail, 1996[2]

It is a truism now that the Central European states' desire to "return to the West" and to be recognized as an integral part of the Western cultural realm is the driving force of their foreign and security policies. This desire is widely considered a more powerful impetus "than mere economic or political motivation could ever be."[3] Indeed, European, Western, or civilizational values are cited across the region as the self-evident and primary bases for a wide range of foreign and domestic policy decisions. Speaking in 1997, the Polish foreign minister, Bronislaw Geremek, stressed that his country had "spared no effort" to "return to the roots of our culture and statehood, to join the Euro-Atlantic family of democratic nations. This is the essence of our aspirations to join NATO".[4] When the Economist asked a Polish government official in 2001 why his country so eagerly pursued membership in the EU, the official replied with surprised laughter, "I have not even thought about that for ten years." The ultimate reason is "civilizational," he then added.[5]

This chapter investigates the working of this identity-based geopolitics. It unravels the ways in which security has been distanced from the notion of military threat and linked to civilizational identity and values, and with what effects. I use Samuel Huntington's civilizational thesis to exemplify the mechanisms and effects of this process. In particular, I show how the civilizational narrative of security and identity reproduces and consolidates the notion of fundamental civilizational insecurity even if no threats are mentioned.

"Like Motherhood and Apple Pie": Culture, Security, and NATO[6]

Samuel Huntington's thesis of civilizational clash is one of the most prominent and most controversial attempts to explain the post-Cold War international system. Put forth first in an article in *Foreign Affairs* in 1993, and then in a best-selling book three years later, the thesis has received much attention in academic, policy-making, and media circles alike.[7] Huntington's vision grows out of post-Cold War geopolitical uncertainty. His starting position is that the contemporary world lacks the "clarity and stability" of the Cold War period, and is thereby akin to a "jungle-like world of multiple dangers, hidden traps, unpleasant surprises and moral ambiguities."[8] Huntington sees culture and identity as the new driving forces of global politics. He posits that conflict lines now run along cultural and "civilizational" rather than political lines. Civilizations are for Huntington the broadest and most enduring possible communities. They are "the biggest 'we' within which we feel culturally at home as distinguished from all other 'thems' out there":[9] Civilizations are "not only real, they are basic."[10]

> In a world where culture counts, the platoons are tribes and ethnic groups, the regiments are nations, and the armies are civilizations. The increased extent to which people throughout the world differentiate themselves along cultural lines means that conflicts between cultural groups are increasingly important; civilizations are the broadest cultural entities; hence conflicts between groups from different civilizations become central to global politics.[11]

The theoretical and empirical problems of Huntington's thesis have received substantial critiques across the social sciences, and I will not repeat them here.[12] The key question here is not whether Huntington's argument has merit, but how it is used in daily politics. And used it is. In the vertiginous field of post-Cold War geopolitics, when many observers wondered what would replace the bipolar world and which enemies to fight, Huntington offered a clear answer. He told his readers where to look for new adversaries, how to interpret their enmity, and how to contain them. He (correctly) highlighted the neglect of culture in traditional realist theorizing, and this observation struck a chord in a world in which ethnic and religious identities seemed to be central to political conflict. The civilizational thesis appears clear and self-evident. Civilization, like culture, is both foundational and infinitely flexible. To evoke it is to cast political conflict as a matter not of political actions but of cultural essences: not of what states do but of who people are. Conflict is taken to the basic level of being human.

Central Europe occupies an important position in Huntington's vision. He recommends consolidating the West by expanding EU and NATO to the borders of Western civilization. For him, the civilizational paradigm answers the question of where does Europe end. "Europe ends where Western Christianity ends and Islam and Orthodoxy begin. This is the answer which West Europeans want to hear, which they overwhelmingly support sotto voce, and which various intellectuals and political leaders have explicitly endorsed."[13] For this reason, Huntington continues, the EU should be made coextensive with Western civilization "as it has historically existed in Europe."[14] It is logical, then, that the civilizational thesis became a central concept in the EU and NATO enlargement discourse. It enabled NATO enlargement to be defined as a process that is ultimately not about military defense but about the Western cultural realm. True, NATO has been legitimized in part on the basis of "Western values" since its inception. Created as a defense alliance against Soviet Communism, NATO was linked to the notions of democracy and freedom from the outset. In the post-Cold War era, as arguments about the Soviet threat lost their political purchase, values became the primary discursive pillar of NATO's existence and enlargement.[15] Starting in the early 1990s, NATO documents began to downgrade the organization's previous focus on military security, and instead framed NATO as a cultural and civilizational entity.[16] They fostered the notion that NATO is "the expression and military guarantor of Western civilization," an organization whose essential identity and cohesion is based upon common cultural and civilizational roots.[17] Over the 1990s, it became commonplace and indeed obligatory to cite NATO enlargement as an example of how identity shapes geopolitics, and how the alliance contributes to "expanding liberal-democratic norms and values" in Central Europe.[18] A "European identity" is in this line of reasoning a precondition for NATO membership. Only when this identity is "truly internalized" can full integration follow.[19] Through "values," NATO was redefined from an entity standing against something—the now defunct Soviet Union—to one that is in favor of something else—civilizational or Western values.[20]

In territorial terms, NATO was reframed as a nonterritorial community of values, an entity that does not have clear insiders and outsiders, but rather a series of more or less complete insiders. Its enlargement is an "element of a broad European security architecture that transcends and renders obsolete the idea of 'dividing lines' in Europe."[21] This enlargement is less an "expansion" and more an "opening" of NATO. The German defense minister Volker Rühe, for example, argued in November 1996 that "The new NATO is opening up eastward. It is not a question of expanding or extending spheres of influence . . . . It is a question of opening up the Atlantic Alliance to sovereign, democratic, and free-market nations."[22] Javier Solana, the secretary general of NATO, reiterated this argument in 1998:

> I would like to erase from our consciousness the words "dividing lines." These are words from the Cold War. They meant that some countries were "in" and some were "out." Today, none are in or out—some are only partly in and partly out.[23]

The next secretary general, George Robertson, stressed once again in 2001 that "joining the alliance is not only about military integration, but also about adopting a system of values."[24] Enlargement does not represent the alliance's moving east, but rather Central and Eastern Europe's moving west.[25] U. S. Secretary of State Colin Powell perhaps best summarized the discursive metamorphosis when he welcomed new members to the alliance in 2004:

> My friends, for most of its existence, NATO has been concerned mainly with the defense of common territory. NATO is now transformed, as only a league of democracies can be, into an alliance concerned mainly with the defense of common values and common ideas.[26] NATO was determined, above all, to prevent aggression. Now it is determined, above all, to promote freedom, to extend the reach of liberty, and to deepen the peace.

As I will show below, a very similar rhetorical metamorphosis occurred in Central Europe.

The reframing of NATO is part and parcel of the broader debate about the changing nature of security and the relationship between security and identity. One of the central questions in this debate is whether distancing security from the military realm and linking it to "soft" societal and cultural issues opens up political debate. There is a substantial body of work arguing that it does, that the broadening of the security agenda into nonmilitary spheres like migration and minority rights makes security policy more responsive to complex social problems that threaten human well-being. In counterpoint to the traditional neorealist visions of security, which treat individuals as citizens of a state, the broadened security agenda views security in terms of individuals' quality of life. Central Europe appears to be a case in point. The very concept of foreign threat is disappearing from the official language and much of the politically correct discourse on European security. The new term of choice is risks, and those are articulated in terms of societal instability rather than in terms of state-sponsored military action.[27] The EU is conceived as a provider of security to Central and Eastern Europe—not in the sense of military defense but rather in terms of societal stability and improved quality of life. NATO has experienced a similar rebranding as an organization increasingly concerned with political cooperation and peacekeeping. These developments may profoundly change the territorial conceptions of security. They scale geopolitics simultaneously downward to the level of individuals and upward to the level of humankind as a whole. Perhaps they cannot entirely eliminate boundaries between "us" and "them," but they can crosscut and blur these boundaries, transforming the norms "we" use when dealing with "them." The conventional conception of security, based on a balance of power and a clear demarcation of inside and outside, is replaced by a more flexible notion that blurs the lines between the threatened "inside" and the threatening "outside." In Central Europe, this replacement may profoundly change the meaning and function of the EU's eastern border and identity politics across that border.[28]

The broadening of the security agenda, however, could also perpetuate and entrench the status quo. Traditionally, a state representative declares an emergency condition when invoking security and claims the need to use whatever means are necessary to block a threatening development. In the NATO enlargement discourse, it is increasingly also "community" or "identity" that is to be secured. But this notion of security simply applies its depoliticizing and dichotomizing effects to other spheres of social life. It redefines these other spheres in terms of existential threats and emergency measures that should be above "normal boring" politics.[29] It construes the identity that is to be secured as unproblematic. It is relatively easy to argue and difficult to dispute that a particular issue or a political actor threatens something as ambiguous as "our identity" or "the way we are or used to be or ought to be to be true to our 'identity.'"[30] By being linked to identity the figure of threat may become not less pervasive or effective, but more so.[31] In the case of NATO enlargement, the "Disney diplomacy" of invoking identity allowed NATO to present itself as an enlightened community representing democratic values, and to present opposition, especially Russian opposition, as a relic from an older and less enlightened era of traditional geopolitics.[32] When Russia complies with "Western values," it is presented as a successful learner; when it does not, it is characterized as backward and non-Western.[33] With NATO as wholesome and good as motherhood and apple pie, it is difficult for any group or state to oppose enlargement, lest it be identified as an outsider to "European values."

Huntington's Handmaidens:
Making Civilizational Maps in Central Europe

Civilizational evocations predated Huntington's thesis in Central Europe. The very concept of Central Europe has a civilizational overtone because it demarcates Central Europe as a cultural entity that is both an integral part and the eastern border of the Western cultural realm. Huntington's thesis reinforced and legitimized that civilizational overtone. Huntington had cast Central Europe not only as an essential part of the West but also as crucial for the West's own security and identity. He had done so from the top of the Western academic establishment, on the pages of a leading Western journal, and then in a best-selling book. His argument nicely complements Central Europe's own versions of the "return to Europe" narrative. It is in some ways even more useful than the "return to Europe" argument, because it ties Central Europe to a unit that is bigger than Europe—that of the West as a whole. It allows Central European states to bypass Europe and appeal directly to transatlantic ties with the United States.[34] The civilizational thesis, or Huntingtonianism as Timothy Garton Ash calls it, quickly became one of the most influential political ideas in the region.[35] Speaking in Riga, a puzzled American colleague observed that "at Western conferences, almost everyone is critical of Huntington. Here, if you criticize him, they look at you as if you were an idiot."[36]

The Huntingtonian or civilizational narrative of security involves two parallel strands in Central Europe. The first is the redefinition of threat from a military and political condition to a more amorphous cultural phenomenon. The second is the recasting of NATO from a political institution to a kind of a cultural association based on common values. In the sections that follow, I explore each of these strands, outlining how they function to uphold the civilizational edifice of security.

Ubiquitous Insecurity, Elusive Threats

Threat is not what it used to be in Central Europe. Numerous primary and secondary accounts, drawing on political documents, speeches, media analyses, interviews, and opinion research, conclude that neither the Central European elites nor the general public perceive the region to be under military threat. Assessments vary as to when external threats subsided or why, or how grave they were in the first place, but by the mid-1990s, most commentators agreed that Central European states were not under an external threat. At least one in-depth study based on focus groups found that in Poland, the Czech Republic, Slovakia, and Hungary, external threats were not an issue even in the early 1990s. In all four countries, researchers found that "people's chief insecurity is the economic and political crisis that they are living through daily." According to the focus groups, the internal crisis of each country was "*by far*, the dominant source of anxiety."[37] When asked, "What does security mean for your country?", the group participants named the internal crisis, "first and emphatically, *every time*."[38] With regard to external threats, respondents mentioned such environmental problems as nuclear disasters as well as (im)migration. By 1998, threat perceptions across Central Europe focused on the "new" threats of minorities and immigrants.[39] Occasionally, surveys indicated concerns about immediate neighbors, such as Germany in Poland or Hungary in Slovakia, but the general trend was clearly moving toward diminishing perceptions of external threat.[40] Official government rhetoric also downplayed the existence of direct external threats.[41]

Yet insecurity has remained omnipresent in Central European politics. Branding oneself as the most pro-security and pro-Western, and thereby vilifying one's opponents as pro-Russian and hence dangerous remained a key political strategy of political parties and individual politicians alike. Although the Russian Federation was not identified as a threat, the Russian card was played at the highest levels of the state to discredit opposition.[42] As recently as 2003, the Russian threat was deployed to justify governmental support of the American-led war in Iraq. In Poland, one commentator explained that Poland supports the United States because the member states of the EU do not understand Poland's security dilemma. "After 50 years of totalitarianism," he says, "the Poles are still terrified of the Russians while Putin is busy killing Chechens."[43] "The Russian threat," Tomasz Zarycki observed, "even if not represented as a direct danger but only as a historical heritage," is fundamental to the legitimization of Polish national identity. It is the Russian threat that makes Poland's behavior on the international scene "coherent and largely predictable."[44] The fundamental insecurity of the Baltic states is likewise a kind of folk wisdom. When a journalist asked three Lithuanian army officers about security threats, all three "glanced down at their feet in unison and fidgeted." After a long pause, one replied, "Just like always." He refused to elaborate.[45]

Political documents and scholarly analyses likewise refuse to elaborate, but likewise treat insecurity as self-evident. They report that the peoples of Central Europe feel a "general and diffuse anxiety" of regional instability emanating especially from Russia and the Balkans. Without necessarily mentioning any specific country, participants in focus groups report that there is an ongoing need for an American presence in Europe to counter any potential instability.[46] NATO is presented as the only guarantor of security. Without it, the argument goes, Central European states would remain vulnerable to "pressure, intervention and destabilization."[47] The absence of military threat, a Polish security expert maintains, "is a felicity that may not endure." "Security is forever a goal to be achieved, not a fate that is guaranteed." Analyses of security customarily discuss various negative scenarios, which usually revolve around the possible reemergence of an aggressive Russia. "It is plain to Poles," a Polish expert says, "that a military threat from the east could arise in the future, should Russia—or just possibly, Ukraine—become an aggressive dictatorship."[48] At the same time, there is little mention of the low likelihood of any of these scenarios coming to pass. Analyses of security typically start by first laying out grim scenarios, then acknowledging that all of them are unlikely, and finally reiterating the importance of NATO as the only guarantor of security.[49] This line of reasoning is extraordinarily consistent. The following two statements by Vaclav Havel illustrate the transition from a clearly localized threat to a less defined notion of insecurity. Havel said in an interview with a German newspaper in 1995 that:

> For reasons of security, being accepted into NATO is indeed more urgent for us than being accepted into the European Union. No-one knows what the further developments in Russia will be like and whether we will not experience unpleasant surprises there. Now time is really ripe to seriously negotiate about our membership in NATO; it alone offers a security guarantee.[50]

Two years later, in 1997, Havel issued a warning that is formulated in far more general terms yet uses more ominous language:

> It [Europe] is a single entity—though it is culturally, ethnically and economically immensely diverse. For the first time in its history, this entity has an opportunity to establish an internal order on the principle of co-operation and equality among the large and the small, the strong and the weak, on shared democratic values . . . . Should Europe fail to grasp this opportunity, we could be heading for a new global catastrophe, a catastrophe far graver than previous ones. This time the forces of freedom would not face a single totalitarian enemy. They could well be drawn into a strange era of all against all, a war with no clear front, a war difficult to distinguish from terrorism, organized crime and other forms of wrongdoing, a war in which indirect and hidden forces would engulf the whole world.[51]

The change of tone in Havel's message reflects the content and tone of security debates in Central Europe. The tone becomes more ominous even as the nature and the location of the threat become considerably more diffuse. Threat comes to be articulated in terms of Europe "failing to grasp an opportunity," in terms of a conflict of "all against all," or a "war with no clear front." This threat is not named and not located.

From Military Alliance to "Community Of Values": the Recasting of NATO

The diffusion of insecurity occurred in parallel with the reframing of accession to NATO from a political strategy of defence to an identity-based pursuit of entry into a cultural and moral community.[52] The discursive metamorphosis of NATO was not handed down to Central Europe from the West; it was also produced in Central Europe. In part as a result of this metamorphosis, the dissolution of military threat did not impede the Central European states from pursuing NATO membership. To the contrary, the net effect of the reframing of NATO was to broaden the legitimation of accession and to redefine the alliance as necessary for *both* security and identity.

Over the course of the 1990s, Central European politicians increasingly began to speak of security in terms of civilizational affinity with the West and to distance foreign and security policies from the notion of threat. By the end of the decade, it was sometimes difficult to find even a mention of defense. Thus Arpad Göncz, the president of Hungary, stated in 1996 that NATO enlargement did not involve an eastward movement of NATO but rather a westward movement of

Central and Eastern Europe.[53] Estonia's then-foreign minister, Toomas Hendrik Ilves, likewise stressed in 1997 that NATO membership would codify "common values—peace, freedom, democracy and welfare— which Estonia values above all."[54] Numerous dignitaries have emphasized that NATO has a cultural "value-based" and "civilizational" identity alongside its geographic and strategic identity, and that this cultural and civilizational role is of primary importance for Central Europe.[55] NATO membership, President Georgi Parvanov of Bulgaria emphasized, is important not only as a security guarantee but also "more importantly" as a recognition that Bulgaria "subscribes to the values of democracy.[56] Within this rhetoric, to be in NATO means to accept and realize the values of democracy, tolerance, and human rights.[57] "I don't see threats coming from the east," said Latvia's former foreign minister, Valdis Birkavs, when asked about Latvia's reasons for seeking membership in NATO. "I see stability coming from the west."[58] "Estonia does not want to join the NATO of the Cold War," Toomas Hendrik Ilves declared in 1997. "In both location and spirit, Estonia is a part of the new Europe and we feel entitled to be constructively involved in the formation of the new European defence arrangement."[59] "In order to think of today's and tomorrow's security," President Ion Iliescu of Romania said in 2002, "we must forget a great deal of yesterday's security rules."[60] It is in part because NATO is perceived as a value-based institution while the EU is seen as an economic institution with complicated bureaucratic procedures that NATO was more popular than the EU throughout Central Europe.[61]

Such pairing of security with culture and Western values is not just a matter of official rhetoric. It percolates through political debate and sets the tone of public utterances. It is operationalized through a wide range of practices throughout civil society—parliamentary debates, news media, entertainment, and education. In all the accession states, the pro-NATO campaigns relied heavily on NGOs. In the regional context, the most prominent civil society actor is the Atlantic Treaty Association (ATA), a Paris-based NATO-affiliated network of forty national Atlantic Associations in Europe and North America.[62] These associations spin off their own NGOs. They seek to serve as catalysts throughout civil society, "working to enhance awareness, to promote discussion and to develop cooperation and partnerships regarding support to Euro-Atlantic values and institutions," to quote the mission statement of Romania's Euro-Atlantic Council. Their activities go far beyond distribution of information. Most of these associations focus on integrating NATO into social life, creating a "politically active society on the road to security and democracy."[63]

Children and youth are a special focus of such activities. Several ATA affiliates have sections of their Web sites devoted to young people. The Atlantic Council of Slovenia, for example, even publishes a quarterly magazine for high school and college students. The Latvian Transatlantic Organisation initiated the publication of a book titled NATO and Latvia's Security, aimed at teachers and students in grades nine through twelve. The Ministry of Education recommends the book to all institutions of general education in Latvia. As about half of Latvia's population is Russian-speaking, the organization also arranged a host of events targeting teachers in Russian-language schools. The chair of Romania's Euro-Atlantic Council emphasized education in the council's newsletter. The "new education" would, in his words, stimulate the "interest and direct involvement of young people" in security matters. The Atlantic Club of Bulgaria organized a program of events intended to foster "Recognizing the Atlantic values as values of the young generation in South-Eastern Europe." The program included a national seminar titled "Methods for use of NATO materials through teaching English language in high schools in Bulgaria" for English language teachers from language high schools. The seminar was supported by the Bulgarian Ministry of Education and Science, the Ministry of Foreign Affairs, and the National Military University, with cooperation from the American Center in Sofia and the British Council. In the Czech Republic, Jagello—the Czech affiliate of ATA—organized a children's drawing competition called "Secure World" in 2002. It later called on the accession states to do the same, and they all complied. Another essay contest aimed at high school students, was also inspired by one held in the Czech Republic in the spring of 2002.[64] The awards in such competitions often included free trips to NATO headquarters or the Prague Summit (in 2002).

Entertainment is likewise a key theme in the activities of the pro-NATO NGOs. In Latvia, the Transatlantic Organisation sponsored a series of events intended to make discussion of NATO "easier" and "friendlier." One particularly successful project was the NATO Road Show, which involved a jeep filled with military technology traveling through Latvia and giving out NATO souvenirs. Along similar lines, the Estonian NATO Association organized several free rock concerts, complete with free pea soup, to attract the youth. In Lithuania, the invitation to join NATO was likewise celebrated with musical events. To warm up those waiting to see President George W. Bush and his entourage on a cold Saturday morning, the government organized a rock concert that featured several popular youth bands, including "a Lithuanian clone" of the Pet Shop Boys.[65] The public relations company BVRG organized another rock concert for the same occasion in an art gallery. The chief executive officer (CEO) of the company explained that "We want to show that Lithuanian youth are capable of celebrating this important political event, and they support it in an enjoyable, joyful, and trendy way."[66]

The snapshot of NATO's Prague summit included in chapter 1 indicates that culture and identity were central themes of that event as well. Delegates from the three Baltic states of Estonia, Latvia, and Lithuania rode to the student summit on the "Baltic Youth NATO Bus."[67] The project, funded by the three states' foreign ministries, several Western embassies in those states, and the Danish Atlantic Treaty Organization, involved a minibus traveling from Tallinn to Prague and picking up young NATO supporters along the way. The chairman of the Estonian NATO Association explained, "We need to realize that a summit is taking place and Estonians are actively participating in it. It is not just the state but the people as a whole, and since we are a people's organization, we will show that the Estonian people are interested in it."[68] The project included a series of events at major stops. The bus was greeted by high-level foreign policy officials and foreign diplomats in all three Baltic capitals. In Kaunas, the bus riders were entertained at a reception hosted by the Polish ambassador to Lithuania. The delegates also distributed information about NATO, talked to "well-wishers," and initiated "face-to-face communication" about NATO. On the way they made a poster: "Next stop—NATO", which featured the handprints of Baltic youth and politicians. In Prague, the poster was exhibited first at the Prague Concert Hall and later at the Student Summit as an expression of Baltic unity on NATO. The bus also carried the Baltic Manifest, a proclamation that presents NATO accession as a matter of values and urges active participation in the alliance and in security more generally (see Figure 1).

The document's concern clearly does not lie with such negative categories as enemy, threat, or discipline. It rather emphasizes "responsible" and "reliable" subjects who together "care" about tomorrow. It imagines a supranational order based on common values.

These are just some examples from the substantial and varied program of events that spanned several years and took place throughout Central Europe. They illustrate the ways in which NATO was made an omnipresent part of the cultural realm. Through such activities, NATO became commonplace, even boring. The characterization of the Slovenian discussion of NATO as a "debate among the convinced" applies to the other accession states as well.[69] There was little or no wide-scale public debate on what NATO entry would mean, nor any realistic discussion of its cost. When public opinion was not sufficiently supportive of

BALTIC MANIFEST

WE ARE THE YOUTH FROM BALTIC NGO'S - ESTONIAN ATLANTIC TREATY ASSOCIATION, LATVIAN TRANSATLANTIC ORGANIZATION AND LITHUANIAN ATLANTIC TREATY ASSOCIATION AND WE ARE GOING TO
NATO PRAGUE SUMMIT BY BUS – *THE BALTIC YOUTH NATO BUS*

We believe that:

- ▫ Peace and security is everyone's responsibility – we must work together, regardless of age, nationality or profession – to secure our future

- ▫ An invitation to join NATO is an invitation to actively participate in protecting our common values securing our future

- ▫ We are reliable allies that will enhance the prospects of peace and stability in the transatlantic area

- ▫ We are the generation that will benefit most from peace and stability – we care about today and tomorrow

NEXT STOP – NATO!
LET'S GO!

Estonian Atlantic Treaty Association	Latvian Transatlantic Organisation	Lithuanian Atlantic Treaty Association

Figure 1   Baltic Manifest

Source: Latvian Transatlantic Organisation, 2002.

NATO accession, the chattering classes simply ignored it in the name of democracy (which was to be achieved and/or protected only by NATO membership).[70] By the late 1990s, arguments in favor of NATO had become essentially cultural ones, based on claims about history, heritage, and cultural traditions. NATO no longer depended on the existence of demonstrable enemies. The actions of the Russian state in a way did not matter because insecurity was attributed to the presumed essence of Russian culture rather than the actions of the Russian state. While stressing that NATO must "open its doors to new European democracies," Havel urged the setting of a definite limit on its possible future enlargement.[71] It is precisely for civilizational reasons, he argued, that Russia is not suited for EU and NATO membership. "It would make no sense," Havel says, to consider Russia for NATO membership because Russia is "a huge Euro-Asian Empire" whose "only relationship with NATO can and will be that of a separate entity."[72] NATO was thus characterized as both a borderless cultural phenomenon and a clearly demarcated civilizational unit.

Border State: Civilizational Geopolitics in Estonia

In August 2003, leading up to the popular referendum on European Union (EU) accession the following month, six widely respected Estonian artists and intellectuals published a joint article in the country's largest newspaper urging voters to say "Yes" in the referendum. Their argument began as follows:

> When one of the world's best-known political scientists Samuel Huntington published his "clash of civilizations" theory in the early 1990s, it touched Estonians' soul. According to Huntington, the border of the European civilization runs exactly along the Narva River [between Estonia and Russia]. Estonians had assured each other of the existence of that border for 50 years, and stood for maintaining it for 5000 years. . . . . For many, that small black-and-white map [in Huntington's book] was a symbolic confirmation that Narva river is the border between western Christianity and Orthodoxy, the Latin and the Cyrillic alphabet, Roman law and Russian lawlessness, democracy and autocracy, not just for us but for the whole humankind. And this is how it will always be.[73]

This proclamation illustrates the civilizational and geopolitical narrative that pervades political debates in Estonia. The influence of this narrative is difficult to overestimate; it is among the key conceptual bases of political speeches, policy analyses, and academic research on foreign as well as domestic affairs. As it lies at the center of the discursive constellation of geopolitics and culture, it serves as a lens through which we can better comprehend the workings and effects of this constellation.

The notion that Estonia is culturally a "kidnapped West" predates the reestablishment of the country's independence in 1991. The mainstream conception of Estonian history posits that the country has been an integral part of (Western) Europe at least since it was conquered by the Teutonic Knights in the thirteenth century. Throughout the period of Soviet occupation, Estonia and the other Baltic states were considered "the Soviet West" by the people in these states as well as by outsiders on both sides of the Iron Curtain. Post-Soviet historiography is premised on a narrative in which the Soviet occupation is represented as an attempt to incorporate Estonia into the "Eastern world . . . influenced by Byzantine culture." The post-Soviet era then represents Estonia's return to its natural place in the Western cultural realm. Referring to the membership of several Estonian towns in the medieval Hanseatic League—a network of trading cities led by Lübeck and other northern German towns and centered on the Baltic Sea—Estonia's president, Lennart Meri, linked Estonia's pursuit of EU membership directly to the Middle Ages:

> Everything new is well forgotten old . . . I would like to say that we in Europe have an experience of a previous European Union. This previous union created a common legal area associating more than a hundred cities, it radiated something which in the current terminology of the European Union and NATO is called common values, and radiated it far beyond its borders.[74]

The "return to the West" narrative is to some extent necessarily a border-drawing practice, since it implies that Estonia has returned to Europe from a place that is not "Western."[75] The intensity of an explicit civilizational overtone, however, has greatly increased over time. It was indeed not until the second half of the 1990s that this overtone began to dominate political debates. In the early to mid-1990s, the conception of Estonia as a gateway between Europe and Russia was also prominent. A strong strand of public debate stressed Estonia's potential to profit from Russia-bound transit—trade as well as travel—because of the country's location and transportation infrastructure as well as Estonians' knowledge of Russia. While NATO membership was always a dominant vision, it was also possible to discuss a form of neutrality akin to the Finnish and Swedish options.[76] The future scenarios developed in the mid-1990s by an interdisciplinary group of experts likewise emphasized the gateway aspect.[77] The catchphrase "return to Europe" had not yet been given a clear civilizational content.

Huntington's thesis inserted clarity into this relatively fluid conceptual space. It supplied an unequivocally articulated prescription from the heights of the Western academy. It recast the sphere of identity in terms of science and thereby reshaped it into a powerful tool in geopolitical arguments. Marika Kirch, a prominent sociologist, discussed the civilizational clash as clearly visible to the naked eye as early as 1994:

> If one supposes hesitatingly that the civilizational border between Estonia and Russia is anachronistic or negligible, one need only stand on the bridge over Narva river . . . and witness carefully the "overt civilizational confrontation" of two cultures: on the Estonian side there is an historic fortress built by the Swedes, Danes and Germans in accordance with the cultural traditions of Western Europe; on the other [in Ivangorod] a primeval fortress as an exponent of Slavic-Orthodox cultural traditions.[78]

The thesis of a clash of civilizations became especially prominent after the publication of a major scholarly volume on Estonia's postsocialist transformations edited by the country's preeminent social scientists. The book, tellingly titled *Return to the Western World*, explicitly used Huntington's work as its conceptual guide.[79] It established Huntington's civilizational thesis as a canonical text in Estonia. In 1999, Huntington's *The Clash of Civilizations* was translated into Estonian, complete with a foreword by Estonia's minister of foreign affairs.[80] On this occasion, Huntington visited Estonia at the invitation of the Foreign Ministry and spoke at a conference together with Estonia's prime minister and minister of foreign affairs. Major newspapers provided extensive publicity for his thesis. *Eesti Päevaleht*, one of Estonia's two principal dailies, devoted two full pages to Huntington's work on civilizations and printed the transcript of a meeting-of-the-minds conversation between Huntington and the foreign minister, Toomas Hendrik Ilves.[81] Hailed as obvious as well as rigorously scientific, the civilizational thesis is regarded as an internationally accepted truth in academic and policy circles alike.[82] Throughout the preaccession years, the thesis functioned as the conceptual, even the "scientific," basis for Estonia's pursuit of membership in the EU and NATO. For Estonia, Prime Minister Mart Laar emphasized in a lecture at the French Institute of International Affairs, Europe is "not a market but a civilization."[83] "If Estonians want to be worthy of their history" proclaims the manifesto that opens this section, we have to believe and say as firmly as Martin Luther: Here we stand—on this side of the border of Europe and we cannot do otherwise.[84] Recognizing that this attitude may seem odd in contemporary Europe, Marika Kirch, a prominent sociologist, explained it by reference to Estonia's special circumstances.

> At Harvard, Huntington is understandably considered a bit strange because in the multicultural society of the United States, his thesis sounds quite uncompelling. In the Estonian context, the opposite is true. The reestablishment of Estonia's independence further underscored the existence and significance of a civilizational border at the Narva-Piirissaare line [in eastern Estonia].[85]

The civilizational narrative is now taught as a part of the middle school history curriculum.[86] Andrei Hvostov, a prominent columnist, observes that the civilizational thesis is not really discussed in Estonia. "These days, the topic of brainstorming is how to get out from between the clashing civilizations."[87]

Civilizational Insecurity

The civilizational narrative defines not only what Estonia is but also what it is not: anything "Orthodox," "Byzantine," "Russian," "Eastern," or "Asian." Just as the narrative locates Estonia unequivocally in the West, it also defines the country as fundamentally different from Russia, on the other side of the putative civilizational fault line. Even beyond explicitly geopolitical arguments, it channels political life into a geopolitical binary of the West and Russia.[88] When urging voters to support center-right political forces in the 1999 general election, President Meri said that Estonia's options were as unambiguous as "a mathematical equation." "On one side Europe, on the other Russia," he continued. "We are on the border, and therefore only a small push is needed to make us fall into one side or rise into the other."[89] Rein Ruutsoo, a prominent academic and public intellectual, emphasized in 1995 that despite Estonia's border location, the country is not "a borderland in the classical meaning of the term." It rather "belongs historically and integrally to the sphere of the so-called Lutheran-German civilization." "For centuries, this has blocked attempts from the East to incorporate the northern Baltics (which include Finland) into the Orthodox-Slavic eastern civilization."[90]

Through the reification of differences, the civilizational narrative generates the notion that Estonia is fundamentally insecure because it is located on a putative civilizational boundary. Geopolitical insecurity, articulated in more explicit terms in the early 1990s and more implicitly toward the end of the decade, is indeed the metanarrative of political debates in Estonia.[91] The country's "historically earthquake-prone," "geotectonically active," "windy" or otherwise insecure dangerous situation is the starting point for a range of claims from foreign and security policy to population and education policies. In the words of Jüri Luik, Estonia's foreign minister at the time (1994), Estonia is "at the frontier of democratic and free-market thinking . . . Some would characterize our position as being between the Devil and the Deep Blue Sea."[92] At the same time, similar to those in Central Europe as a whole, Estonian security discourses underwent a clear "cultural" turn in the 1990s, whereby references to external threat were replaced by a more amorphous and flexible notion of insecurity.

This amorphous insecurity is framed in terms of civilizational identity. It is still linked to Russia but not necessarily to the policies of the Russian state. Rather, insecurity is framed in terms of Russian identity and culture—Russianness as such. It is less direct but more fundamental. For within the civilizational framework, policies change but civilizational identities remain constant. Thus, although statements about an immediate Russian military threat were the staple of government rhetoric in the early to-mid-1990s, when Russian troops were still stationed on Estonian territory, these had all but disappeared from mainstream political debates by the late 1990s. While the National Defense Policy Framework stated in 1996 that the main sources of threats to Estonia are "aggressive imperial ambitions and political and/or military instability,"[93] the minister of foreign affairs maintained a year later that "Estonia sees no specific threats to regional security."[94] The National Security Concept developed in 2000 indeed posited that Estonia perceived no military threat to itself from any other state. The document articulated Estonia's security concerns in terms of risks rather than threats, listing "possible instability and politically uncontrollable developments in the international arena as well as international crises" as Estonia's prime security risks.[95] With regard to Estonian-Russian relations, government officials allude to a steady improvement. In 2003, the National Security Concept was revised again, and the notion of territorial defense was removed altogether. The government's explanation was that Estonia no longer faced a territorial threat, and territorial defense was therefore no longer important.[96] Governmental security rhetoric indeed changed so much that it was criticized for mimicking the language of Western countries and neglecting Estonia's existential insecurities. During parliamentary debates of the National Security Concept in early 2001, several members of parliament from both the ruling coalition and the opposition prodded Ilves, then the foreign minister, on the allegedly vague definition of security.[97] The subsequent version of the National Security Concept from 2004 resulted in a broader and at times acrimonious debate as to whether the departure from territorial defense gave adequate consideration to the country's insecure geopolitical situation. The concept's critics maintained that given Estonia's "unpredictable neighbour," the country should maintain the principle of territorial defense. The government did not budge, stressing that Estonia faced no foreign threat. By the late 1990s, security had become articulated not through images of an invading army but through the more opaque notions of "the gray zone" or "unpredictable neighbour."

Yet this change did not dissolve or even diminish the sense of threat. While references to a military threat declined over the second half of the

1990s, references to security actually increased during the same time period.[98] "Whenever Russia or Serbia consider adopting western ways they must go outside and give up parts of themselves," says Rein Taagepera, a well-known liberal intellectual. "In contrast," he continues, "when Estonia or its Baltic neighbours (Latvia and Lithuania) adopt western ways, they only have to reach deeper and actually recover parts of themselves."[99] Commentators on foreign policy frequently caution against "emotionalism" in relations with Russia. "Seemingly intelligent and democratic politicians or analyst can unexpectedly express positions that are oddly reminiscent of 'old thinking'".[100] Estonia's policies must therefore be based on a "crystal clear understanding that the Russian threat is not a matter of diplomatic talk but a true fact of the ruthless world."[101] Russia is thus treated as essentially unchanging—a power that can pretend to a certain Westernness, and even fool Westerners with it, but a power to whom Western values are ultimately alien. Enn Soosaar, a prominent columnist and respected cultural figure, posited in 2003 that "Russia is Russia is Russia."[102] The West, President Meri said in his European of the Year acceptance speech in 1999, underestimates Russia's "immense historic inertia":

> Russian history is full of . . . top-down perestroikas, as dramatic as the melting and breaking of ice on the big rivers of Siberia in Spring. Peter the Great beheaded fifty-four conservative streletses with his own hand and had their remains left on the Red Square for six months. Yet the modernization of the state does not begin from the emperor's axe, but from the citizen, his attitude, his preparedness for his duties and rights.[103]

This persistent evocation of cultural insecurity explains in part why the goal of NATO accession became more entrenched in political debates despite the softening of security rhetoric. By the mid- to late 1990s, neutrality came to be evaluated as a dangerous policy that would make these countries more vulnerable, presumably to malevolent foreign influence.[104] A course in state defense was introduced as an elective in secondary schools. The textbook for the course was approved by the Ministry of Education but published by the Ministry of Defense. Estonian media report that 78 percent of Estonian high school students consider it necessary to teach state defense to all high school students, and 94 percent support NATO accession.[105] Throughout the accession process, pro-EU commentators argued that any problematic aspects of EU membership, such as bureaucratic policy-making and the loss of national sovereignty, must be put aside in the face of the Russian threat. "We should not forget," said Soosaar in his "midway report" of Estonia's return to the West, that:

There are undoubtedly individuals and interest groups in today's Estonia who would support integration with the East, and even though they are in a clear minority, they may become active (possibly as a result of foreign inspiration). They do not have to play with open cards. It suffices, for example, to mask as ones looking for a "third way." If Estonia's integration with the West is hampered, we will be sucked sooner or later . . . into the CIS or another similar association.[106]

Even in late 2002, Mart Laar—a troubled prime minister who faced growing domestic opposition at the time—circulated a letter warning his Pro Patria party of a possible repetition of 1939.[107] His successor as prime minister, Siim Kallas, used foreign threat as a key argument in political debates even on the eve of accession to the EU. If the referendum fails, he argued before the EU accession referendum in 2003, Estonia would slide "dangerously close" to Russia, with its discernible "wish to restore the Stalin-era empire."[108] The rationale for supporting the United States' invasion of Iraq—an unpopular action that more than half of the population did not support—was the Russian threat. Prime Minister Kallas raised the specter of "Stalin junior" coming to power in Russia, and implied that opposition to the war in Iraq was tantamount to "bowing to" Russia or the Soviet Union.[109] He likened the opponents of the war to Vladimir Zhirinovski (a Russian ultranationalist) or the Estonian leftists who were sympathetic to Communism in the 1940s.[110] In this context, argued Mart Helme, a former ambassador to Russia and a prominent foreign affairs commentator at the time, Estonia should support the United States because "exaltedly flag-waving Americans" offer Estonia better protection than "[European] bureaucrats soaked in Brussels-style cleverness."[111] Late that year, just a few months before accession to the EU and NATO, Justice Minister Ken-Marti Vaher likewise warned that "the much-feared threat from the East has not disappeared."[112] Even after EU and NATO accession, the country's politicians as well as media commentators argued that Estonia should attempt to "correct" EU policy toward Russia, to make it more "realistic," based on a better understanding of Russia.[113]

Estonian political debate is not monolithic, of course, and the foregoing examples do not capture the whole range of opinion. Parallel to the polls that showed widespread perceptions of Russian threat, other surveys indicated that most ethnic Estonians did not consider the country to be threatened from the outside. As early as 1998, more than 95 percent of Estonian residents said that the country does not face any real military threat from another country; more recent poll numbers point in the same direction.[114] One could argue that insecurity is no longer a significant feature of Estonian identity construction.[115] Pami Aalto reported that Estonian (and other Baltic) political elites see the EU less as a shelter from insecurity and more as a facilitator of Estonia's cooperation with Russia.[116] Since the turn of the decade, it has become increasingly possible to argue publicly against Russophobia and for closer contacts with Russia.[117] Poor relations with Russia were reportedly among the most consistent criticisms of Foreign Minister Ilves. There has been considerable discussion of a new and more pragmatic policy toward Russia, especially from the political groups most sensitive to business interests.[118] Responding to the civilizational manifesto that starts my account of Estonia, Jaan Kaplinski, a preeminent poet and public intellectual, pointed out that five thousand years ago, there were no Estonians, Slavs, or European spirit. There was no [Western] Christian or Orthodox faith, Latin or Cyrillic alphabet.[119] The Russophobic positions that were considered commonsensical and even patriotic ten years ago are viewed as impractical and even distasteful now. The politicians who stressed the fundamentally non-European character of Russia in the early 1990s were speaking of Russia as an integral part of Europe by the end of the decade.[120] It is possible as of 2007 to joke about Estonian-Russian relations, and there is indeed a small counterculture that mocks the official essentialist rhetoric.[121] An editorial that appeared in *Eesti Ekspress*, the country's main weekly, on February 25, 1999, the day after the seventy-first anniversary of the Republic, offers a glimpse into the irreverent side of the Estonian political debate. The tongue-in-cheek editorial announces jovially that by 2050 Estonia will be a "happy state." It has been greatly strengthened due to the "over-abundant ethical substance of the ethnonational body," a substance that Estonia now exports to Europe as well. This ethical substance, the editors continue, makes Estonia a "core" state of Europe and a kind of conscience of Europeanness. The irony is explicitly geopolitical, playing with the officially sanctioned civilizational narrative. "The first step in our moral ascent," *Eesti Ekspress* says, was "the restoration of the territorial unity that is the basis of the enthonational unity." This restoration meant that Estonia reclaimed portions of its territory from Russia, parts that were important because they were "the well-known location of Viking Truvor's grave, which is important in the development of contemporary European geopolitics."[122]

Some observers see these developments as signs of a "gradual erosion" of the linkage between security and identity, a trend toward more inclusive identities that are no longer premised on the trite binaries of Europe/non-Europe and security/threat.[123] It is not so simple, however. The occasional critical or irreverent comments do not destabilize the received wisdom that Estonia is a threatened border state. The public sphere—including national media, academic writing, and public political pronouncements—is dominated by the Huntingtonian logic of explanation. In the public sphere, calls for a more flexible policy toward Russia have not challenged the civilizational framing of public policy. It is possible that this framing does not represent the private opinions of most Estonians, but it does structure public political debate. Particular Hungtingtonian statements may be criticized, but the assumptions on which these statements and actions rest remain unchallenged. A threat is not always present but it is always available for activation. By the late 1990s, Estonian politics had become a "monomania" in which all politics was reduced to security—itself defined in cultural terms—and all security issues were reduced to entering the EU and NATO. In this monomania, culture became "a slogan for security policy" and "the workhorse that should pull [Estonia's'] wagon into the EU and NATO."[124] Security still lies at the center of Estonian political debate as of 2007, and the civilizational narrative is still the force that holds that centre together.

Cultural Geopolitics

The persistence of (in)security as a key theme in Central European politics is remarkable, when we consider that the region is stable, its economies are growing steadily, its relations with Russia have improved, and its membership in the EU was widely anticipated for years before it happened. This chapter argues that the rhetoric of security has persisted in Central Europe because it has acquired cultural connotations. Insecurity has metamorphosed into something that is based on culture and identity rather than threat. Security policies therefore no longer depend on an external threat for legitimation but only on allegiance to "Western identity" and "Western values."

The civilizational narrative makes security simultaneously vaguer and more fundamental. Like culture, (in)security is at the same time nowhere and everywhere. The whole of social life becomes available for securitization. The cultural framework functions not as a cast-iron framework but as a flexible enabling tool. It does not suppress debate completely; rather it channels debate into the civilizational framework. The Huntingtonian logic of political debates does not necessarily indicate the presence of vehement anti-Russian sentiment among the elites or the population. It rather forms the glue that links security and geopolitics to culture and identity, and holds that complex at the center of political debate. It denies the ambiguous and hybrid nature of identity. It also enables political actors to discredit any argument, person, or political group simply by assigning them "Eastern," "Russian," or "Byzantine" characteristics. The gravity or character of a threat is debated, but the underlying assumptions about cultural tension and conflict are rarely questioned. Within the civilizational narrative, a conception of cultural difference as a security risk emerges *logically*. If European and national security are conceived in terms of a civilizational fault line, then any manifestation of Orthodox civilization can *only* be conceived as a problem. It is ultimately cultural differences that are the source of insecurity. One does not have to be a Russophobe; most of those who speak about the essence of Russian identity do not regard themselves as such. Securitization happens at an earlier point, when security is tied to a reified concept of identity. The significance of the civilizational narrative lies less in what it explicitly prescribes than in what it implicitly enables.

Sovereignty for Security?

The enormous hardships that have been imposed . . . by the transition from central planning and state ownership to market-based economies make it difficult, if not impossible, for governments to win popular support on the basis of the material benefits they can deliver. The declaration of "sovereignty," the establishment of cultural supremacy, or even the threat of military action are promises more easily delivered than an improvement in the standard of living. Moreover, such acts strengthen the state's power far more effectively than efforts to institutionalize civil liberties . . .

Steven Burg, 1996[1]

Europe and Homeland

The sovereignty of the nation-state is a prominent theme in Central European political debates, especially debates on European integration. Throughout the region, a key argument for membership in the EU and NATO was that such membership would provide the accession states with security guarantees and thereby protect their sovereignty. A key argument against EU membership—NATO was left out of that one— was that it would reduce the security of the Central European states by eroding their sovereignty. Both pro-and contra-EU arguments firmly link security and sovereignty. Such bundling of the two concepts was not unique to Central Europe, but it was especially visible there. Sovereignty pooling was and is a particularly sensitive issue in the region because the political struggles of previous decades were based on establishing or strengthening national sovereignty. A particularly defensive ethos toward national sovereignty is deeply rooted in the political cultures of this former buffer zone, and narratives of Europeanization have to compete with entrenched imaginaries of nation-building and national exceptionalism.[2] In the words of Vladimir Tismaneanu, "for reasons which are both psychological and cultural, many politicians and intellectuals in east-central Europe have reservations about the supranational, cosmopolitan globalized vision of the European Union."[3] The Polish Euroskeptics' slogan, "Independence Before Interdependence" is indicative of these reservations.

This chapter examines the workings of the conceptual bundle of sovereignty and security. My question is not how European integration affects the sovereignty of the Central European states or how that effect is popularly perceived. The question rather concerns how the concept of sovereignty functions in political debates and how it enables particular territorial conceptions of security. The chapter foregrounds the deeply territorial conceptions of identity and illuminates the geopolitical logic that animates Euroenthusiasm and Euroskepticism in the region. Euroskepticism, I argue, is not a vestige of an earlier nationalist era or an aberration from the new Europeanized identities. Rather, Euroskepticism is an integral part of the production of security and identity in Central Europe.

European integration has always had an uneasy relationship with the various European nationalisms. The claims that EU regulations contradict and undermine national traditions have been used for decades by the left and the right alike.[4] Right-wing populist movements in particular view the EU as a force of top-down globalization and rootless cosmopolitanism, one that erodes the essential links between lands and peoples that is the basis of European identities.[5] As Simone Weil put it in 1942, to be rooted "is perhaps the most important and least recognized need of the human soul."[6] This view is made possible by three widely accepted assumptions about territory: first, that identities are territorially defined; second, that they are internally homogenous and externally distinct; and third, that national identities can be fully contained within a state.[7] These assumptions produce a territorial imaginary of a "horizontal grid of culturally particular units in which a state is authorized to protect the identity of the titular nation."[8] They define states as actors with distinct identities as if they were the equivalents of individual persons. They privilege the relationship between the individual and the state, and they abstract political identity from the myriad of other relationships in which political identity operates. The result is a desocialized view of the state that implies an essentially transcendental persona making itself. This view turns sovereign states into naturalized abstract individuals that can then be inscribed with the moral authority of their own personhood.[9] Within this territorial imaginary, cultural differences within the nation-state—for example, cultural minorities—logically emerge as a security problem.[10]

Europeanization as a process in which economic, political, and cultural processes are shaped by the norms and standards of the EU fits uneasily with this territorial imaginary.[11] Although the nation-state maintains a decisive role in matters of justice and home affairs, including immigration, citizenship, and minority rights, EU regulations play an important role in *how* the nation-state regulates these issues. This role cannot be easily measured, but according to the *Economist*, over 50 percent of national legislation in the member states is framed in Brussels.[12] Furthermore, legislative change is not the only or even the primary mechanism of Europeanization. The process involves more than the technical transplantation of EU standards and procedures; it also transforms economic, political, and social processes. It not only regulates behavioral and policy outcomes but also reshapes the processes by which subject positions are produced. Europeanization is ultimately a process of the production of subjects.[13]

This subject-producing effect was felt especially in the most recent round of enlargement, in part due to the marked power differentials between the member and the accession states. The speedy adoption of EU standards led the Central European electorates and even the political elites to feel that they had lost control over legislative change. While the elites unwaveringly supported EU accession, the general populations were more ambivalent. On the one hand, support for a foreign policy of "return to the West" was exceptionally high. Foreign policy goals were never a topic of intense domestic debate, and domestic constraints on foreign and security policies were weak. On the other hand, problems did arise when foreign policy goals necessitated revisions in domestic legislation on sensitive issues like minority rights.[14] Throughout Central Europe, initial euphoria gave way to a more complex picture in which support was mixed with apathy and disillusionment. Vaclav Havel observed in 2001 that:

> Today's talk about identity and sovereignty is often rather gloomy. Both are allegedly endangered: by an EU that wishes to assimilate "us" as much as possible; by the European Commission with its standards; by NATO, the International Monetary Fund and the World Bank; by the United Nations; by foreign capital; by Western ideologies; by Eastern mafias; by American influence; by Asian or African immigration; and by God knows what else.[15]

The president of Latvia, Vaira Vike-Freiberga, highlighted a similar air of discontent in 2005. "On the streets of some countries we see increasing disillusionment, social tensions, intolerance and a return to nationalistic tendencies. More and more people are reverting to their nation-state as the lynchpin of their identity."[16]

This disillusionment, and the Euroskepticism it engenders, often does not represent a clearly articulated opposition to European integration as such, but rather a broader distrust of national governments and market reforms. Polling data indicate that although concerns over sovereignty and culture play a part in Euroskepticism, they rank well below prices, jobs, and other bread-and-butter issues.[17] Poll numbers are fickle and sometimes contradictory, however, and do not necessarily reflect the political weight of the notion of national sovereignty. For example, the very same Eurobarometer poll that states in one section that only 12 percent of Central European voters associate the EU with the loss of cultural identity, reports in another section that 27 percent of these very same voters fear the loss of their national identity and culture within the EU.[18] Furthermore, EU membership has not necessarily decreased, but in some cases increased identification with the nation. The percentage of those citizens of the accession states who identified themselves only with their nationality increased by 12 percent between the fall of 2003 and the spring of 2004, from 36 to 48 percent 2004.[19] Such different numbers, sometimes within the same poll, exemplify the amorphousness of the concept of sovereignty. Regardless of whether the majority of the electorate "really" fears the loss of national sovereignty, Euroskeptic arguments are often articulated through the trope of national sovereignty and culture. Sovereignty becomes the rhetorical touchstone for expressing discontent and frustration with national governments, the EU, and the West more generally. It enables the malcontents to selectively cast the EU as another Soviet Union of sorts, with the principal difference being that prescriptions come from Brussels rather than from Moscow.[20] As an Estonian official casually put it, "The EU is just another empire. We are going from one empire to another."[21] The EU is presented as an imposition of global (Americanized) pop culture and globalized hybridity on nation-states that still need to strengthen their sovereignty and national identity.[22] This cultural conception of sovereignty enables hyperbolic arguments about values and culture. A telling example is the Slovak Parliament's decision in 2002 to adopt a special declaration aimed at preserving the country's sovereignty in regard to such "traditional values" as opposition to abortion, euthanasia, or same-sex marriages. The Polish prime minister, Jaroslaw Kazynski, likewise made sovereignty an important theme of his first statements as the head of government in 2006. Poland, he proclaimed, "will demand full sovereignty in moral matters." [23] Ironically, such issues as abortion or same-sex marriage are largely in the domain of the nation-state anyway.[24]

The political purchase of the concept of sovereignty is especially visible in the sphere of minority rights. This is so in part because of extensive Western monitoring of the rights of Central Europe's ethnic minorities throughout the 1990s. According to the European Commission's data from 1999, minorities account for 44 percent of the population of Latvia, 38 percent of Estonia, 20 percent in Lithuania, 18 percent in Slovakia, 14 percent in Bulgaria and 13 percent in Romania.[25] The Organization for Security and Co-operation in Europe (OSCE), the Council of Europe (CE), and the EU all have directly or indirectly monitored minority rights in the CE and made recommendations for amending national laws. In several Central European countries, including the Czech Republic, Slovakia, Hungary, Estonia, and Latvia, the EU and the OSCE played substantial role in the design and implementation of citizenship and minority rights laws.[26] True, the OSCE does not so much undermine state policies as it supports and legitimizes the authority of the state. It is an intergovernmental organization whose primary concern is the stability of the state system. It conducts its business through silent diplomacy with national governments, silent in order to avoid embarrassing the governments and to prevent the media from sensationalizing sensitive issues. The OSCE's pressure on Central European states has been political rather than legal, based on the promise of EU membership rather than international law.[27]

Notwithstanding its state-centric mission, however, the OSCE was undoubtedly an important player in the management of minority-state relations in Central Europe. The accession states' desire to be seen as legitimate actors in the international arena was a powerful incentive in policy-making and provided domestic actors with a platform from which to demand legislative change or better implementation of existing laws.[28] The following observation by Rudolf Cheme, a former Czechoslovak, and later Slovak, ambassador to Hungary, illustrates the perceived link between minority rights and European or pro-EU credentials in the minds of policy-makers too:

> Around the treaty [The Hungarian-Slovak Treaty on Good Neighbourly Relations and Friendly Cooperation] a certain myth developed: One who is for it is pro-European while one who is against it is anti-European. At the same time, the treaty pleased neither the oppositional socialists nor the liberals, nor the Christian democrats; they recognized it as bad, as dangerous

for Slovakia. But in the face of the spread of this myth, the oppositional parties had no choice. Gritting their teeth, they voted for ratification (with the exception of a portion of socialists)[29]

As I will show in the context of Estonia, minority rights can become a kind of marketing tool whereby the accession states seek to showcase their European credentials.

Whether the Western gaze did substantially change the identities of national actors is another matter. Some observers argue that Europeanization has affected not only policy but also notions of (sovereign) nation- and statehood. Others note that internationalizing these traditionally domestic issues can result in legislative amendments that do not in fact reflect a change in popular attitudes. This process can lead to "displays of tolerance without the real thing."[30] It can furthermore feed the perception in the accession states that they are obliged to choose between legislation they deem important to protect their culture on the one hand and legislation that complies with EU standards on the other. This perception in turn has fueled resentment against the EU and enabled Euroskeptics to selectively frame the union as a national security threat.[31] Central European Euroskepticism thus highlights the disjuncture between the rhetoric of "returning to Europe" and the equally strong ethnic conceptions of state- and nationhood. The concept of national and state sovereignty became the lynchpin by which this disjuncture is played out in the public sphere. Its importance lies less in its legal content than in its political utility. This utility results from the concept of sovereignty being tied to national security and national identity in political debates.

From One Empire to Another? Sovereignty in Estonia

At yet another parliamentary discussion of the OSCE-recommended amendments to Estonia's citizenship laws in November 1998, Jüri Adams, a member of the parliament's Constitutional Affairs Committee, explained how his committee processed such amendments. The committee first considered the recommendations made by the OSCE High Commissioner on National Minorities, Max van der Stoehl, and drafted changes to Estonia's laws on this basis. It then faxed or e-mailed the proposed changes to van der Stoehl, and this process sometimes led to several rounds of corrections and negotiations. Only after van der Stoehl's office had approved the proposed amendments did the committee forward them for parliamentary discussion. Adams noted sarcastically that he had never anticipated that the parliament of a sovereign country would adopt legislation in this way.[32]

Adams's sarcasm illustrates the widespread discontent in Estonia over the pronounced influence of international and supranational organizations, especially the OSCE and the EU, on Estonia's citizenship and minority rights legislation. When Estonia applied for EU membership in 1995 and became the first former Soviet republic to be invited to accession negotiations in 1998, it was becoming a state while also becoming a member of the EU. Virtually every domestic policy issue became a foreign affairs issue as well. When presenting unpopular legislative amendments to the parliament, government officials routinely invoked the need to harmonize Estonian legislation with the EU. The Ministry of Foreign Affairs became a key player in domestic policy-making. Sovereignty was institutionalized while simultaneously delegated to the EU. Similar processes have taken place throughout Central Europe, but they were more rapid in Estonia.

Estonia's official policy as well as much of the debate among elites has been unequivocally pro-EU throughout the post-Soviet era. Popular opinion, however, started to waver as membership became a realistic option in the late 1990s. Throughout the accession negotiations, support for EU membership in Estonia was among the lowest in the candidate countries.[33] The portion of the electorate who said that they would vote for EU accession in a referendum declined from 44 percent in 1995 to 26 percent in 1998, although it subsequently rose again to 46 percent by 2000 and then hovered around 50 percent throughout the early 2000's.[34] On the eve of the accession referendum in September 2003, Estonia was once again among the most skeptical accession states, with fewer than 50 percent of voters supporting accession.[35] Sovereignty was not the only concern but it was an important one. Approximately 40 percent of voters said that Estonia's independence would be worse off inside the EU than outside. Furthermore, the loss of sovereignty was a principal concern for those who said that they would either vote against EU accession in a referendum or would not vote at all.[36] Pollsters explain this finding as the result of Estonians' apprehension of joining another union so shortly after gaining freedom from the Soviet version. Although the referendum finally passed with 67 percent of the 63 percent of eligible voters who participated voting in favor of accession (33 percent voted against it), state and national sovereignty have remained high-profile issues in political debates.[37] As elsewhere in Central Europe, Euroskeptic arguments do not necessarily reflect a deeply held opposition to European integration or the EU. In many cases, they rather represent a political strategy selectively deployed for short-term political goals. It is an effective strategy, however, and we therefore need to understand how it works.

As elsewhere in Central Europe, sovereignty was a key trope in both Euroenthusiastic and Euroskeptic arguments in Estonia.[38] The mostly pro-EU political elites presented EU membership as a way to secure Estonia's sovereignty by strengthening its security. Andres Tarand, chairman of the parliament's Foreign Affairs Committee, stressed in 2001 that EU membership provides the irreversible guarantees for Estonia's independence, language, and culture that Estonia *cannot obtain in any other way*.[39] The EU is framed as a necessary condition for the continuation of the Estonian state, not only as an option for the sovereign state but also as a prerequisite for state sovereignty.[40] The Euroskeptic arguments are no less grand. They indeed start with Estonia's constitution. The inalienable sovereignty of the Estonian state is a central pillar of that document. Paragraph 1 of the constitution states that that the independence and sovereignty of the Estonian state are timeless and inalienable.[41] The paragraph was designed specifically in reference to the Soviet annexation of Estonia in 1940. On August 6 of that year, a Soviet-installed government formally declared that Estonia would "join" the Soviet Union. Paragraph 1 of the 1991 Constitution was designed explicitly to rule out such a scenario. It makes it unconstitutional for the Estonian government to enter into a treaty that jeopardizes the country's sovereignty.[42] Euroskeptic arguments cite Paragraph 1 as clear evidence that EU accession is unconstitutional. The symbol §1 appears in the center of the opening page of the Estonian Euroskeptics' home page.[43] During the referendum campaigns, the Euroskeptics wore T-shirts with the §1 symbol.[44]

The constitutional emphasis on sovereignty is so important that a high-level expert committee convened by the Ministry of Justice in 1995 to analyze the constitutional impact of EU accession devoted a whole chapter of its report to Paragraph 1. The committee starts by explaining that sovereignty is a more important concept in the Estonian constitution than in many other European constitutions. It elaborates that the principle of independence means that the Republic of Estonia must continue to exist as a state, while the principle of sovereignty means that Estonia as a sovereign state may not subjugate itself to the laws of any other state or institution. Estonia may integrate with international organizations and ratify international treaties, as these are an inseparable part of a sovereign state. It must not, however, accede into such supranational institutions as the EU because in that case Estonia would permanently transfer its sovereignty to EU law (*acquis communautaire*).[45] The committee concluded that the Estonian constitution does not allow membership in the EU because accession would violate the principle of inalienable independence and sovereignty. The point of the report was not a political statement against the EU, but a clearly defined legal position. The committee left the door open to constitutional changes, but it also reconfirmed and reinforced the central position of sovereignty in Estonian political debates.

Ethnic Sovereignty

Underneath the legal arguments, the dynamic that animates the pro- and contra-EU evocations of sovereignty is cultural. Weaving together legal, geopolitical, and cultural arguments, it is premised on the special relationship of the ethnically defined Estonian nation with Estonian territory. It exemplifies the territorial imaginary on which the securitization of state sovereignty is based. To understand how this dynamic works, we must start with the Estonian constitution once again. The preamble of the constitution states that guaranteeing the preservation of the Estonian nation [*rahvus*] and culture is the primary responsibility of the Estonian state because the state has been founded on the principle of national self-determination.[46] Although the constitution defines "the people of Estonia" [*Eesti rahvas*] as the subject of sovereignty, the constitutionally codified linkage between the Estonian nation and the Estonian state is invoked in political debates to mean that the nation is the ultimate subject of sovereignty in the Estonian nation-state.[47] The authority and legitimacy of the Estonian state is thereby grounded in the nation. The continuation of the nation is the central mission of the state and the sovereignty of the state is the existential prerequisite for the survival of the nation. Through this nexus between the state and the nation, sovereignty is constructed not only, and not primarily, through the political category of the state, but also through the cultural category of the nation.[48] Furthermore, the Estonian state is construed in even more specific terms as the expression of the Estonian ethnos, or nation in the ethnic sense. Although the Estonian term *rahvus* is usually translated into English as "nation"/"nationality" in the sense of a civic political community, *rahvus* in Estonian political debates customarily refers to an ethnic group. The more context-sensitive translation of the term *rahvus* would be "ethnos/ethnicity." Indeed the English term nationality refers not to citizenship but to ethnic background in Estonia.[49] The state's primary responsibility therefore is, in more precise terms, to ensure the continuation of the Estonian ethnos.[50] It is the undivided sovereignty of not simply the state or nation but of the ethnos that is cast as the prerequisite for the survival of the state and the ethnos itself.

The primacy of the ethnos as the subject of sovereignty (and security) is reinforced through assumptions and claims about territorial roots, homeland, and indigenous culture. The status of "the oldest nation in Europe," one that has occupied its territory for seven thousand years, is a fundamental pillar of such claims.[51] Even a primary school textbook from 1994 emphasizes that: "There are few peoples in Europe, whose direct descendants have lived in the same territory for so long."[52] In this argument, the long-term settlement of Estonians on Estonian territory gives ethnic Estonians special moral authority regarding Estonian territory. That authority is not a formal legal entitlement but a more nebulous yet deeper-running cultural one.[53] Conversely, the state must nurture the roots of the Estonian nation in Estonian soil. Any erosion of the special relationship between the two poses a security risk to the Estonian state. The *Estonian Human Development Report* contends that it is the responsibility of the nation-state to ensure "that the cultural environment is shaped by the ethnos [*sic*] that founded the nation-state."[54]

This contention makes ethnicity and, by extension, the rights and responsibilities of ethnic minorities a security issue. Ethnic composition is indeed often the first issue mentioned in analyses of contemporary Estonia. I will not review the voluminous literature in depth, but the contours of the usual narrative are worth sketching.[55] In 1934, the last census before Estonia was illegally annexed by the Soviet Union in 1940 reported that about 88 percent of the country's population was ethnic Estonian. The remaining 12 percent included Russians (8.2 percent), Germans (1.5 percent), and members of various other ethnic groups. During the Soviet occupations of 1940–41 and 1945–91, Estonia experienced mass emigrations and deportations as well as an influx of non-Estonians—mostly ethnic Russians, Ukrainians, and Belorussians—from other parts of the Soviet Union. As a result, the country underwent a significant demographic shift. By the last Soviet census, which was taken in 1989, the proportion of ethnic Estonians in the country's population had decreased to 65 percent. The northeastern part of Estonia was predominantly Russian-speaking, and the capital city of Tallinn was about 50 percent Russian-speaking. This demographic shift and the Russification policies of the Soviet Union fueled intense concerns and existential angst among ethnic Estonians about the survival of their culture and language. Upon the reestablishment of Estonia's independence, the affirmation of the ethnos and ethnic homeland metamorphosed from a move of resistance to a virtually unexamined foundation of political arguments. Jaan Kaplinski, one of the very few critics of that foundation, said fittingly in 1999 that "Estonia is not simply a state. Estonia is a state in which one must believe. Estonia is simultaneously a state and a state religion."[56]

The legal framework on which the Republic of Estonia was reestablished in 1991 codified the link between the state and the ethnic majority. In legal terms, the Republic of Estonia that established its sovereignty in 1991 is the restored Republic of Estonia that existed *de facto* from 1918 to 1940 and *de jure*, represented by a government in exile, from 1940 to 1991. That republic was reestablished in 1991 after having been illegally held in abeyance for over fifty years. Because the Soviet annexation of Estonia was illegal according to international law, the Estonian Soviet Socialist Republic had no standing—it was indeed never recognized by several western countries, most notably the United States. Directly following this restitutionist logic, only citizens of the Republic as it had existed in 1938 as well as their descendants were eligible for automatic citizenship in the restored Republic of Estonia. This stipulation meant that although Estonian citizenship is not based on ethnicity in legal terms, in actual effect, the citizenry of the restored state was overwhelmingly ethnic Estonian. All others, regardless of how long they or their parents had lived in Estonia, could obtain Estonian citizenship only through naturalization. In legal terms, they were classified as immigrants according to international law because they had crossed an international border when they moved to Estonia. Consequently, most Russian speakers—nearly half a million people (494,000 individuals)—were rendered stateless in 1992 when Estonia restored the 1938 citizenship law. They could continue living in Estonia, but they were not eligible for automatic citizenship.[57] They were rendered stateless since the Soviet Union no longer existed and they did not qualify for Estonian citizenship. As Estonian residents, they could opt for Russian citizenship because the Russian Federation had assumed the legal responsibilities of the Soviet Union, or they could seek naturalization in Estonia. The latter, however, has been a slow process. The number of persons naturalized declined from 20,000 a year between 1994 and 1996 to 3,425 in 2000.[58] By 2000, nearly a decade after the reestablishment of independence, about 12.4 percent of Estonia's legal residents (approximately 175,000 individuals) were still stateless, according to the Citizenship and Migration Board.[59] The situation has changed very little since that year. The number of stateless persons, or "persons with undetermined citizenship" in official terminology, decreased from 12.4 percent of the population in 2000 to 12 percent in 2003.[60] Citizenship is crucial in this context because in the European legal tradition, most states consider only citizens of the state as members of national minorities.[61] In Estonia, then, stateless Russian speakers are effectively a part of the Russian-speaking linguistic minority but are not considered members of a national minority under international law.[62] Estonian citizenship is not necessarily a marker of Estonianness either. The Non-Estonians Integration Foundation (NEIF), a government-funded NGO responsible for coordinating and managing integration-related programs, states that the "vast majority" of the country's non-Estonian population are not "fully integrated into the mainstream of Estonian political, social, and cultural life."[63] This statement refers to nearly a third of the country's population. The logic of citizenship is cultural and geopolitical, premised on the link between individual identity and national territory. Alexander Astrov, a Russian-Estonian academic, observed with soft irony in 2005 that any Russian-speaker who studies the Estonian constitution recognizes immediately that it is not the rule of law that is the basic principle of the Estonian state. Rather, the Russian-speaker finds that he has no other choice but to put himself at the service of the cultural principle codified in the preamble of the constitution—preservation of the Estonian culture.[64]

Although the West fully accepted the legal logic of restitution, it paid anxious attention to the treatment of Russian speakers in Estonia. The OSCE had a mission in Estonia from 1992 until 2002, and the European Commission, among others, keenly followed its work. This issue was all the more sensitive because Russia consistently maintained that the civil rights of Russian-speakers were being violated or at least jeopardized (although such accusations were not corroborated by any international organization). As a consequence, Estonia has been under considerable international pressure from East and West alike to liberalize its citizenship and language laws, to naturalize non-Estonians, and to thereby integrate them into Estonian society. The government appointed a minister without portfolio for ethnic affairs in 1997 and founded NEIF the following year.[65] In 2000, the parliament approved the *Integration in Estonian Society 2000–2007* document, the principal policy framework of ethnic integration. The West gave substantial financial support to the enterprise. Foreign funds, mostly from the EU Phare program, the Nordic countries, Canada, the United Kingdom and the Open Estonia Foundation, constituted over one-half (53 percent) of the funds allocated for ethnic integration in Estonia in 2000.[66] It is important to note that what motivates this aid is not just concern for the Russian speakers, but also, and at least as importantly, concern for the stability of the interstate system. This fact was not lost on the Estonians. One official wryly noted that "Sweden is, of course, interested in [ethnic integration] because they don't want our Russians showing up on their shores."[67] As Gregory Feldman points out, Western monitoring of Estonia's ethnic integration is itself based on the territorial imaginary of an interstate system based on distinct cultures.[68]

In response to Western recommendations, Estonia has taken a number of steps to facilitate ethnic integration. It adopted all of the over 30 legal amendments recommended by the OSCE, and has complied with European legal norms on citizenship and minority rights at least since the late 1990s.[69] Various monitoring missions, as well as European Commission reports compiled throughout the accession negotiations, found no systematic infringement of minority rights in Estonia. Pressure from the OSCE was not legal but political; it relied on the carrot of EU membership rather than the stick of international law—which gives considerable freedom to sovereign nation-states anyway.[70] Ethnic relations within Estonia are peaceful, and most residents of the country characterize them as positive.[71] In 2005, only 16 percent of ethnic Estonians considered Russian speakers a threat to the survival of the Estonian nation.[72] Most harbor a "relaxed attitude" toward Russian speakers.[73] Over the 1990s, the keywords of minority rights debates changed from decolonization and purification to integration and multiculturalism.[74] Elena Jurado noted that by the late 1990s, calls for improved minority education in Estonia no longer evoked the negative implications of a different course of action ("what the EU might do"), but instead relied on moral arguments about the proper treatment of minorities. "The motivations of Estonian decision-makers," Jurado said, "experienced a full circle, evolving from ethnocentric (identity) considerations to strategic ones and back to identity considerations (based on multiculturalism)".[75] Indeed, Katrin Saks, the minister of ethnic integration, summarized ethnic integration in terms of "one state, several cultures."[76] In recognition of this transition, and in preparation for the EU's invitation to membership, the OSCE closed its mission in Estonia in 2002. That event, together with Estonia's subsequent accession into the EU and NATO, effectively removed ethnic integration from the political radar screen. It is not a major issue as of 2007 in Estonia's foreign relations, in the policy priorities of the government, or in public political debate. Some observers argue that the Russian minority is now included in the Estonian collective Self. Indeed, as I argued in the previous chapter, explicit Russophobia no longer has the political cachet it enjoyed in the early 1990s. Even many ethnic Estonians are getting increasingly tired of the the stuffy ethnic state and its archaic self-conceptions. For these individuals, "The question isn't just the Russians. The question is whether there will still be oxygen to breathe" in Estonia.[77] Alongside a certain opening of Estonian identity narratives toward more inclusive conceptions of

Estonianness, however, the territorial imaginary of a cultural homeland has become normalized and further entrenched in Estonian political life. The notion that the Estonian state protects the "Estonian cultural realm" has become solidified.[78] This solidification was made possible through linking the concept of cultural homeland to national security.

Notwithstanding the eventual withdrawal of Western monitoring, ethnic integration was a key foreign and domestic policy issue in the preaccession period. It enjoyed the spotlight because it was considered necessary for Estonia's accession into the EU. One commentator aptly noted in 1997 that the newly appointed minister of ethnic integration was a key person in taking Estonia into Europe.[79] The political groups that favor ethnic integration—both Estonian liberals and the ethnic Russian parties—likewise link ethnic integration and EU accession. They argue that membership in the EU strengthens Estonia's sovereignty because it ensures the state's external security and internal stability. As Ando Leps, a center-left member of parliament (MP), put it in 1998, changes in the citizenship law are issues of "first, whether we want to accede into the EU, and second, and this is most important, whether we want to accede into NATO".[80] The President's Academic Council, an advisory body of sixteen prominent academics, journalists, and cultural figures, made a similar point in a public letter to the Estonian people in 1998. More liberal citizenship policies, the Council said, will have to be introduced as a result of pressure from large states anyway. To preclude such impositions and to avoid conflicts with "European humanistic principles," Estonia should liberalize its citizenship and language laws.[81] Government officials likewise depicted integration not in terms of submission to crude Western pressure but in terms of Estonia's demonstration of its true European identity and values. Foreign Minister Ilves's remarks during a parliamentary discussion of election laws offer a brilliant example of this. Questioning plans to erase the legal clause stipulating that candidates for local office must command the Estonian language, Villu Reiljan, an MP from the opposition, asked rhetorically which OSCE document makes such a demand of Estonia. Foreign Minister Ilves responded,

> The OSCE does not have such a document. Simply, it is very clear, they have said so to us, that if we fulfill the so-called guidelines that still remain, the mission will leave. This was confirmed publicly in a television interview last week by [OSCE] Representative Doris Hertram (sic.), and I think that this was confirmed yesterday also in an interview by the representative of the European Union Mrs. Bonnier, Ambassador of Sweden. . . .

[T]he decision is whether we wish to be European or not. The question is not that if we do this, the OSCE mission will leave, which it will do, but this is not the issue. The question is that if we all want to go into Europe, if we want to be NATO members, we have to follow common values, we must adopt them. If we do not, nobody is going to force us, nobody is going to say that you must do so. They are saying to us that if you want to be with us, this is one condition, but you do not have to be with us.[82]

Answering a similar frustrated question from another MP a few minutes later, Ilves put it in more figurative—and explicitly civilizational—terms; "I repeat once again that nobody is making prescriptions, that we ourselves decide whether we want to be Europeans or we want to be in Byzantium."[83]

Geographies of Threats to Sovereignty

The controversies over Western recommendations regarding citizenship and minority rights have clear geographical and territorial underpinnings. The recommendations are controversial for two reasons: first, because they are seen as eroding the link between the Estonian nation and the Estonian homeland' second, because they are seen as serving the interests of Russia. In both cases, individuals are presumed to be essentially cultural beings aligned with a particular homeland.[84] The *Integration in Estonian Society 2000–2007* document indeed starts from the premise that there are two distinct societies in Estonia—Estonian and non-Estonian—and that this "may become dangerous both socially and from the point of view of security policy."[85] Crucially, Russian speakers are identified as a security problem not because of their actions but because of their lack of roots in Estonia.[86] It is their presumed rootlessness that arguably makes them less able or even unable to fully accept Estonian culture or be loyal to the Estonian state. This line of argumentation was especially visible in the early 1990s, when the non-Estonian population was frequently represented as a fifth column that Russia could use to destabilize Estonia.[87] Likewise in later years, the fifth-column metaphor popped up whenever Russian speakers expressed opinions that differed from those of ethnic Estonians on such issues as NATO accession or NATO's 1999 action in Kosovo.[88] Mart Nutt, an MP and one of the principal authors of Estonia's aliens and citizenship legislation, invoked Huntington by calling it "a ruthless fact" that a Russian considers a Serb as a brother while an Estonian will remain an alien. "Blood is thicker than water," Nutt continued, "and this holds true also for the Russian who, according to some sociologists, has been integrated." Jüri

Saar, a professor of psychology at the Academy of State Defense, echoes this essentialist argument when he claims that:

> civilizational conflict exists as a reality in all of these persons here who still have to adapt to new values and norms. I think that it would be extremely short-sighted and silly to speak of Estonia as a territory with two peoples who speak different languagess but whose civilizational background is both unnecessary and impossible to distinguish.[89]

Most mainstream arguments certainly do not insinuate the actual presence of a fifth column in Estonia. They still assume the existence of distinctive Estonian and non-Estonian mentalities, however. This assumption logically centers the debates on whether and how quickly an "Estonian mindset" can take root among non-Estonians and ensure their loyalty to the Estonian state.[90] In the words of a high school history textbook from 1999, among the "aliens" who had settled in Estonia, "there were and are numerous nomads who have lost their nation, language, roots, and homeland, and who are, on top of it, even proud of it."[91] Without the Estonian mindset, this line of reasoning continues, non-Estonians will ultimately remain a source of instability in the Estonian state. Perhaps the clearest example of the assumption of distinct Estonian and Russian mentalities with definite geopolitical implications is provided by a sociological survey, designed by a team of prominent sociologists in 1997, that had a "loyalty index" as a measure of such a mindset.[92] The index was based on thirteen indicators derived from thirteen yes/no questions. These questions concerned non-Estonians' optimism regarding Estonia's future development, support for Estonia's accession to the EU and NATO, cultural similarity to Estonians, and whether or not non-Estonian respondents felt they had been offended on the grounds of ethnicity in Estonia. Those who reported that they were optimistic regarding Estonia's future development, supported Estonia's membership in the EU and NATO, considered themselves culturally similar to Estonians, and felt that they had never been offended on the grounds of ethnicity in Estonia, scored high on the loyalty index. Those who answered otherwise were classified as more or less hostile to Estonia. As a part of non-Estonians' loyalty to Estonia, the survey also measured their attitudes toward Russia. Attitudes toward Russia were measured by questions as to whether relations between Estonians and Russians are (or are not) exacerbated by Russia's "continuous attacks" against Estonia, and whether Russia is (or is not) a "dangerous neighbor for Estonia."[93] According to that classification, a mere 17 percent of non-Estonians are "loyal Estonian-minded." A whole 19 percent, on the other hand, are hostile to Estonia ("Russia-minded separatists"), with the remaining 64 percent falling somewhere in between. The study concluded that a substantial portion of non-Estonians "do not consider Russia a potential threat" and therefore "accept and consider normal Russia's potential malevolent actions against Estonia." [94]

This conceptual framework identifies Estonia as an insecure state that must protect its sovereignty to preserve its culture. Commenting on the government's decision to simplify the naturalization of children of stateless residents, Sirje Endre and Mart Laar, both prominent politicians (the latter served as prime minister twice in the 1990s), stressed that changes in citizenship policy could have an "unpredictable" impact on the "psychology of the indigenous people." "It is unlikely that Estonian society will calmly look at the violations of its rights," they said, because "Estonia is too small to accept the new citizenry that would emerge overnight." [95] Peeter Vihalemm and Marju Lauristin, eminent sociologists, likewise argue that multiculturalism in Estonia can work only on the basis of "Estonian cultural dominant." This is so because:

> for small nations . . . the multinational solution could be a source of future permanent insecurity. Even when they have their own states, the small nations remain vulnerable to the political and cultural expansionism of big nations, especially if they have enclaves of these big nations on their own territory. [96]

The argument proceeds in terms of the special relationship between ethnic Estonians and the Estonian territory rather than in terms of Russia or Russian speakers. Yet Russia is a key part of the argument. Western recommendations on minority rights are cast as potential security threats in part because they are seen as a kind of Trojan horse for the Russian threat. [97] Within this narrative, Estonia's sovereignty is threatened not only by Western institutions themselves but also by Russia, which, having understood that Estonia unconditionally follows all recommendations from the West, puts pressure on Estonia through Western institutions. These institutions either misunderstand Estonia's "critical demographic situation," or practice a malevolent form of *Realpolitik* in which Estonia is sacrificed in order to secure amiable relations with Russia. The OSCE might, in this argument, turn into "a weapon against Estonia" if larger states want to use small states as scapegoats to distract attention from their own problems with minority rights. [98] Mart Nutt said that "OSCE recommendations" should be read as "Russia's demands." [99] "If we in our euroflattery campaign do not consider our security," Nutt continues, "then accepting Estonia might bring such security risk to the

EU that it might abandon us."[100] The sanctions imposed by EU member states against Austria in 2000 after the right-wing anti-immigrant party led by Jörg Haider joined the governing coalition were promptly used in Euroskeptic arguments as an example of the EU's constraining the sovereignty of the member states.[101] "It reminded me of the Prague Spring," said Robert Lepikson, a prominent Euroskeptic. "Only Russian tanks were missing."[102]

The arguments described above do not emanate from the right-wing fringe; they come from the center-right (by Western European standards) mainstream that has dominated Estonian politics since the reestablishment of independence. Within that mainstream, both liberals and conservatives share the assumption that the national majority must maintain a privileged position in the state in order to protect itself.[103] Political elites countered the popular concerns over sovereignty by a two-pronged argument. They first stressed that Estonia is already a part of Europe and that Estonians are fundamentally Western (i.e. not eastern) already, so that no loss of sovereignty will occur. Second, they invoked the Russian threat, essentially threatening the Euroskeptics with Russia. The refrain of the pro-EU arguments was that "a 'no' to the EU is a 'yes' to Russia"[104]. "If we reject the EU," said Jüri Luik, a leading politician and Estonia's ambassador to the United States at the time, "we'll quietly but surely sink toward Russia."[105] Unwillingness to relinquish some sovereignty to the EU, concurred Marko Mölder, a prominent Russia-watcher, would be "catastrophic to the long-term survival of the state."[106] Estonia would in fact not give up its sovereignty, said Rain Maruste, a constitutional and human-rights judge, but rather make a "final decision between civilizations." The only reason not to accede to the EU, Maruste continued, is "if we prefer remaining alone and belonging to the eastern civilizational sphere. Then we could contently twist off the cork of the moonshine bottle, cut up the cheap sausage and send the whole eurothing to hell."[107]

An ironic twist here is that because of the overwhelming emphasis on security, those who advocate the necessity of liberalizing citizenship and language laws necessarily invoke threats to Estonia's sovereignty to legitimize their arguments. They effectively threaten Estonia with Western displeasure, which would put Estonia into the Russian sphere of influence. In so doing, they frame their arguments in terms of the Russian threat and thus reinforce the nationalists' emphasis on maximal sovereignty of the nation-state to withstand that threat. The Russian threat then becomes crucial for Estonia's pursuits of EU membership, as the elimination of that threat would also eliminate the urgency for European integration. One commentator tellingly noted that "Estonians' decision on the future Euroreferendum depends on Russia." It may well take poor relations with Russia, she noted, to increase Estonians' enthusiasm for the EU.[108] Because fears of the loss of sovereignty are construed principally through the Russian threat, these fears are also necessary for pro-EU arguments.

Conclusion: Cultural Sovereignty

The logic of explanation that links culture, sovereignty, and security in the ways that I have detailed here is not peculiar to Estonia or Central Europe. Its influence extends far beyond the issues of citizesnhip and minority rights. State sovereignty and the right of the national majority to a privileged relationship with the state are conventional and banal pan-European assumptions.[109] They logically lead to securitizing culture as an issue that must remain under the jurisdiction of the nation-state. In Central Europe, it is often not just the state and not even the nation, but the ethnos, that functions as the subject of sovereignty in political debates. It is also Europe. Sovereignty is to be protected in part because national sovereignty protects the state's Europeanness. It retains the links among territory, culture, and politics that are seen as a hallmark of European states. The spatial imaginary underpinning the uses of sovereignty is simultaneously a traditional nationalist one and also a civilizational one.

The securitization of sovereignty in Central Europe therefore does not represent simply a generalized fear of supranationalism that would subside once the electorates are "educated" about the benefits of EU membership. It is not a vestige of a bygone nationalist era. Neither is it merely an empty trope of elite manipulation uttered to cover the lack of substantive arguments. Rather, it is central to the construction of security. It is principally through the notion of sovereignty that the concept of security serves not only to oppose but also to promote European integration. Whereas in nationalist arguments, any deviation from the absolute undivided sovereignty of the nation-state is a loss, in liberal arguments it may be a gain in terms of security. Conversely, it is largely through security discourses that the concept of sovereignty enters public debate. In other words, sovereignty is important because it is threatened. Claims about threats to sovereignty therefore do not constrain but form the preconditions for state sovereignty in Central Europe. Such particular issues as minority rights enter and leave the political spotlight, but the cultural conception of sovereignty retains its mobilizing effect. Continued debates around the rights of ethnic and sexual minorities in Central Europe indicate the continued salience of the cultural-territorial conception of security in the region.

5

Cultural Geopolitics and Cultured Geopoliticians

Nowhere else in modern times has there developed such a deep belief in the well-nigh magical power of the word and of cultural symbols in general.

Zygmunt Bauman, 1987[1]

[Lennart] Meri . . . embodies in his person the concentrate of Europe. Writer and polyglot, he knows the history of our continent better than anyone else. When this tall, thin, and elegant man reminds us (in French) that Estonia has been "the eastern border of Europe" for ten centuries already . . . one wonders how was it possible to ignore such an obvious fact for so many years.

Le Figaro *interview with Lennart Meri, 1997*[2]

Zygmunt Bauman's analysis of Central European intellectuals and *Le Figaro's* interview with one of them—Estonia's two-term President Lennart Meri—illustrate the key role of intellectuals in the geopolitical scripting of Central Europe. Bauman stresses the role of cultural and intellectual capital in Central European politics, and *Le Figaro* illustrates the effectiveness of that capital in putting Central Europe onto Western mental maps.

Accounts of Central Europe, especially those penned in the 1990s, often mention the intellectual aura of the region's political elites. They usually cite it as an exotic flavor before proceeding to a more "serious" analysis. This chapter focuses on that intellectualism. It examines how the cultural and moral capital of Central European elites works in geopolitical discourses; in particular, the ways in which it consolidates and legitimizes the notion that geopolitics is fundamentally a matter of culture and identity. The chapter goes beyond analyzing the framing of culture in political debates to investigate those who do the framing. In so doing, it provides a more "peopled" account of the production of geopolitics and clarifies the function of human agency in this process. The chapter does not depart from the noninstrumentalist approach to power, in which individual agency is not external to discourse but is constituted within it. My analysis is not a "what great men think" account of geopolitics. It rather examines the political and cultural resources that make particular geopolitical claims effective. I maintain that in order to understand the success of the grand statements about centuries-old struggles and belongings in Central Europe, we must consider how these statements are legitimized by the cultural capital of the speakers. My argument is not about causality (cultural capital causes actions) but about conditions of possibility (cultural capital makes certain actions politically legitimate).

The chapter will proceed by clarifying the relationship between intellectuals and foreign policy in Central Europe. To anchor my analysis in a particular context and to do justice to the colorful personalities that I study here, the chapter will then focus on one individual, Lennart Meri (1929–2006). An erudite writer and filmmaker, Meri was highly successful in putting Estonia onto Western maps. He did it especially through the strategic use of his spectacular erudition and artistic accomplishments. Meri was the master shaman of Estonian foreign policy, and his evocative speeches offer rich insights into the formidable role of cultural capital in the making of cultural geopolitics.

Cultured Politicians

Although the practices of the modern state are highly diffuse and dispersed, security and foreign policy are relatively concentrated realms. The practices of specialized elites in specific places in state structures have a disproportionate influence on these realms. These practices are not homogenous, and neither are they necessarily accepted by the population at large. They do, however, define the terms and establish the parameters of public debate. They furnish the claims of geographical certainty and scientific truth on which security discourses rely.[3] They create the intellectual and cultural climate in which particular foreign and security policies come to be seen as necessary, feasible, culturally authentic, and morally right.[4] At the same time, foreign policy is also firmly anchored in popular narratives of geography and identity. Even though official policy-making relies on "expert" knowledge, the categories of Self and Other, community and identity, are formed on the popular level.[5] The influence of foreign policy elites is derived in large measure from resources beyond their formal positions, from the ways in which these statements fit into broader notions of identity, culture, and geopolitics. In today's media-saturated political climate, these elites include a wide array of commentators and pundits far beyond officials in foreign and defense ministries. Analyses of intellectuals of statecraft must therefore closely consider the broader societal context in which geopolitical discourses are produced. We must move beyond elite statements and closely examine the societal context that makes their statements legitimate and effective. We must capture the dual character of geopolitics as at once both highly elitist and firmly populist. My focus on intellectuals of statecraft—the politicians, intellectuals and pundits who regularly comment on, participate in, and influence the activities of statecraft—is intended to do that. I recognize the concentration of legitimate expertise in a few select loci like foreign ministries, but I also investigate the ways in which that expertise draws from and depends on popular conceptions of geopolitics.[6]

Central Europe is widely conceived both internally and externally as a region in which culture and identity are especially important influences on politics. In Milan Kundera's influential formulation, "Central Europe. . . . is a culture or a fate."[7] Such elevated rhetoric about culture, identity, and European values is not new in the region. Central European intellectuals have a long tradition of political engagement.[8] At least since the nineteenth century, they have regarded themselves as a secular group of "chosen ones" with a political and moral mission, rather than a simple status group or class fraction.[9] In the words of Garton Ash:

> In the "abnormal" conditions which have actually been normality for much of Central Europe over much of the last two centuries, intellectuals have felt been called upon, or have felt themselves called upon, to take roles that they did not take in the West . . . . The writer as priest, prophet, resistance writer, and substitute politician.[10]

These are not simply highly educated professionals, but more specifically, individuals with backgrounds in the humanities and arts, who are often among the most luminous public figures in the region. During the Cold War, the realm of culture was an important site of resistance to what was widely regarded as an imposed non-Western political and cultural system.[11] Indeed, the very concept of Central Europe, as it emerged in the 1980s, was produced by Central Europe's writers and philosophers.[12] Intellectuals played a key role in bringing down the socialist regimes, and Central Europe's postsocialist political elites include many of them. Their "pastoral moral authority" within civil society and their ability to narrate a compelling story of deep-rooted memory and identity were especially important in a time of rapid societal change and geopolitical vertigo.[13] As the conduct of politics was defined first and foremost in terms of the pursuit and defense of certain values rather than the mastery of certain procedures, the moral capital based on distance from the former regime was a key requirement for success.[14] Katherine Verdery notes that culture and politics were so closely intertwined, and elites moved back and forth between intellectual and political work with such frequency, that the roles of politician and intellectual were indistinguishable.[15] Being an outsider to formal politics—an intellectual rather than a politician, a former dissident, a returning émigré, or even a relatively young person supposedly less tainted by collaboration with the toppled regime—was an important source of legitimacy. Cultural capital remained an important source of power, prestige, and privilege in postsocialist societies.[16] Anatol Lieven coined the term "cultural politicians" to denote the new political elites with backgrounds in the arts and humanities.[17] Literary ability, imaginative use of language, profound knowledge of "high" culture were and still are a key part of their popular appeal. The region's political parties, parliament, and public administration were "packed by PhDs, reputed scholars, and university graduates who, lacking the skills of decision making, bargaining, negotiating and conflict resolution, were forced to be involved in bitter ideological battles over symbols and values."[18] Yet it would be a mistake to dismiss these intellectuals as simply inept politicians. Their cultural arguments made possible the distinctive cultural flavor of Central European geopolitics.

Following Bauman and Verdery, I identify Central European intellectuals by the kinds of claims and resources they employ in social struggles—claims to a monopoly on knowledge, competence and truth.[19] Intellectuals are individuals who make claims to knowledge and moral values, and who gain some degree of social recognition for these claims. They occupy a site that is privileged in forming and transmitting discourses. Their claims to "culture," "science," "truth," and related values function as boundary-maintenance practices by which certain segments of the privileged classes set themselves off from the rest of society, including—perhaps especially—other segments of the elite. Cultural capital here refers to the intellectuals' legitimacy to speak about culture and identity—legitimacy conferred by their status as intellectuals. This kind of cultural capital can be converted into political capital, but it is initially based on distance from formal politics. This definition of cultural capital differs slightly from Pierre Bourdieu's conceptualization in his seminal *Distinction*.[20] It accentuates a humanistic background and artistic credentials, and it emphasizes the practices that explicitly defend prior definitions of cultural value. Although all highly educated professionals are in a privileged position to have their version of "culture" accepted by broad segments of the society, my argument here focuses on the kind of cultural capital derived from legitimacy to speak in the name of national culture. I thus omit individuals with backgrounds in fields commonly associated with high-level state positions—political science and international relations, economics, and law—as well as engineering and the natural sciences.[21] Although these individuals undoubtedly possess high cultural capital in Bourdieu's terminology, they do not exercise legitimacy in the sphere of culture and identity in the way that writers or historians do. In Central Europe, it is cultural capital in this narrower sense that constitutes the important albeit often overlooked resource in geopolitical discourses.[22]

Examples of leading politicians with arts and humanities backgrounds—which in many cases include earned doctoral degrees—abound throughout the region. Playwright Vaclav Havel, who served two terms as the president of the Czech Republic, is perhaps the most prominent of them. Other such literary politicians include the writer Arpad Göncz, who served two terms as President of Hungary;[23] the historian, writer, and filmmaker Lennart Meri, who served as Estonia's foreign minister and then president for two terms, and the professor of musicology, Vytautas Landsbergis, who was a leading politician in Lithuania in the early 1990s. Bulgaria's former two-term President Zhelyu Zhelev—a former dissident—holds a doctorate in philosophy; that country's president as of August 2006 is Georgi Parvanov, who holds a doctorate in history; and the president of Latvia, Vaira Vike-Freiberga, has a PhD in psychology. On the ministerial level, Jaroslav Šedivy, Mihai-Razvan Ungureanu, Bronislaw Geremek, and Wladyslaw Bartoszewski, former foreign ministers of the Czech Republic, Romania, and Poland (the last two) respectively, all hold doctorates in history. Dmitrij Rupel, who served twice as foreign minister of Slovenia, holds a PhD in sociology. Andrei Gabriel Plesu and Sandra Kalniete, the former foreign ministers of Romania and Latvia respectively, are art historians by training—and

Plesu holds a doctorate in history. These examples are limited to the upper levels of the foreign policy establishment, excluding important institutions like parliaments and other government structures as well as the media and academia. When assessing the importance of intellectuals and intellectual capital, however, we need to consider that these individuals bring in close associates: former academic colleagues, dissidents, and fellow students.[24] In Estonia in the 1990s, for example, the foreign ministry was staffed with (youngish) historians to the extent that it raised grumbles even in that highly corporatist country. The influence of a background in the humanities therefore percolates through the country's foreign policy apparatus. It is not icing on the cake, so to speak; it is rather an ingredient in the cake itself, namely the practice of foreign policy.

Many of these cultural politicians had established public reputations as intellectuals before they were elected or appointed to high offices. In a context in which politics is highly individualized, their popularity frequently rests on their prepolitical personal image rather than their formal political position. Their speeches use philosophical ruminations and evocative language, mixing references to high culture and scholarly works with traditional arguments about geopolitics and national interest. Their literary and academic credentials are emphasized in interviews, speeches, and biographical blurbs.[25] They see themselves as intellectuals and emphasize their distance from traditional interstate power politics. Havel stated unambiguously in 1992 that his foreign policy derived from his dissident past. "Just as our 'dissidence' was anchored in . . . moral ground," he says, "so the spirit of or foreign policy should grow and, more important, continue to grow from it."[26] True, Havel and other former dissidents had to adjust their idealist beliefs and bohemian casualness; as a result, their policies represented pragmatic politics as well as ethical convictions.[27] Their public image at home and (especially) abroad, however, continued to revolve around their (dissident) intellectual past. When Estonia's defense minister, Jaak Joerüüt, was addressed as "Mr. Minister" by his secretary during one of his first interviews after taking office, Joerüüt—a former writer—swiftly corrected her: "What minister? A writer!"[28] In many cases, it is precisely the intellectuals' backgrounds in the arts and humanities and their *lack* of experience in statecraft that have bolstered their legitimacy as experts on statecraft.

The "cultured" intellectualism of Central European political elites has affected not only the domestic legitimation but also the conduct of their states' foreign policy. Especially in the early 1990s, Westerners were sometimes baffled by Central Europe's "disorganized" political scene, in which the movers and shakers were not trained politicians and managers but a seemingly *ad hoc* group of bearded intellectuals (and they were mostly men) who were better at philosophical pontification than diplomatic etiquette.[29] Observers of the Prague castle of the early Havel era noted that Frank Zappa and Lou Reed were welcome consultants there, "pranksters whizzed through the castle corridors on children's scooters," and the décor of the Communist state was replaced by works of modern art.[30] It was not only Central Europe but also the West that experienced geopolitical vertigo and needed maps to make sense of erstwhile enemies. The Western media needed representative heroes of postsocialist countries in order to present these countries in immediately recognizable form, with "progressive" movements opposing "reactionary" forces.[31] The cultural politicians often fit the bill. They were admired by representatives of Western media not simply by virtue of their position, but also for their presumed ability as formerly dissident intellectuals to truthfully articulate the identities and interests of the Central European countries. The cultural capital of these politicians functioned to authenticate their statements. Vaclav Havel is an excellent example of this authentification effect. Analyses of Central Europe often rely heavily on statements by Havel, not only because of his former formal position as a head of state, but also because of his moral authority as a former dissident. After Havel's famous speech to a joint session of the U. S. Congress in 1990, the *Washington Post* wrote that Havel had "provided stunning evidence that his country, far from being only an inheritor—let alone borrower—of the European intellectual tradition, is a prime source of it."[32] The writer Milan Kundera and the publisher Adam Michnik are other good examples of cultural figures whose political success is based in part on their intellectual credentials. In both cases, it is precisely their positions as intellectuals that give them the license to make geopolitical claims. The cultural politicians thus played a key role in putting Central Europe on the mental maps of Westerners.[33]

It is easy to romanticize these intellectuals, to elevate them as agents of resistance to traditional geopolitics. In this romanticized view, intellectuals speak truth to power. In the post-Cold War era, however, Central European intellectuals for the most part do not bear out their romanticized image. They have moved from the politics of resistance to the hallways of power. The point here is not to eulogize them, although their individual accomplishments are certainly impressive. It is rather to place in the foreground some nuances that are normally delegated into footnotes or excluded altogether. True, politics in Central Europe has certainly been professionalized since the early 1990s; the leading politicians are now less likely to come from intellectual and artistic circles. The democratic reforms of the post-Cold War era have undermined the special political status of intellectuals. Professionalization has been the order of the day for well over a decade. As state subsidies to higher education, scholarly research, and the arts are dwindling, the economic and social capital of the intellectuals is diminishing as well. This trend has created disillusionment and even bitterness among the humanistic elites. "There was this myth among dissidents in communist times that ordinary Czechs were secretly reading Proust," says Vladimir Zelezny, a former Czech dissident who has since turned to private television business. In reality, Zelezny continues, the Czechs aren't interested in Proust. They are "beer-drinking, working-class Catholics, rather like Belgians but less cultured."[34] Zelezny's fellow intellectuals seem to agree: many have left formal politics altogether, and there is a heavy dose of nostalgia for the heady days of the late 1980s and early 1990s[35] As Barbara Falk points out, however, "The myth of the dissidents re-marginalizing themselves through their political ineptitude or annoying moral superiority is just that, a myth."[36] Cultural politicians have had an enormous impact on Central Europe's political climate, and they continue to wield influence. They created the master narratives of EU and NATO accession. They put into place the vocabulary of culture and geopolitics that has framed foreign and security policies in Central Europe throughout the post-Cold war era. They put postsocialist countries on Western mental maps and interpreted foreign affairs to the domestic audiences throughout the 1990s. These were intellectuals in a very direct sense who made the return of geopolitics possible by participating in its conduct and legitimation. Even today, Central Europe's foreign ministries and foreign representations are staffed with appointees from the 1990s. It is still possible to undermine political opponents by implying that their educational background is inferior. Influential commentators on foreign policy still include many literary and academic figures with no background in international affairs and little experience in formal politics.[37] In the small corporatist states, intellectuals and artistic networks still matter. As recently as the NATO Prague summit in 2002, Western military experts shared the lavish banquets with former dissidents.[38] We still cannot understand Central European political debate without close attention to the past and present roles of intellectuals.

". . . Which Brings Out the Long-lost Historian in Me": The Cultivated Geopolitics of Lennart Meri

The French weekly *La Vie* interviewed the president of Estonia, Lennart Meri, in his home in late 1998. The article starts by describing the milieu:

> Outside, in the vast shimmering light, the horizon is silent and still: the frozen Baltic Sea . . . Estonian President Lennart Meri receives us . . . at a remote retreat—perched between the forest, the sea, and the sky—where he likes to withdraw for weekends. Gazing at the sea, he notes the proximity of Finland and Sweden. Polite manners and aristocratic charm are complemented by refined humour. And moments of silence that dot speech full of lyric detours. It belongs to an intellectual, who has long been a writer.[39]

Interviews with Meri often start with a discussion of his artistic accomplishments. The son of an Estonian diplomat, Meri started his education between the two world wars in the elite private schools of Berlin and Paris. Given his father's position in the First Republic, the family was deported to Siberia upon the Soviet annexation of Estonia in 1940—a fact that Meri occasionally mentions in his speeches. After the family's return in 1946, Meri studied history and made a career as a writer and filmmaker. His books and films are based mostly on ethnographic material about Finno-Ugric peoples that he collected during extensive travels in Siberia, from the Kola Peninsula to the Bering Strait. Meri's 1976 book *Silver White*, a poetic reconstruction of the history of the Finno-Ugric tribes, became a bestseller in Estonia and Finland, while his 1977 film *The Winds of the Milky Way* won a silver medal at the New York Film Festival.[40] Meri became active in the Estonian independence movement in the late 1980s. He served as the Republic's first foreign minister, then as Ambassador to Finland, and from 1992 to 2000, as its two-term president. When Meri died in March 2006, the *Economist* said that he will be remembered not only for his political accomplishments but also for his "unusually amiable and cultivated" manners.[41]

Meri's public persona was that of an erudite, witty, and eccentric intellectual with a "unique skill" of making history vivid and exciting.[42] Photos of Meri in his exotic filmmaking trips or writing his speeches late at night in a cloud of cigarette smoke were an integral part of his image. Meri's interviewers typically delighted in his "infectious" intellectual curiosity.[43] The *Economist* described him as "formidably well read" and "fluently caustic and charming in five languages."[44] In the political scene in which "former Communists and members of the new Right (often of course one and the same) often vie with each other in the crude and provincial narrowness of their attitudes," Meri represented "an older and nobler past."[45] Meri flaunted his reading, frequently combining historical vignettes with ruminations on themes ranging from cultural anthropology and geography through etymology and semantics to genetics and physics. He presented his arguments as "theses" and wrapped up his speeches with a "bouquet" of conclusions. He wove in touching and often funny details of his interactions with the little-known Finno-Ugric peoples of Siberia. He cited Molière and de Maupassant to French audiences and Martin Luther to German ones. Meri's self-description as a "long-lost historian" that opens this section comes from a speech given in Finland, in which Meri, speaking on European integration, quoted extensively from the diary of Juho Paasikivi, one of Finland's leading politicians throughout the first half of the twentieth century.[46]

Meri's audacity and "very great" personal charm did much to raise Estonia's profile in the West; Anatol Lieven's account of his 1991 interview with Meri, who was Estonia's foreign minister at the time, gives a good sense of both. The interviewee "quickly overran the fifteen minute appointment allocated by his staff."

> An hour later, the Minister was cheerfully recounting the story of an expedition to Yakutia in which he ended up eating his own horse. He then whisked me off in his official car to an exhibition of Russian culture in Estonia under the First republic, a subject in which he is conspicuously knowledgeable.[47]

Meri took a similarly casual approach during his first encounter with U.S. President George H. W. Bush. He walked up to Bush during a summit meeting of the Commission for Security and Cooperation in Europe in Helsinki in 1992, when Meri was Estonia's ambassador to Finland. Addressing President Bush as "George," Meri informed him that his administration had neither a Russian nor a Baltic policy. An American diplomat later confided to Lieven that "before that, Bush hardly remembered that the Balts existed. Now, thanks to Meri, he is furious with them." Meri's appreciation of Russian high culture and his ability to quote Aleksandr Pushkin—Russia's beloved poet—"at the slightest provocation" eased diplomatic exchanges with Russia even when relations between the two countries were cool at best.[48] Peeter Olesk, a prominent literary scholar and a personal friend of Meri, described Western audiences' surprise at encounters with Estonia's President:

> The foreign audience . . . is expecting another reformed member of the Central European nomenklatura, one who speaks in broken English, reads his speech, complains about the sorry fate of his state and its current economic difficulties, opines that the world owes his country something, and finally—to put it figuratively—asks for a ten [rouble note].
>
> But everything turns out differently. Meri is late. Sometimes a lot. His arrival causes a commotion because he differs from the former apparatchiks

almost anthropologically. When he starts speaking, it becomes apparent that he is fluent in several languages. He does not repeat the lame statements, common in such situations, about democracy, tolerance, minorities, multiculturalism, European Union, etc., etc., but he offers a message that is carefully crafted specifically for these people specifically for today.[49]

Ronald Asmus, the deputy assistant secretary of state for European affairs in the second Clinton administration, said that he came to view Meri, with whom he had extensive personal contact, "as a kind of Havel of the north."[50]

Throughout his presidency, Meri put his artistic language and spectacular breadth of reading into the service of a compelling geopolitical narrative of Estonia's long-established links with Western Europe. His opening remarks at a concert devoted to Estonian classical music in Munich in 1993 give a sense of his skillful interweaving of history, culture, and geopolitics.

> We have defended our identity with arms, but even more with traditions . . . [We] have defended our identity primarily in order to remain in Europe, to remain Europeans, and to help Europe defend the phenomenon of Europe—the diversity of her cultures. . . . We opened our concert season, if my memory does not fail me, on 3 June 1583 when the City of Tallinn hired a musician for 52 thalers, 114 poods of rye, and 10 cubits of wool cloth to offer professional music to the city dwellers year round.[51]

In Meri's geopolitical imaginary, Estonia's participation in Europe's economic system dates from the late Roman Empire. It was the Roman historian Tacitus, Meri pointed out, who mentioned Estonia in the forty-fifth chapter of his Germania in 98 A.D. already. "The closeness of Estonia and Europe," Meri said, "did not start then; it had achieved such dimensions already that it required documentation. Tacitus did not discover the Northern Dimension. He was the first chronicler of a functioning northern dimension."[52]

As many of Meri's foreign audiences knew little else about Estonia other than its location next to Russia, or even "in" Russia, his speeches were often designed to overwrite that image with well-crafted examples. "Do you know," he asked *Politique International*, a French magazine, that "the first Catholic bishop assigned to the lands of Estonia in the twelfth century, Monsieur Fulco, was from France? . . . The city of Tallinn had a long correspondence with Martin Luther." "We staged Molière during the lifetime of Molière." It was a Frenchman, Léouzon Le Duc, who wrote in 1855 that "Estonia's national independence is only a question of time."

"Our European identity is so obvious," Meri said to *Politique International*, "that it saddens me to hear that Estonia has made a decision to belong to Europe. We are not an aimlessly floating island that tries to hook itself to something. We have belonged to Europe since the Roman Empire. We in fact bear witness to Europe's return to lands from which it had withdrawn before World War II." To speak of Russian influence on Estonian culture, Meri noted, is the same as tracing such influence in Finland or Schleswig-Holstein, which also belonged to the Romanovs at one time.[53]

Meri's mapping of Estonia relied on the notion of culture and values. Toasting the secretary general of NATO, Javier Solana, in 1996, he emphasized that "For Estonia, unlike Otto von Bismarck, Europe is not a mere geographical concept. For Estonia, Europe means an endlessly expanding process of shared values. Let it be compared to Fred Hoyl's expanding universe."[54] When asked for clues to Estonia's successful integration with the EU—"the best pupil in the Baltic class or perhaps even among all candidate countries" as *La Vie* put it—Meri invoked geography:

> Do not forget the key role of the Baltic Sea. Since prehistoric times through the era of Hanseatic trade to today, the Baltic Sea has always been a uniting factor. During the Soviet times, the narrowness of the Gulf of Finland never let us to be cut off from the contemporary world.[55]

In another speech on Estonia's rapid economic transformation, Meri used his knowledge of the indigenous peoples of Siberia. Large countries are slow by nature, he implied, while small countries can adapt quickly. Estonia, he said, is fast and flexible like an Eskimo's kayak. While a tanker ship needs sixteen nautical miles to turn, he told his American audience, a kayak can turn on the spot.[56]

As a part of adding Estonia to the mental picture of European values and civilization, Meri erased Russia from that same picture. Estonia's eastern border, he stressed in his 1993 Independence Day address, has "through centuries been the eastern border of the European legal system, and will so remain . . . . Our border is the border of European values."[57] In a speech to the Center for Strategic and International Studies in Washington, D.C., Meri employed anthropology to challenge the argument that admitting the Baltic states would put NATO into the "ancient" Russian sphere of influence.

> Friends, nothing is further from the truth. I am personally deeply interested in cultural anthropology and have for years made films about Finno-Ugric people on the vast Eurasian continent. This interest emerged when I was deported to Siberia as a child. I can confirm that Estonians have lived

on their corner of the Baltic Sea for 5,000 years and in historical terms, Russia has put down its foot only for a few passing moments . . . Moreover, it is the end of the twentieth century now. Unless I am deeply mistaken, talking now about spheres of influence, historic territories, and other such things is at least anachronistic and politically profoundly perverse.[58]

When Meri spoke of Siberian rivers, he did not obtain the image from books but rather from firsthand knowledge of the mighty waterways of Siberia. The mention of the emperor's axe was all the more effective because it did not come from a Russophobe; quite the contrary, Meri's deep appreciation of Russian high culture was well known. When asked by *Die Welt* about solutions to the conflict in Chechnya—a subject on which Estonia has been among the staunchest critics of Russia—Meri evoked just that high culture. The problem, he noted, is that neither Russian conservatives nor Western politicians understand the Chechens' historical quest for independence. These groups "share a dislike of Griboedov, Pushkin, Lermontov, and Tolstoy [nineteenth-century Russian writers], who wrote with great sympathy about Chechens' struggle for self determination in the nineteenth century already."[59]

Meri's intellectual flair worked better for foreign than for domestic audiences. At home, many considered Meri erratic, paternalistic, and snobbish. One of his popular presidential nicknames was Lennart I. He was elected by the parliament rather than by popular vote. Even his critics, however, conceded that Meri's diplomacy was very effective. *Le Vie* reported that interviewees in Tallinn's cafes characterized Meri as "our Vaclav Havel," "our moral authority," and "our best export article." Tõnu Õnnepalu, a writer, corroborated *La Vie's* assessment, saying that Meri "gave depth and grasp to the history of the people, discovering its roots and its mythology." Rein Veidemann, a fellow cultural politician, put the matter in equally strong terms, stating that Meri represented "an ideal symbiosis" of national pride and European culture.[60] "We cannot help it," Veidemann said even during Meri's tenure in office, "that Meri is more a myth than a person already. He is a part of the Estonia-myth, and *Estonia is a part of Meri as a myth*."[61] Veidemann's statement is hyperbolic, of course, but it pinpoints the pivotal role of individuals like Meri in the scripting of geopolitics. The story of the post-Cold War Estonia is indeed indistinguishable from Lennart Meri as the master shaman of that story.

Intellectuals and Statecraft

The cultural narratives of geopolitics do not emerge mystically from some kind of national psyche. They are made possible by the cultural resources employed by specific individuals in select nodes of political debate. In Central Europe, the cultural capital of the region's humanistic intellectuals is central to these resources. The realm of culture has high political purchase because it has been put into the center of political debate by intellectuals of statecraft who derive their authority from that realm. This kind of cultural capital operates differently from that of their Western counterparts like Henry Kissinger, Condoleezza Rice, or Samuel Huntington. True, the authority that comes with the more traditional credentials of statecraft, such as training in international relations, is important in Central Europe as well. In addition to this specialized professional knowledge, however, the Central European scene also favors the kind of cultural capital linked to a background in the arts or humanities. That kind of capital works through "artsy" ruminations, lyric detours, and scattered vignettes about philosophy and literature rather than through the vocabulary of state and strategy. It is less authoritative than the traditional language of statecraft, but is equally effective. It is indeed more effective at times, because its political effect is coated with the speaker's emotional language and humanistic credentials. To quote *Le Figaro* again, "When this tall, thin, and elegant man reminds us (in French) that Estonia has been 'the eastern border of Europe' for ten centuries already . . . one wonders how was it possible to ignore such an obvious fact for so many years."[62] Although the cultural capital highlighted here is not the sole reason for the success of cultural geopolitics in Central Europe, it is nonetheless a very important reason meriting close attention. Making cultural capital visible is important for destabilizing and overcoming the exotic image of Central Europe as a particularly "cultural" place and foregrounding the processes that underlie cultural geopolitics.

6

The Ritual of Listening
to Foreigners

I had recorded what I later would call the Poles' *ritual of listening to foreigners*, in which the naïve but self-assured Westerner would encounter the shrewd Pole, who deftly charmed his guest while revealing nothing of what he truly thought . . . Many Poles had mastered the sophisticated art of impressing westerners while maneuvering to get what they wanted.

Janine Wedel, 2001[1]

A friend of mine . . . once said that an author coming from Central and Eastern Europe to the West will find an ideal literary situation there. He can narrate fantastic stories about his country, about his part of the continent, can sell them as nothing but the truth and can then retire comfortably because his stories will never be verified. This is possible, on the one hand, because the public thinks that just about anything could indeed happen here; on the other hand, because these countries remind the West more of literary fiction than of actually existing states.

Andrzej Stasiuk, 2003[2]

Janine Wedel pinpoints the widespread assumption in Western accounts of EU and NATO enlargement that Central European states, eager to integrate with the EU and NATO, closely follow Western policy recommendations. Accounts of security in particular presume that as these states seek security from the West, they gradually adopt Western conceptions of security. This chapter destabilizes the convenient imagery of obliging Central Europeans. It underscores that the geopolitical scripting of Central Europe involves more than Westerners analyzing the region; it also involves local intellectuals of statecraft providing the data for these analyses. Taking a hint from the above remarks by Wedel and Stasiuk, I suggest that Central Europeans' apparent receptiveness is illusory. The region's intellectuals of statecraft do not simply adopt but also construct the Central Europe that emerges from Western security studies. Listening to foreigners is not simply a process of learning; it is also a strategy of telling Westerners what they want to hear so as to attract or retain Western attention and money. These are indeed Western stereotypes of Central Europe as "not yet" fully mature or European that allow, and indeed necessitate, that strategy. It is because of Western ignorance that Central European intellectuals of statecraft can assume the role of expert interpreters and storytellers.

To flesh out the role of Central European intellectuals of statecraft in shaping security discourses in the region, this chapter accentuates not the information that Western experts gather, but rather the data that their Central European colleagues supply. In particular, I highlight the practice of Central European elites impressing and flattering their Western counterparts while discreetly guiding these Westerners' interpretations of Central Europe. In so doing, I throw light on the citational practices through which geopolitics is constructed—the circulation and reverberation of assumptions, claims, and modes of analysis between Western and Central European intellectuals of statecraft. It is in such reverberation that some conceptions of security are coated with ever more layers of legitimacy while others are gradually marginalized. My account is based on secondary data, specifically on a close and careful rereading of the primary and secondary accounts of the interaction between Western and Central European intellectuals of statecraft in the 1990s. Such accounts have become numerous in recent years, as present and former high government officials like to reminisce about the challenging and exhilarating times of the early 1990s. My rereading does not reveal any previously unknown information. It rather highlights details about settings, contexts, and personal idiosyncrasies that have been there all along, so obvious as to be almost invisible.

The chapter substantiates the work that destabilizes the gently patronizing framework of a one-way power relationship in which security is fashioned in the power centers—Washington and Brussels—and then imprinted on the margins—Central Europe.[3] It accentuates the ways in which security is constructed on the margins of the Western security establishment. True, intellectuals of statecraft from the core states have disproportionate influence over the writing of geopolitics and security. Their accounts of Central Europe carry more clout than local ones and are more easily accessible internationally. They have the power to represent global politics in particular ways and make peripheral states adopt these representations. Western intellectuals of statecraft define the parameters of what qualifies as security or threat, Europe or non-Europe. Central Europeans' power position vis-à-vis the West is weak. Most discursive analyses of geopolitics and security therefore rely empirically on elite representational strategies in the core states. By focusing almost exclusively on the core states, however, these analyses skate over the question of the manner in which intellectuals of statecraft in the relatively peripheral or marginal states participate in security discourses. They thereby tend to strengthen, not weaken, the cliché that geopolitics is written in the concert of great powers and then handed down to the smaller states. To emphasize the agency of Central European intellectuals of statecraft is not to deny the hegemony of the core states, but rather to argue that looking only at the core states is not enough. Local experts do not simply bear witness to the "odious mixture of ignorant goodwill, hypocritical rhetoric and indifference" that has characterized the West's approach to Central Europe.[4] They also use it to their own advantage. This chapter examines how this process operates: *how* particular Western claims are appropriated and used by intellectuals of statecraft in Central Europe. It does not downplay the expertise of Western intellectuals of statecraft; it rather balances the emphasis on the West with a closer attention to Central Europe.

Translators and Transactors

As I have argued in earlier chapters, the neglect of the local context of security discourses is an integral part of transitologist conceptions of societal change in postsocialist Europe. These conceptions assume that it is both desirable and possible to convert Central Europeans into Western ways of thinking.[5] The transition from socialism to a market economy was to change not only processes of production but to also transform persons. It was to make East Europeans more like Westerners, to make them Western subjects. Although there was never one monolithic "Western" approach to Central Europe, Western experts tended to assume that if their Eastern counterparts listened and nodded, they were learning. This assumption was often incorrect, however. Central Europeans sometimes painted a rosy picture of learning to give Westerners a sense that they were being successful and their advice was correct. Alternately, they conjured up grim images of local ineptitude to play to the Westerners' inflated view of their own usefulness.[6] Elizabeth Dunn's study of privatization in Poland gives an especially telling example of such practices. When Alima, a Polish manufacturer of baby food, was sold to the American company Gerber, American managers attempted to make Alima's management and production process similar to Gerber's. The Polish managers of Alima appeared to be acquiring the skills that the Americans bestowed on them. They hosted the Americans very well and made them feel comfortable. "Every meeting was a coffee break, a tea party." The Poles also gave as little information about their own experience and objectives as possible, and indeed routinely misled their American counterparts. They listened to Gerber's directives, "nodding and acquiescing, and then doing whatever they had originally planned on." Two of Alima's directors used to "leave board meetings and go behind their office door and giggle, because [another executive] was piling it on so thick and the Americans were just nodding along. It was either laugh or vomit."[7]

A similar problem of oversimplifying local contexts and local networks plagues security studies. Most accounts of security in Central Europe conceive the matter in terms of a one-way process: produced in Western power centers and imprinted on or adopted by the margins. Both journalistic and academic accounts of Central Europe rest on the assumption of a feeble Central Europe wooing the West in order to gain NATO membership. The following remark illustrates the general tone:

> All know that, notwithstanding the criteria for entry announced at the EU's Copenhagen Summit in 1993, it will not be by [the Central European countries'] own efforts, but by acts of grace in Brussels and Washington that they will be raised to what they perceive to be the twin paradise of EU and NATO membership.[8]

Encounters between Western and Central European politicians and government officials thereby come to be viewed in terms of their "pedagogical component."[9] Central European administrators who come into contact with Western institutions arguably "gradually internalize the values" reflected in their daily operations.[10] Most studies surely recognize that the process is not smooth or linear, but they nonetheless adhere to the notion of learning by socialization. Especially before their membership in the EU and/or NATO, the Central European states were assumed to have little maneuvering space vis-à-vis Western norms, even less than either the member states or such "inescapable outsiders" as Russia.[11] Their elites were merely to bear witness to the transition and to learn the craft from their Western counterparts.

Although Central European experts corroborated Western assessments, however, they did not necessarily follow Western prescriptions.
Changing opinions and identities were certainly among the effects of
their listening to foreigners. There were also other effects, however, like
keeping Western attention and money—including Western research
grants, exchange visits, and other such perks. Because Central European
states depended on Western money and were directly or indirectly monitored by several Western institutions throughout the 1990s, a great deal
of their foreign policy rhetoric was directed to Western audiences.[12] The
stories told to foreign audiences did not necessarily reflect domestic
debate but served as sales strategies. The listening ritual was in part a performance *for* western audiences.[13] The Estonian writer Tõnu Õnnepalu's
reflection of the climate of Western didacticism and Central European
cynicism is telling.

> As a true East European I sat bright-eyed and listened to his outrageous
> ideas about freedom . . . Why not? Especially for the promise of a delicious
> supper in the luxurious ambience of ancient Europe. . . . From govern-
> ments and university professors on to the last paperboy [East Europeans]
> are all ready to listen to wonderful speeches about democracy, equality,
> whatever you please, whatever the customer wishes! As long as he pays.[14]

Intellectuals of statecraft were also the gatekeepers in Western interactions with Central Europe. They were pivotal in interpreting and trans-
lating (figuratively and literally) Central European contexts to the West.
This gatekeeping function is especially prevalent in security studies,
because Western security studies were isolated from Central European
social science circles during the Cold War.[15] These are not simply
Western views, but a very narrow range of Western views that are influential in Central Europe. These views do not present themselves to the
people in the marginal states; they are translated, literally and figuratively, by local intellectuals of statecraft. We must therefore analyze how
some Western views become "state-of-the-art" and other views do not
even reach political debates in the margins. We need to reexamine the
interpretations and translations to bring out the agency of those who
performed them. In so doing, we can offer an account of how particular
articulations from Central Europe came to function as authentic ones.

   There is now an emerging interdisciplinary literature that exposes and
problematizes assumptions of a passively receptive Central Europe.[16] It
shows that the narrative of the learning process was so prevalent in part
because Central Europeans supported it. Their obliging nodding was an
integral part of the "actually existing transition." A great deal of Central

European research that appears in Western journals and the working papers of Western institutions supports the notion that these states still need to learn from the West.[17] The key concepts of transition, such as civil society, return to Europe, Western superiority and Eastern inferiority, would not have persisted without it. Postsocialist transformations thus involve a highly selective appropriation of some parts of Western rhetoric and the rejection of others by specific groups in these states rather than wholesale adoption of Western norms by the candidate states.[18] Janine Wedel's work on transactors is especially useful here. Wedel shows how government officials in Poland and Russia pleased their self-assured Western benefactors while discreetly guiding these benefactors' interpretations of how aid money was spent in the recipient states. These local officials not only swayed the administration of Western aid in the recipient states but also influenced the design of aid programs in the donor states. Their influence was effected through close-knit flexible relationships among a small elite group—whom Wedel calls "transactors"—that included representatives from both donor and recipient states. Transactors were in part the West's own doing. In the West's search for representative heroes of transition, Western journalists and consultants relied on a handful of individuals whom they depicted as particularly competent and reformist. These individuals were promoted largely because of their Western experience, Western dress code and mannerisms, and fluent use of Western rhetoric—an ability to parrot the slogans of "market," "reform," and "democracy," and name recognition by well-credentialed fellow Westerners.[19] They made up the "dream teams" of transition. In both donor and recipient states, these persons became progressively more entrenched in the administration of aid, to the point where they effectively became the only legitimate representatives of each side. They were able to claim privileged access to the "other" side as their key advantage over other groups, and thereby advance their version of the interests of the other side. Both advice and money was thereby channeled to and filtered through these small groups of transactors, while dissenting voices on both sides were marginalized as backward and incompetent.[20]

Huntington's civilizational thesis illustrates a kind of intellectual transactorship in the scripting of geopolitics. His thesis would not be as influential in Central Europe if it were not actively promoted by influential individuals in the region. Conversely, being cited at the putative civilizational fault lines has greatly enhanced the standing of Huntington's thesis in the West itself. It is Havel's observation that "cultural conflicts are increasing and are more dangerous today than at any time in history," that Huntington quotes to substantiate his claims.[21] Huntington situates his argument explicitly in the context of European proclamations. The civilizational thesis, Huntington claims, offers the answer about the borders of Europe that various European intellectuals and political leaders have explicitly endorsed.[22] Conversely, Central European arguments about civilizational borders have been greatly strengthened and legitimized by Huntington's position at the center of the Western security establishment. Huntington offered an easy package of explanation to Central Europeans: they no longer had to convince their Western counterparts of civilizational conflict, they could instead simply refer to Huntington's work. When asked by a Western researcher about the cultural differences between Estonians and Russians, Mart Nutt, a conservative Estonian MP, chuckled and said, "They are well known. In general, it's religion, language, how the individual relates to the state, there are many differences . . . . If you read Huntington, it applies to Estonia."[23] In the West, claims about Central Europeans' "natural" fears of Russia are often accepted as authentic in part because Central European politicians, intellectuals, journalists, and pollsters say that they are to Westerners, and say so over and over again. In order to grasp the prominence of the concept of civilizational clash in Central Europe, one must therefore consider its influence in Western governmental, academic, and intelligence circles *as well as* its high-level promotion in Central Europe. It is through the combined clout and mutually lent legitimacy of Western and local intellectuals of statecraft that the notion of civilizational clash has been given mythical proportions in Central Europe.

The persons who are best positioned to impress Westerners are those with fluent English and extensive Western experience. In the early to mid-1990s, as the Central European states built up or strengthened their foreign ministries and diplomatic corps, returning émigrés were well placed for this role. Among high elected officials, Latvia's president, Vaira Vike-Freiberga; Lithuania's president, Valdas Adamkus; Estonia's president Toomas Hendrik Ilves; and Bulgaria's former prime minister, King Simeon II, are all returned émigrés. There are also numerous émigrés at the ministerial level. The former Latvian ambassador to Washington, Ojars Kalnins, was a public relations executive from Chicago, and Ilves was Estonia's foreign minister before he was elected president in 2006.[24] The former U. S. assistant deputy secretary of state Ronald Asmus tells a story of meeting a man who appeared at the headquarters of the RAND Corporation wearing a Hawaiian shirt and speaking English with a West Coast accent, who turned out to be Lithuania's defense minister. Émigrés were also hired by Western embassies in Central Europe. One could have conceivably had a situation in which a diplomatic meeting between representatives of, say, the United States and Estonia involved two people who were ethnic Estonians, had grown up in the United States, and were fluent in both English and Estonian. Anatol Lieven noted that American embassies in all three Baltic states regularly employed members of the diaspora in the early 1990s. In the domestic politics of the Baltic states, these individuals functioned both as representatives of the United States and as members of the titular nation. According to Lieven, they tended to lapse carelessly into "complete identification" with the Balts. A Western diplomat in Riga remarked to Lieven, "The Western diplomats here generally don't speak Russian and have never worked in Russia. They socialize entirely with Latvians, have Latvian girlfriends, and often seem to be competing to see who can be the biggest Latvian nationalist."[25]

To underscore the agency of Central European intellectuals of statecraft is not to imply the existence of a Central European conspiracy or Central European exceptionalism. It is rather to emphasize that power relationships between Westerners and Central Europeans are *two-way*; that problematizations of security in North America and Western Europe are not only constitutive of security discourses elsewhere, but are also in part constituted by these other discourses. I wish to emphasize that we need to examine closely the "multiple and shifting intersections of power and agency especially visible during moments of social discord."[26] Peter Van Ham is correct in stating that "one of the most challenging tasks of the foreign policy agenda of central European countries has been to *carve out* a place on the mental map of European and American policy-makers."[27] This fact necessitates a precise rethinking of the role of Central European intellectuals of statecraft in the making of geopolitics. If Western policymakers have little understanding of the Central European states, it does matter how these states are carved out *for* their mental maps *by* local intellectuals of statecraft. We need to examine how such broad politically charged categories as security, identity, and geopolitics are problematized and used by different groups in different circumstances. We need to ask not only what images are evoked but also more pointed questions, namely, through what interactions and representational practices these images are woven into daily political practice.

"Those Goody-goody Estonians"

Estonia exemplifies the key role of local intellectuals of statecraft in the scripting of geopolitics especially because it enjoys an image of a particularly successful learner. Estonia was the first Soviet republic to be invited to accession negotiations in 1998. The *Economist* labels it the "most hyped" of all the post-Communist countries of Eastern Europe.[28] The skill of Estonian intellectuals of statecraft is only a small part of that success but, as I will argue below, it is a significant part. The *Economist* characterized the country's "disarmingly candid" two-time foreign minister, Toomas Hendrik Ilves, as one of the most successful foreign ministers in Europe in the late 1990s.[29] President Meri, "charming in five languages," was elected European of the Year in 1998.[30] The two-time prime minister Mart Laar was the only Baltic politician selected among Europe's fifty most influential leaders by *Business Week* in 2001.[31] This is how one high official of the European Commission explains Estonia's success at the Commission to Andres Tarand, a leading Estonian politician:

> You [Estonians] should not become too full of yourselves. You come from you-know-where. But one thing that has especially impressed us and why we chose you from the Baltic states [to start accession negotiations in 1998] was that your people know already how to talk to us, while the Lithuanians don't and the Latvians often don't exist.[32]

In part because of Estonia's "star pupil" image, its small size, and the fact that the Estonian language—a Finno-Ugric tongue very different from the Indo-European languages—seems impenetrable to most foreigners, Western views of the country have tended to be bird's-eye perspectives. The former foreign minister Jüri Luik says that for a small state like Estonia, "its diplomat is often the state's only representative, only sign. The world's decision-makers, be it politicians, businesspeople, or other diplomats, frequently know only one or two Estonians. This is the limit of their knowledge."[33] Especially in the 1990s, Western experts were not accustomed to paying attention to Estonia—and to the Baltic states more generally. Many indeed obtained their information about the Baltics from the Russian-language press.[34] Their opinions of Estonia were often formed on the basis of the "Western" feel of Tallinn's Old Town, which dates from the Hanseatic period, and the Western mannerisms of their Estonian hosts. The managing director of the Saatchi and Saatchi Group for the Baltic states, Ukraine, and Belarus, put it in this apparently well-meaning comment:

> Estonia is like a drive-through zoo where you can look out the window from the safety of your car. If you go to Russia or the Ukraine, you have to climb into the cage with the animals. Estonia provides an environment where it is possible to learn something and yet not get your feet dirty.[35]

In addition to its success-story image, Estonia is interesting also because of the substantial Western monitoring of its postsocialist transition. In the early to mid-1990s, there was considerable international concern about the rights of Estonia's Russian-speaking population, and various intergovernmental organizations and NGOs regularly monitored Estonia's policies in these spheres. Consequently, a great deal of domestic policy-making was directed to Western audiences. Estonia revised its initially inflexible stance toward its Russian-speaking minority and adopted legislative changes in line with OSCE and EU recommendations. At the same time, given the context of intense domestic concern with the country's newly reestablished sovereignty, Estonian politicians also had to be careful to appeal to this popular sentiment. They had to perform a careful balancing act between sufficient nationalism and "bravery" vis-à-vis Russia for domestic audiences and sufficient Russia-neutral multiculturalism for foreign audiences. In sum, then, Estonia offers fresh insights into the construction of security, habitually considered the domain of the powerful, precisely because the country is so small and powerless. As Estonia seems so self-evidently an eager apprentice of the West, it offers a particularly telling example of how local intellectuals participate in the making of the Western norms that they seem to simply adopt.

How to Entertain the Nuncio

The foregoing subtitle is borrowed from Andrei Hvostov, a prominent Estonian columnist. Hvostov used it in a newspaper article to underscore the efforts of Estonian foreign policy professionals to present a favorable image of the country to Western audiences. The phrase also illustrates how these professionals project different narratives of security to (elite) foreign audiences and to (popular) domestic audiences, depending on the expectations of these audiences. Such maneuvering is an integral part of Estonian security discourses, resulting in a discrepancy between (domestic) security debate and actual security behavior, a discrepancy that has been present since the mid-1990s.[36] In order to understand Estonian security discourses, we must understand how this discrepancy works.

In formal political statements, virtually no high-ranking government official has depicted Russia or the Russians as a threat to Estonia since the mid-1990s. Official proclamations construe security as a sphere of democratic values in the new borderless Europe rather than a matter of military defense. They emphasize "constructive engagement" with Russia—this phrase has indeed been the official policy line since 1994.

For foreign audiences, government officials invoke images of the New Europe and vibrant cooperation in the Baltic Sea region. They applaud multiculturalism, allude to rapid ethnic integration, and suggest major improvements in relations with Russia. They frame Estonia as a Nordic upstart and give any threat from Russia a scant mention.[37]

The Ministry of Foreign Affairs is central to this narrative, as it is that ministry in particular that projects this narrative to the domestic arena. The ministry's role was discernible throughout the 1990s, but it became especially visible after Estonia started negotiations for accession to the EU. Yet the position of the ministry or its key professionals on some hot issues, such as Estonian-Russian relations or minority rights, was not necessarily in line with the position of the parliament. For example, a key breakthrough in Estonian-Russian border negotiations took place around 1994, when Estonia abandoned the position that the border must follow the Tartu Peace Treaty of 1920. This breakthrough resulted from "improvisations" by key foreign policy professionals.[38] These professionals, however, did not always coordinate their statements with those issued by the parliament or even the foreign ministry. Thus, when Prime Minister Andres Tarand announced at a press conference in Helsinki in 1994 that Estonia had dropped its insistence on the Tartu Peace Treaty, he did not necessarily have domestic political backing for such a step. Tarand describes the Helsinki press conference in his signature folksy style:

> The Helsinki adventure was entirely improvised. I think that had I tried to touch this topic in the government, I would have gotten nowhere. For especially Pro Patria [a leading nationalist party] was a bit stuck, imprisoned by its own "brave" grassroots. We did not have coordination even with the foreign ministry, except that I knew [foreign minister Raul] Mälk's thinking. At that time, Estonian politics was improvisational anyway. As soon as the Finnish journalist posed the question, I commenced my storytelling. The soil had been hoed and prepared and it all came out spontaneously.[39]

From the mid-1990s onward, Estonia's foreign ministers have also promoted pragmatic policies toward Russia in their editorials, published in national newspapers. Foreign Minister Ilves, for example, reproached Estonian politicians as early as 1997 for the "un-European behavior" of fuelling unconstructive fear of Russia.[40] He insisted that Estonians should abandon the cliché that if someone talks about compromise, it is an immediate threat to Estonia's independence. As I showed in chapter 4, the foreign ministry has been among the strongest supporters of the liberalization of citizenship and language laws, consistently arguing that such liberalization would strengthen Estonia's image as a mature

European country. Even when not taking explicit positions, various foreign ministers, especially Ilves, have emphasized the need to show the West that Estonia subscribes to "Western values." Commenting on an important speech by Ilves at the Humboldt University in Berlin in 2000, Andrei Hvostov praised Ilves' diplomacy:

> Finally, an important rule of salesmanship is to not say what the potential buyers do not want to hear. It is not a good tone to remind western politicians of Huntington's civilizational thesis. When Moscow claims that the expansion of western organizations to the east pushes Russia out of the common European forest, then the East European candidate states should argue the opposite to avoid further complications.
>
> Which is what Ilves did in Berlin. Answering a question about the mood of the nearby bear, he announced calmly that we have no problems with the bear.
>
> Not a word about the bear wanting to eat someone or displaying unpredictable behavior. As if he was talking about a panda. And this is how the European Union came a step closer to us.[41]

While the ministers of foreign affairs conjure images of cooperation in the New Europe, however, the domestic Estonian-language press operates with images of an unstable and immature Russia lapsing back into imperial fantasies as the thaw in Europe is coming to a close.[42] These images commonly invoke Russia as a threat and frame foreign policy as a realm of survival. Estonia's only option in such accounts is to quickly integrate with the EU and NATO, and to subcontract security to these organizations.[43] Even though the EU is seen as an important provider of "soft" security, Estonia ultimately covets the "hard" security provided by NATO.[44] Even as NATO recast itself in cooperative terms, most Estonian were not so interested in the "new" NATO. They much preferred the old NATO, with American military bases on their eastern border.[45] Commenting on the National Security Concept, Aap Neljas, a member of the working group that developed the concept, said that it contains a contradiction between "Euro-Atlantic rhetoric" and the "actual evaluation of risks." He noted that this contradiction is common among NATO candidate states that must work within the rhetoric of NATO while pursuing membership in the alliance. As the National Security Concept is primarily directed toward an international audience, he jokes, those who do not know the Estonian context may not understand that when Estonia says "teddy," it means "bear."[46]

The foreign ministers' Western-directed rhetoric was not always popular at home. Ilves, for example, was hailed internationally as one of the most imaginative Estonian politicians, but was criticized domestically for allegedly directing even the speeches delivered in the Estonian parliament to the foreign diplomats and press rather than to the domestic electorate. Thus, in parliamentary discussions of the National Security Concept—a 2001 document that states that Estonia faces no threat—several MPs paid left-handed compliments to the foreign ministry for having developed a document that pleases the West. Ilves was repeatedly asked to clarify and specify Estonia's security risks, and he repeatedly circumvented these requests.[47] When Ilves reminded the parliament later that year that more liberal language laws would help Estonia's integration into the EU, Uno Laht, an opposition MP, noted that Ilves' remarks "give an impression as if we get responses some European bureaucrat who defends Europe not Estonia."[48] The issue is more complex, however, than a divergence of opinions among Estonian politicians. Whereas Ilves's statements abroad allude to improving relations with Russia, his interviews in the Estonian media express disbelief that Estonia could improve relations with Russia.[49] To use Hvostov's metaphors, while statements to foreign audiences mention no bear, "as if talking about a panda," statements to domestic audiences operate with a dangerously unpredictable bear.

To highlight these incongruities between foreign and domestic as well as formal and informal policy rhetoric is not to treat any of these rhetorical strategies as monolithic, to search for a "true" underlining position, or to imply that Estonia's foreign policy is designed to purposefully mislead any specific audience. I cannot infer and am not interested in any politician's intent. My point rather is that security debates in Estonia do not illustrate a contest between authentic and ready-made positions. They rather function as a malleable discourse in which different images and associations—New Europe, historical legacies, cultural affinities and so on—are deployed flexibly and strategically. The significance of this positioning to different audiences is not that it exists—it is always a part of political practice. The significance rather is that its frequency and effects are frequently underestimated.

Don't Forget the Estonians . . . They Are the Best of Europeans

In early 1997, then-foreign minister Ilves began a speech at the European Commission representation in Bonn by quoting Dr. Otto von Habsburg of the European Parliament. Von Habsburg had visited Tallinn in 1992 and had been presented with the original brass name plate of the interwar Tallinn office of the Pan-European Union. The plate had been kept hidden during the entire half-century of the Soviet occupation. Von

Habsburg remarked later, "Don't forget the Estonians. . . . They are the best of Europeans."[50]

Ilves's gesture of using a statement by a member of the European Parliament to explain Estonia to the European Commission illustrates how Estonians use utterances by Westerners to make claims about Estonia to Westerners. This section examines such a strategic use of Western authority and, more broadly, the reverberation and circulation of geopolitical claims between Estonian and Western intellectuals of statecraft. In so doing, I point to the capacity of intellectuals of statecraft on the Estonian side to influence Western conceptions of Estonia.

Due to the paucity of most Westerners' knowledge of Estonia, local experts are instrumental in writing the country onto their mental maps. Most Westerners rely on local experts to point out data sources, help with contacts, and provide insights into Estonian politics.[51] The circle of these experts is small and tightly knit. A local joke suggests that in order to understand Estonian politics, one must know those who were desk-mates in primary school.[52] Visiting Western consultants, journalists, scholars, and students proceed through a well-established routine of appointments. The individuals whom they interview are chosen because of their institutional location, language skills, savvy with Westerners, existing contacts in the West, even office location (preferably in the capital city of Tallinn). These are the same persons who attend seminars in the West and thus have the credentials that Westerners recognize. They are deeply involved in policy advice, policy-making and policy monitoring; they are not separate from but belong to the state apparatus. They are also highly mobile: they circulate in high government positions in Estonia and abroad, thereby acquiring extensive experience working with international organizations and foreign governments. It is through these individuals, virtually all of whom know one another, that Westerners gain access to Estonian society. The acknowledgment lists and endnotes of research concerning Estonia indicate the few dozen of Estonians consulted for most Western accounts of the country. In many cases, these consultations leave no trace in the final Western account beyond the initial polite acknowledgement of assistance.[53]

The influence of key Estonian intellectuals of statecraft is exercised not only through public statements but also through informal conversations with their Western colleagues over many years. The recollections of both Estonian and Western officials speak fondly of colorful picnics, saunas, and walks in the Old Town. President Meri was known for his penchant for giving personal tours to foreign dignitaries in Tallinn's renowned medieval Old Town. Strobe Talbott, the U. S. undersecretary of state for European affairs, made his acquaintance with Meri on just such a tour. Talbott was on his first visit to (then) Soviet Estonia in the late 1980s. Meri took Talbott under his wing and showed him around in Tallinn, and they subsequently had a long, informative, and enjoyable conversation about Estonia.[54] Meri's relationship with the former secretary general of NATO, Manfred Wörner, likewise featured a memorable stroll in 1990. Wörner had been deeply impressed with the Old Town, remarking that the medieval quarter was Estonia's "best diplomat."[55] Ronald Asmus, Talbott's deputy at the State Department, likewise spoke of the hospitality and erudition of his Baltic counterparts, "especially . . . Meri and the Estonians." He spoke fondly of the day that he and Talbott spent at Meri's retreat on the Baltic coast—taking a sauna, swimming, and talking politics into the small hours of the morning. "You know," Talbott later remarked to Asmus, "we talk more openly to these guys than even some of our current allies."[56] Former two-time Prime Minister Mart Laar stressed the importance of Robert Frasure, the first American ambassador to re-independent Estonia. Frasure was, according to Laar, so "engaged with Estonia's joys and worries," that "it sometimes remained unclear whether he represented the United States in Estonia or Estonia in the United States."[57] When Graham Avery, an advisor of the European Commission directorate for enlargement, visited Estonia, Foreign Minister Ilves, knowing that Avery was a fan of the world-famous Estonian composer Arvo Pärt, saw an opportunity to impress him. Ilves organized a casual drop-in at a rehearsal of the Estonian Philharmonic Chamber Choir, which was rehearsing Pärt. This kind of activity is easy to organize in Estonia: the city's main concert hall is within a five-minute walk from the Foreign Ministry and Ilves—naturally in the Estonian context—knew Tõnu Kaljuste, the conductor of the choir. Avery was very moved, saying, "You are not joining Europe; Europe is here already."[58]

Western monitoring of Estonia's ethnic integration policies offers perhaps the best examples of the skillful use of Western rhetoric by Estonian intellectuals of statecraft to make statements about Estonia to the West. When responding to Western concerns regarding minority rights in Estonia, Estonian intellectuals of statecraft do not make claims about Estonia but cite suitable Western claims about Estonia. Thus Foreign Minister Luik defended Estonia's citizenship laws by invoking remarks that the vice president of the United States, Al Gore, had made during his 1993 visit to Estonia—"In demonstration of [inter-ethnic] tolerance, Estonia is a model for the rest of the world."[59] Or consider this retreat, in which Estonian government officials had to explain Estonia's use of substantial Nordic funding for ethnic integration to the Nordic ambassadors. Far from reporting on Estonia's progress, Katrin Saks, the minister of ethnic affairs, successfully bypassed the ambassadors' inquiries about the government's long-term plans. She did so by stressing that ethnic integration was "a learning process," which was therefore necessarily slow and difficult (and which needed financial support from the West). She did it with a smile conveying polite assertion, not embarrassment. It is perhaps needless to add that Western funding continued; Western money paid for about half the ethnic integration programs around the turn of the decade.[60] One Estonian official later said that the whole state program for ethnic integration "is good only for raising money. We can show it to whomever."[61] The OSCE mission in Estonia, customarily viewed as a Western watchdog of Estonia's minority rights policies, was appropriated by Estonia to legitimize Estonia's policies. OSCE approval has indeed been crucial in convincing the West that Estonia is a stable state fit for membership in the EU and NATO. As a government official put it, "I think [that] OSCE is good for Estonia because they say, 'Well, Estonia is not Kosovo.' It's pretty peaceful and so they give their approval to the European Union, which Estonia wants to join."[62] The foreign ministry indeed used to bus various Western journalists to Ida-Virumaa, a predominantly Russian-speaking county in northeastern Estonia, to "facilitate" their reporting about the region. This observation is not to deny OSCE's and other Western institutions' watchdog function, but to point out that in addition to the monitoring role, OSCE's presence has also functioned to justify and promote Estonia's citizenship and language policies. The notions of Western norms and the learning process, central to Western rhetoric about minority rights as a component of state security, are therefore not simply imposed on Estonia by the West but also used by Estonia to deflect Western criticism.

Close contacts between Western and Central European intellectuals of statecraft are neither rare nor problematic. Western intellectuals of statecraft are shrewd professionals whose opinions are not necessarily swayed by swimming and sauna. Talbott and Asmus enjoyed the conversations with Meri, but they also insisted on policy changes to build a multiethnic democracy in Estonia.[63] There is likewise nothing odd about Estonians wanting to make a favorable impression on foreign guests. Given the lingering negative stereotypes of this "post-Communist" or "post-Soviet" country, they have no choice but to try to counter these stereotypes directly. It is also possible that political memoirs written nearly a decade after the events they describe embellish the story. For many Estonian intellectuals of statecraft, the 1990s was a fascinating time, "like childhood, with its comic and emotional facets."[64] My point is very specific: to place in the foreground the fact that Estonian intellectuals of statecraft *take an active part in* the production of Western accounts about Estonia. This is the context in which Estonia's image of a stellar pupil emerged, a context of statements about open European politics in which borders unite rather than divide were uttered in good English—consider that Meri and most foreign ministers were fluent in English, and Ilves is a native speaker of the language—often in the lovely Germanic settings of Tallinn's Old Town. Estonia's success cannot be viewed apart from that context. This point does not mean that Estonian intellectuals of statecraft impose their views on their Western counterparts. There may have been some deliberate misleading on the part of Estonians, but that is not the issue here. The issue is that Western accounts of Estonia have been made possible in part by the information, interpretation, and other assistance provided by Estonian intellectuals of statecraft. Talbott's interpretations of Estonia are not Meri's, but Meri has contributed to them even when the two men disagree. What I wish to dispute is not the contacts but the assumption that what happens during those contacts is Central Europeans learning Western norms while in no way influencing their production. The interaction between Western and Central European intellectuals of statecraft is an integral part of the construction of security in Central Europe. Only if these interactions vanish from the final analyses are we are left with seemingly uncontested and unproblematic "Estonian" or "Western" views, which are then inserted into familiar accounts of the "other" side.

Writing Geopolitics from the Margins

This chapter foregrounds the agency of Central European intellectuals of statecraft—that is, their capacity to not simply adopt or learn, but also to strategically appropriate Western narratives of security. Delineating the patterns of such appropriation, the chapter shows that these intellectuals play a key role in producing the conceptions of security that are considered most accurate and authentic, in Central Europe as well as in the West. Western security discourses are not simply bestowed on the region but are also in part crafted in the region. The watertight narrative of security that emerges as Western and local experts repeat the same claims has been made possible through circulation and reverberation of particular claims and modes of analysis between Western and Central European intellectuals of statecraft, and the mutual conferral of legitimacy between them.

Although the charming hosts who gladly and expertly explain the local situation to visitors do not cause specific accounts, they are an integral part of the settings in which some accounts are made plausible and others implausible. The host intellectuals function not only as translators but also as gatekeepers between the Central European countries and the West.

It is therefore not enough to presume a generalized learning process through which Western norms come to be adopted in Central Europe. We must examine closely *how* this happens—how Western concepts are interpreted and implemented in Central Europe, and how Central Europe is marketed to the West. This examination involves investigating the manner in which security discourses in the center and at the margins of the Western security establishment are mutually constituted. The question is not who causes certain constructions of security, but rather what conditions make certain accounts possible and others impossible. The capacity of the margins is perhaps not one of direct influence but rather one of indirect tinkering with Western discourses through the strategic use of Western research, Western rhetoric, and Western name recognition. It involves help with and suggestions regarding whom to interview and what books to read. Although Western intellectuals of statecraft have an enormous power to define which Central European voices are deemed authentic and relevant and which ones are ignored as irrelevant, their Central European counterparts likewise have considerable power to define the information about the region that is presented to Western experts as authentic and correct. The task is not to weigh the relative importance of each side but to underscore that *both* are vital for discourses of European security.

How Many Threats and How Many Europes?

Security . . . is not a noun that names something, it is a principle of formation that does things.

Michael Dillon, 1996[1]

Geopolitics Unbound

Commenting on the political situation in Ukraine, Vaclav Havel said in March 2006 that:

Ukraine belongs to a united European political entity; the values that Ukraine endorses and that are embedded in its history are European to the core . . . Much the same is true for Ukraine and NATO. Partnerships based on shared rules, standards, and values are the heartbeat of modern security.[2]

With this comment, Havel shifts Ukraine from its customary position in "Eastern Europe" into "Europe" and holds out a clear possibility for the country's political and security integration with the West on the basis of its European identity and values. His comment illustrates the continued political utility of invoking identity and values to explain complex political processes like security. It also testifies to the highly amorphous and flexible character of these categories.

Whereas the previous chapters examined how the discursive constellation of security and identity works in Central Europe, this concluding chapter foregrounds the broader theoretical and political significance of that constellation in contemporary European politics. Whereas the earlier chapters focused empirically on the period leading up to EU and NATO enlargement in 2004, here I look at the period since 2004 and into the future. Enlargement here does not refer to an increase in the numbers of EU member states. It rather denotes a process that expands the EU's normative space—the space in which the discourses of European security and European identity influence political practice. Defined in this way, Europe's eastern enlargement operates beyond EU and NATO member states. It is a process that produces a particular kind of geopolitical space.

Security discourses in Central Europe involve a seeming paradox. For years, accession to the EU and NATO was presented as a rite of passage that would complete the region's postsocialist transition, fulfill its dream of "returning to Europe," and finally free its states from security concerns. Yet the figure of (in)security has neither faded away nor lost its mobilizing function in political debates. Although claims of military threats were gradually expunged from mainstream political discourse, insecurity has retained its key position in this discourse. Most of the practices cited in this book come from the late 1990s or later, when very few commentators seriously argued that the Central European states were under a foreign military threat. This persistence of insecurity is not simply a matter of inertia, of Central European states still adjusting to being secure. Rather, insecurity has persisted because of its productive functions; because it produces community and consent.

There are three related but nonetheless distinct facets to this productive process. The first concerns what David Campbell calls the requirements of enmity, the ways in which otherness is a necessary part of identity construction.[3] Security discourses do not simply rehearse negative images of what "we" fear and what "we" are not. They also function as positive projects of the construction of "our" identity and interest. External threat produces a domestic society that the state can claim to protect. The figure of threat actively mutes debate and mobilizes the population for action. As much of Central European politics has revolved around efforts of nation-and state-building, external threat has played an important part in these processes. Security still serves to consolidate the European and national identities to be secured, to reify Russia as essentially un-European, and to frame complex political issues in terms of emergency measures that should be above or beyond normal political debate. The entailments of identity which are satisfied by security claims are still in place.

The construction of security and geopolitics—in Central Europe and beyond—is therefore part and parcel of the production of political subjectivity. It operates through references to responsible and reliable subjects, the proclamations of a new beginning, freedom, and openness, and the calls for proactive participation and emotional involvement in security. On the collective level, it produces membership in the EU and NATO as a state's precondition for being—as a requirement for being recognized as a modern, mature Western subject. On the individual level, it constitutes EU and NATO membership in terms of individual responsibility and individual emotions. Accession is defined not as something that happens to the electorate for reasons of state. It is rather defined as a positive process that happens through the active participation of individuals and social groups. The enlargement discourse is moralistic, affective, and adamantly nonterritorial. It emphasizes not territories but universal values. In it, individuals and groups can acquire Western credentials if they participate in demarcating and securing the West. Even in 2007, voters are reminded that they have been recognized as mature Western subjects and must now prove that they are worthy of the trust. The enlargement discourse is not concerned merely with putting individuals into the service of (state) security, but rather seeks to integrate individuals into the very functioning of security discourses. It works not against but through the creative efforts of individuals.[4]

The second reason for the persistence of insecurity stems from the ubiquitous presence of identity and culture in security discourses. Security continues to be an effective trope because identity is an effective trope. The cultural conception of security, whereby security claims are discussed in terms of deeply rooted cultural idenitities, has continued since the double enlargement. When the Central European countries expressed their support to the U.S. war in Iraq, politicians throughout the region justified this step by evoking the moral dimension of foreign policy. For example, Sandra Kalniete, the foreign minister of Latvia, explained her country's position in terms of its "responsibility and moral obligation" to share its "experience and knowledge of successful transformation and transition process from a totalitarian regime to a democratic society."[5] Mart Laar, the former prime minister of Estonia, observed that identity and values as bases for foreign policy are *more* important in Central Europe than in Western Europe, and that this is why Central European countries are less receptive to "European Realpolitik" than Western European states.[6] As security is linked to identity and values, it is unbound from specific threats and shifted explicitly to the realm of identity politics. As culture is omnipresent, so is security. Just as political decisions are framed in terms of identity and morality; they are also framed in terms of security.[7] The effect is to elevate rather than decrease the political import of security. Security discourses in Central Europe thus testify to the complexities of broadening the security agenda to cultural issues. In particular, they show that the political effects of such broadening cannot be deduced theoretically. The enlarged "cultural" definition of security is not necessarily more progressive or more backward than the traditional military concept of security. Its political effects can be teased out only through a context-sensitive empirical inquiry.

The third reason for the continued effectiveness of security in Central European politics has to do with the naturalizing and legitimizing effects of geographical assertions and assumptions. True, security claims are increasingly based on more diffuse cultural categories, such as cultural spheres, frontiers, and homelands rather than on the territories of states. Geopolitics is decoupled from state territoriality and transferred into the realm of cultural difference and moral values. It appears to be unbound from geographical markers. At the same time, the cultural discourse of geopolitics converts difference into distance. It acknowledges difference as such and reifies it as a core aspect of identity and an attribute of place.[8] Although politicians like to talk about the eclipse of geopolitics, the practice of locating places in terms of Europe—in the center, on the margin, in the East, in the West—has retained its key position in the enlargement discourse. Thomas Diez notes that the construction of European identity has shifted from temporal othering, in which alterity was constituted not in terms of a geographically demarcated area but in terms of Europe's own nationalist past, to spatial othering, in which Europe and its Others are constructed in geographical terms.[9] To understand this process, we must look beyond the formal political arena; that is, beyond official speeches and the EU's formal interaction with nonmembers. We rather need to foreground the othering *logic of explanation*, according to which places are on the slope of West and East, Self and Other, inside and outside, security and threat.[10] That logic is manifested far beyond the formal political arena, in the mundane ideological habits of discussing social and political life in terms of Europeanness. It is effective precisely because it is the commonsense encasing of political debate.

The key change in the 1990s, then, was not the amount or extent of insecurity but the specific functions of the category. The practices that designate threat and prescribe responses to it have become more commonplace and less noticeable over the last decade. Arguments that still carried connotations of particular interest and particular perspective a dozen years ago are today presented as truisms that appear to emanate from nowhere. The circular reasoning in which security, identity, and the double enlargement were all explained in terms of one another is so well rehearsed and commonsense as to no longer require evidence or elicit reaction. This reasoning works not through grand statist rhetoric but through unremarkable habits in which places are problematized on the basis of commonsense cultural borders and hierarchies. An ironic twist here is that invoking culture and identity in the narrative of Europe's eastern enlargement makes the enlargement argument dependent on these concepts. Across Europe, as EU bureaucrats evoke identity and values to promote the EU, neonationalists use these same terms in anti-EU and anti-immigrant arguments.[11] Likewise in Central Europe, the notion of a culturally defined homeland is used as much against as for the EU.

Security and geopolitics have thus become normalized and banalized. Yet as Hannah Arendt has pointed out, banal is not synonymous with benign.[12] To speak of the banality of geopolitics, then, is not to imply triviality or benevolence but rather to specify its mechanisms of operation. It is to underscore the need to pay attention to daily practices beyond the formal arena of the state—practices in schools, in the popular media, and in the cultural sphere more broadly. Likewise, to label security as banal is not to downplay the military connotations of the concept. Security has not been detached from its military connotations. Military expenditures were the key measuring stick for a country's readiness for NATO membership throughout the preaccession period. The cultural turn in security discourses has diffused these military connotations through the political debate.[13] The challenge, then, is not to expand the security agenda in the belief that the more issues are framed in terms of security, the better. Rather, we should seek less security—that is, less framing of complex societal issues in terms of security. As Giorgio Agamben puts it: "It is the task of democratic politics to prevent the development of conditions which lead to hatred, terror, and destruction—and not to reduce itself to attempts to control them once they occur."[14]

Margins and Edges

As geopolitical imaginaries in Europe rely less on fixed entities like states and more on fluid categories like identity, the number of margins proliferates. Noel Parker observes that Europe is "getting edgier"; that is, there are ever more actors who see themselves as in some sense marginal in the European project.[15] Etienne Balibar likewise notes that borders have not been eliminated in Europe; rather, all of Europe appears to be on the border.[16] This proliferation of borders and margins is part and parcel of the diffusion and fragmentation of security and identity. In debates on security, there appear to be no threats—there are only multiple crosscutting layers of insecurity. In debates on identity, the geographic demarcation of the East has undergone a similar diffusion and fragmentation. Although the East still exists as a repository of negative connotations, it functions not as a place but as a characteristic or a feature of a place. Security discourses endow places with lesser or greater Europeanness or Eastness. In the mid-1990s, for example, as the process of eastern enlargement slowed down and wars in the former Yugoslavia fueled concern about ethnic conflict in Central Europe, the region was shifted back into the East.[17] In the terminology of this book, the former Yugoslavia was not simply shifted eastward; rather, it was endowed with greater Eastness and less Europeanness. The East is detached from clear geographical connotations and transformed into a generalized marker—Eastness—in European identity construction.[18]

As the EU and NATO edge closer to their traditional Easts of Russia and Turkey, questions about the borders of Europe and Europeanness will become more visible and more consequential in the enlargement discourse. Up to the 2004 enlargement, the EU's and NATO's influence on its neighbors involved the carrot of eventual membership. It appears that no such carrot will be offered to today's outsiders.[19] Rather, the EU's practices toward the East rely increasingly on blurring the lines dividing EU members, potential members, and those who are not even potential members.[20] The EU's relations with the outside increasingly deploy the argument of "all but membership," as Romano Prodi put it: the operation of EU norms without formal membership.[21] Such "flexible partnerships" are increasingly used by NATO as well.[22] As the administrative mechanisms of accession negotiations will not be available to "discipline" these outsiders, including and excluding states and regions via discourses of Europeanness, culture, and values will gain importance. It may well be that nobody is completely "outside" the shifting contours of Europeanness, but nobody is completely "inside" either.[23] Everyone can be included to a degree, but everyone can also be excluded to a degree as well. They can be included in the logic of explanation that has exclusionary effects on them. Turkey or Ukraine, for example, can be either included or excluded on the basis of the cultural and geographical claim that they are not within the realm of European identity and values. They are included in the proliferation of Europes and the East, but the specific inscription of Europeanness and Eastness varies depending on the specific argument. The East-West slope can thus remain simultaneously conspicuous and ambiguous.

The proliferation of margins multiplies the number of marginal actors and highlights the need to understand their capacity to act. Within

European and Western security discourses, Central European intellectuals of statecraft are such actors. Their role in the construction of geopolitics is not simply one of expressing their states' identities and interests. In the context of their inferior power position with respect to their Western colleagues, they must please not only the domestic electorate but also the West. Yet they do not simply learn Western conceptions of security either. They strategically adopt and appropriate Western narratives, carefully maneuvering between the Central European states' "own" interests and their Western partners' expectations. To highlight such maneuvering is neither to hint at a Central European conspiracy nor to imply that the practice is unique to Central Europe. It is rather to point out an important nuance that has hitherto not received due attention.

It is still too early as of 2007 to assess the impact of the double enlargement on Central European security experts' capacity to act within the enlarged EU and NATO. On the one hand, EU accession has given them greater incentives to follow EU policies even when these contradict domestic interests. Although national politics remains an important arena for these foreign policy professionals, their careers depend greatly on their success in Brussels. If there is a discrepancy between domestic sentiments and foreign expectation, they have less incentive to follow the former and more to gain by responding to the latter. On the other hand, membership in the EU and NATO also gives Central European states more room to negotiate and maneuver. Being a part of the EU's formal policy-making process gives them an opportunity to strengthen their voice in the enlarged Union. The new member states are actively engaged in bilateral and multilateral relations with the EU's eastern exterior. For example, Poland is developing closer contacts with Ukraine and Belarus, Romania promotes itself as a regional power around the Black Sea, and Bulgaria and Slovenia frame themselves as important actors in distributing EU norms to southeastern Europe.[24] Some of the incentives for "performing" for the West are no longer there or are not as strong. In November 2006, Poland vetoed the launch of a new framework agreement between the EU and Russia.[25] This was the first time that a new member state blocked an important EU initiative. It indicates that Central European states are starting to exercise their power within the EU. Such newly relaxed attitude toward Western expectations has been noted in NATO as well. Even before the latest enlargement, one senior figure in European security remarked in 2002 that "Hungary has won the prize for most disappointing new member of NATO, and against some competition."[26] Moreover, as Central European intellectuals of statecraft (among others) staff the agencies that manage the Union's exterior, they are in a good position to speak about the EU to the East and vice versa. Their interpretations of European norms as well as their practices of preaching and practicing these norms in the EU's external relations will become more influential. Central Europe's relationship with the EU's eastern exterior is in some ways substantially different from Western Europe's relations with that exterior. Central Europe is closer to the outside, but it it also in greater need of distinguishing itself from that outside. Central European intellectuals of statecraft can invoke not only their European and Western credentials but also the insights gained from being the "formerly kidnapped West." As Central Europe is becoming a part of "normal boring" Europe, the agency of Central European intellectuals of statecraft in shaping European geopolitical discourses will be greater as well as more insidious.

Jan Zielonka recently asked whether the EU's new geographic reach is demanding and producing a new geopolitics on the continent.[27] His answer is affirmative: that Europe does need a new geopolitics based on overlapping neomedieval spatialities, and that this geopolitics is coming into being. I agree with Zielonka on the need for new spatial conceptions of European politics, but I am more skeptical of the new reframed geopolitics that is operational today. Although Europe's eastern enlargement appears to illustrate a more inclusive neomedieval geopolitics, one in which the concepts of security and Europe shed their exclusionary territorial functions, the process is still underpinned by a series of flexible exclusions. This geopolitics is an amorphous geopolitics of identity and values. It is a geopolitics that denies that it is one. Although identity rather than politics appears to be Europe's defining feature, the concern with the European cultural realm is also a concern with the borders of that realm. Geographical and geopolitical assertions and assumptions sneak in through the back door just as they appear to have been eclipsed by identity. Thus, as long as the enlargements of the EU and NATO are construed as a way to secure European values, a certain amount of insecurity and un-Europeanness is needed as a yardstick against which to measure the success of this process. Enlargement reconfigures the specific borders or characteristics of the dangerous outside, but it still requires that outside to hold up the discursive architecture of enlargement. This continuous production of insecurity underscores the need to investigate the category of security in terms of its political functions rather than its level or degree. The task is to shift analyses from intentions to effects, from institutions to practices, from what security means or will mean or could mean or should mean or is intended to mean—or when it is going to fade—to how it is actually used in daily (geo)political practice.

Notes

Preface

1. Václav Havel. "Redefining the West." *Project Syndicate*, October 2001, http://www.project-syndicate.org/print_commentary/havel22/English (accessed August 10, 2006).
2. Jan Zielonka, *Europe as Empire: The Nature of the Enlarged European Union*. Oxford, UK: Oxford University Press, 2006, 12.
3. The Visegrad cooperation started formally in 1991, when Poland, Hungary, and Czechoslovakia signed a cooperation agreement in Visegrad, Hungary. When Czechoslovakia split into the Czech Republic and Slovakia, Visegrad became an association of four countries. For more information, see the Visegrad Group at: http://www.visegradgroup.eu/main.php?folderID=925 (accessed March 15, 2007).
4. Janine Wedel, *Collision and Collusion: The Strange Case of Western Aid to Eastern Europe*, 2nd ed. (New York: Palgrave, 2001).

Chapter 1

1. Robert. B. J. Walker, "The Subject of Security," in *Critical Security Studies: Concepts and Cases*, ed. Keith Krause and Michael C. Williams (Minneapolis: University of Minnesota Press, 1997), 63.
2. Dinah Spritzer, "Praguers Wary of Terrorist Attacks," *Prague Post*, November 20, 2002.
3. Martin Simecka, "The Havel Paradox," *Transitions Online*, March 21, 2003, http://www.tol.cz (accessed May 20, 2005).
4. The Czech National Security Council performed background checks on more than 4,300 people—everyone from the congress center janitors to hotel managers. Jennifer Hamm, "City Locks Down for Summit Safety," *Prague Post*, November 20, 2002. Authorities advised citizens to leave the town; about 200,000—more than 10 percent of the city's population—heeded the advice. Alfredo Azula, "NATO Summit 2002 Ends," *Prague Post*, November 22, 2002. Schools were closed. The Czech Interior Ministry posted a 10-point "good conduct" list on its Web site, advising citizens to

avoid conversations with activists distributing leaflets, follow police directives without question, avoid discussions with "radicals," and shy away from "confused situations" that might attract police attention. Adam LeBor, "The Other Big Brother in Prague," *Budapest Sun* 10 (November 28, 2002). The borders of the Czech Republic were tightened to "keep out protesters with a history of violence." The cost of the security arrangements was approximately 620 million kronas, up from the 113 million spent during the International Monetary Fund (IMF) meeting in 2000. Hamm, "City Locks Down for Summit Safety." Martin Simecka, a former Slovakian dissident—at the time a summit delegate, however—noted that the empty streets of Prague reminded him of the 1980s, "when it was like this every night. However, on 20 November 2002, it was late morning." Simecka, "The Havel Paradox," 1.

5. Timothy Garton Ash, "Love, Peace and NATO," *Guardian*, November 28, 2002.

6. Vaclav Havel, opening speech at the conference on "The Transformation of NATO," November 20, 2002, http://old.hrad.cz (accessed July 12, 2004).

7. Quoted in Martin Simecka, "The Havel Paradox."

8. Vaira Vike-Freiberga, speech delivered at the NATO summit in Prague during the meeting of the North Atlantic Council (NAC) and the seven invited countries (Brussels: NATO, November 21, 2002).

9. Kärt Karpa, "Suursaadik Kannike kuulas NATO otsust pisarsilmil" [Ambassador Kannike listened to NATO's decision with teary eyes], *Eesti Päevaleht*, November 22, 2002. Note on translations: Unless otherwise noted, all translations from the Estonian language are mine.

10. BBC News, "Newcomers' Joy at NATO Invitation," November 22, 2002. Reactions in Western European newspapers hardly mentioned the new member states and instead focused on the transatlantic rift that had occurred in regard to the United States' policy toward Iraq. See BBC Monitoring, "Roundup of West European Press Comment on the NATO Prague Summit," November 25, 2002.

11. Ben Schiller, "International Students Gather for Summit Simulation," *Prague Post*, November 27, 2002.

12. Garton Ash, "Love, Peace and NATO."

13. Joseph Fitchett, "Meanwhile: Havel, a Class Act, Exists with Humor," *International Herald Tribune*, February 4, 2003.

14. The artists involved did not necessarily intend to promote NATO. Jiri David, the Czech artist who had designed the blinking heart, said that "it's a profane, banal, kitsch symbol. But at a specific place, it gains unique character . . . . Coincidentally, the heart will be lit on the event of the NATO summit. But I'm not an artist for NATO." Jan H. Vitvar, "Prague Castle Holds Up Its Heart for All to See," *Prague Post*, November 21, 2002. Some accounts suggested that Havel himself was fully aware of the ironies of the event. Simecka, "The Havel Paradox."

15. Garton Ash, "Love, Peace and NATO." For a more in-depth analysis of the symbolism of the Prague summit, see Merje Kuus, "'Love, Peace and

NATO'? Imperial Subject-Making in Central Europe," *Antipode* 39 (2) 2007: 269-290.

16. Robert W. McColl, "A Geographical Model for International Behaviour," in *Pluralism and Political Geography*, ed. N. Kliot and S. Waterman (London: Croom Helm, 1983), 284–94; quoted in Simon Dalby, *Creating the Second Cold War: The Discourse of Politics* (New York: Guilford, 1990), 33. For informative analyses on the history of geopolitics, see also *Geopolitical Traditions: A Century of Geopolitical Thought*, ed. K. Dodds and D. Atkinson (London: Routledge, 2000); Gearóid Ó Tuathail, *Critical Geopolitics: The Politics of Writing Global Space* (Minneapolis: University of Minnesota Press, 1996); and Geoffrey Parker, *Geopolitics: Past, Present, and Future* (London: Pinter, 1998).

17. Adam Daniel Rotfeld, "Borderless Europe and Global Security," address given at the Ron Brown Fellowship Programme Alumni Conference, Kraków, September 26–28, 2003.

18. Accounts that explicitly evoke geopolitics in the European context include Colin Gray and Geoffrey Sloan, eds., *Geography, Geopolitics and Strategy* (London: Frank Cass, 1999); Peter J. Katzenstein, *A World of Regions: Asia and Europe in the American Imperium* (Ithaca, NY: Cornell University Press, 2005); Ola Tunander, Pavel Baev, and Victoria Ingrid Einagel, eds., *Geopolitics in Post-Wall Europe: Security, Territory and Identity* (Oslo: International Peace Research Institute, 1997); and Jan Zielonka, *Europe as Empire: The Nature of the Enlarged European Union* (Oxford: Oxford University Press, 2006).

19. The journal *Geopolitics* has published extensively on these issues. See especially Pami Aalto, Simon Dalby, and Vilho Harle, "The Critical Geopolitics of Northern Europe: Identity Politics Unlimited," *Geopolitics* 8 (2003): 1–19; and Sami Moisio, "EU Eligibility, Central Europe and the Invention of Applicant State Narrative," *Geopolitics* 7 (2002): 89–116. See also Christopher Browning, "The Internal/External Security Paradox and the Reconstruction of Boundaries in the Baltic: The Case of Kaliningrad," *Alternatives* 28 (2003): 454–581; Barry Buzan and Ole Wæver, "EU-Europe: the European Union and its 'Near Abroad,'" in *Regions and Powers: The Structure of International Security*, ed. B. Buzan and O. Wæver (Cambridge and New York: Cambridge University Press, 2003), 352–76; Thomas Diez, "Europe's Others and the Return of Geopolitics," *Cambridge Review of International Affairs* 17 (2004): 319–35; Bahar Rumelili, "Constructing Identity and Relating to Difference: Understanding the EU's Mode of Differentiation," *Review of International Studies* 30 (2004): 27–47.

20. Przemyslaw Grudzinski and Peter van Ham, *A Critical Approach to European Security* (London: Pinter, 1999), 154.

21. Diez, "Europe's Others and the Return of Geopolitics," 319. For Diez, geopolitics is the traditional geopolitics of interstate pursuit of primacy.

22. Zielonka, *Europe as Empire*.

23. Václav Havel, "Europe: Twilight at Dawn," *Project Syndicate*, December 1996.

24. For recent analyses of these geopolitical thinkers, see Klaus Dodds and James D. Sidaway, "Halford Mackinder and the 'Geographical Pivot of History': A Centennial Retrospective," *Geographical Journal* 170 (2004): 292–97; Bruce Kuklick, *Blind Oracles: Intellectuals and War from Kennan to Kissinger* (Princeton, NJ: Princeton University Press, 2006); Ola Tunander, "Swedish Geopolitics: from Rudolf Kjellén to Swedish 'Dual State,'" *Geopolitics* 10 (2005): 546–66. For reviews of the resurgence of geopolitics, see Klaus Dodds and David Atkinson, eds., *Geopolitical Traditions: A Century of Geopolitical Thought* (London: Routledge, 2000); and David Newman, "Geopolitics Renaissant: Territory, Sovereignty and the World Political Map," *Geopolitics and International Boundaries* 1 (1998): 1–16.

25. Samuel P. Huntington, *The Clash of Civilizations and the Remaking of the World Order* (New York: Simon and Schuster, 1996); Robert D. Kaplan, *The Coming Anarchy: Shattering the Dreams of the Post Cold War* (New York: Random House, 2000).

26. Gearóid Ó Tuathail, "Displacing Geopolitics: Writing the Maps of Global Politics," *Environment and Planning D: Society and Space* 12 (1994): 531.

27. Nicholas Spykman, "Geography and Foreign Policy, I," *American Political Science Review* 32 (1938): 29.

28. David Atkinson and Klaus Dodds, "Introduction to Geopolitical Traditions: A Century of Geopolitical Thought," in *Geopolitical Traditions*, 3.

29. Sami Moisio, "Competing Geographies of Sovereignty, Regionality and Globalisation: The Politics of EU Resistance in Finland 1991–1994," *Geopolitics* 11 (2006): 440.

30. See James F. Brown, *The Grooves of Change: Eastern Europe at the Turn of the Millennium* (Durham, NC: Duke University Press, 2001); and John O'Loughlin, "Ordering the 'Crush Zone': Geopolitical Games in Post-Cold War Eastern Europe," in *Geopolitics at the End of the Twentieth Century: The Changing World Political Map*, ed. Nurit Kliot and David Newman, 35–56 (London: Frank Cass, 2001).

31. The West here refers to the core states of North America and Western Europe; East-Central Europe refers to the postsocialist countries of the former Soviet bloc; and Eastern Europe refers to the discourse of Eastern Europe. I capitalize all words because the terms refer at once to places as well as to discourses about these places. Eastern or Central Europe here refer not to clearly located places but to political and intellectual projects. To differentiate between Eastern, Western, and Central Europe in this manner is not to essentialize the differences between different parts of Europe, but to acknowledge their different power positions in European security discourses.

32. Quoted in Vladimir Tismaneanu, "Discomforts of Victory: Democracy, Liberal Values and Nationalism in Post-Communist Europe," *West European Politics* 25 (2002): 91.

33. Stefano Guzzini, "'Self-fulfilling Geopolitics'?, Or: The Social Production of Foreign Policy Expertise in Europe," Paper presented at the joint convention of the Central Eastern European International Studies Association and the

International Studies Association in Budapest, June 26–28, 2003. Guzzini also points out that this renaissance of explicitly realist geopolitical thinking occurred just as the end of the Cold War seemed to herald the superiority of nonrealist approaches in western IR theory.

34. See Derek Averre and Andrew Cottey, "Introduction: Thinking About Security in Postcommunist Europe," in *New Security Challenges in Postcommunist Europe*, ed. A. Cottey and D. Averre (Manchester: Manchester University Press, 2002), 1–25; Charles Krupnick, ed., *Almost NATO: Partners and Players in Central and Eastern European Security* (Lanham, MD: Rowman and Littlefield, 2002); and Richard Smoke, ed., *Perceptions of Security: Public Opinion and Expert Assessments in Europe's New Democracies* (New York: Manchester University Press, 1996). These studies provide detailed overviews of the Central European states' security policies and thereby make valuable contributions to our understanding of the region. They tend, however, to define the problematic of security in overly narrow, static, and commonsensical terms.

35. For lucid discussions of narrative as a methodological tool, see Andrew R. Sayer, *Method in Social Science: A Realist Approach*, 2nd ed. (London: Routledge, 1992), 259; and Hayden White, *The Content of the Form: Narrative Discourse and Historical Representation* (Baltimore, MD: Johns Hopkins University Press, 1987).

36. Guzzini, "'Self-fulfilling Geopolitics'?" 1.

37. Ó Tuathail, *Critical Geopolitics*, 7.

38. Martin W. Lewis and Kären E. Wigen, *The Myth of Continents: A Critique of Metageography* (Berkeley, CA: University of California Press, 1997), ix.

39. Hugh Gusterson, *People of the Bomb: Portraits of America's Nuclear Complex* (Minneapolis, MN: University of Minnesota Press, 2004), xxi.

40. Gearóid Ó Tuathail and John Agnew, "Geopolitics and Discourse: Practical Geopolitical Reasoning in American Foreign Policy," *Political Geography* 11 (1992): 190.

41. Simon Dalby, "Critical Geopolitics: Discourse, Difference, and Dissent," *Environment and Planning D: Society and Space* 9 (1991), 274. Simon Dalby was a pioneer in critical geopolitics. Dalby, *Creating the Second Cold War*. See also John A. Agnew and Stuart Corbridge, *Mastering Space: Hegemony, Territory and International Political Economy* (New York: Routledge, 1995); Simon Dalby, *Environmental Security*, Minneapolis: University of Minnesota Press, 2002); Jennifer Hyndman, *Managing Displacement: Refugees and the Politics of Humanitarianism* (Minneapolis: University of Minnesota Press, 2000); O'Tuathail, *Critical Geopolitics*; and Joanne Sharp, *Condensing the Cold War: Reader's Digest and American Identity* (Minneapolis: University of Minnesota Press, 2000). Critical geopolitics is not monolithic; the above works disagree on a number of theoretical and methodological points. I treat critical geopolitics as a coherent body of work because of its central concern with the ways in which international politics is conceived and practiced spatially.

42. Anatol Lieven, "Against Russophobia," *World Policy Journal* 17 (Winter 2000/2001): 2; Katherine Verdery, "The 'New' Eastern Europe in an Anthropology of Europe," *Provocations of European Ethnology*, American Anthropologist 99 (1997): 715–17.

43. Timothy Garton Ash, *The Uses of Adversity: Essays on the Fate of Central Europe* (New York: Random House, 1989), 180.

44. Richard Ned Lebow and Thomas Risse-Kappen, "Introduction: International Relations Theory and the End of the Cold War," in *International Relations Theory and the End of the Cold War*, ed. Richard Ned Lebow and Thomas Risse-Kappen (New York: Columbia University Press, 1995), 3.

45. Sayer, *Method in Social Science*,143.

46. Katherine Verdery, "Post-Soviet Area Studies?" *NewsNet* 3 (2003): 7–8. See also Karen Dawisha, "The Social Science and Area Studies: Never the Twain Shall Meet?" *NewsNet*.43 (2003): 3–5. I will come back to these issues in chapter 2.

47. Hugh Gusterson, *Nuclear Rites: A Weapons Laboratory and the End of the Cold War* (Berkeley, CA: University of California Press, 1996), 6.

48. Clifford Geertz, *Local Knowledge: Further Essays in Interpretive Anthropology* (New York: Basic Books, 1983), 92; quoted in Liisa Malkki, "National Geographic: The Rooting of Peoples and the Territorialization of National Identity among Scholars and Refugees," *Cultural Anthropology* 7 (1992): 26.

49. Ó Tuathail and Agnew, "Geopolitics and Discourse," 193. On the relationship between ideas and materiality, see John A. Agnew, "Regions on the Mind does not Equal Regions of the Mind," *Progress in Human Geography* 23 (1999): 91–6. Agnew reminds us that "an object and an idea about that object are not the same and in the world that humans inhabit the distinction is crucial" (Ibid., 92).

50. Content and structure (what is said and what rules govern utterances) cannot be neatly separated. I make this point to distinguish the book from studies that rely on opinion polls or content analysis.

51. Michel Foucault, "Polemics, Politics, and Problemizations: An Interview with Michel Foucault," in *The Foucault Reader*, ed. Paul Rabinow (New York: Pantheon Books, 1984), 381–91, 389.

52. For an argument that emphasizes the importance of such attention to the messiness of foreign policy practice, see Iver B. Neumann, "Returning Practice to the Linguistic Turn: The Case of Diplomacy," *Millennium: Journal of International Studies* 31 (2002): 627–51.

53. For further explanation, see Jutta Weldes and Diana Saco, "Making State Action Possible: The United States and the Discursive Construction of 'The Cuban Problem', 1960–1994", *Millennium: Journal of International Studies* 25 (1996): 361–95; Sayer, *Method in Social Science*, 103–16.

54. Hugh Gusterson, "Missing the End of the Cold War in International Security," in *Cultures of Insecurity: States, Communities, and the Production of Danger*, ed. Jutta Weldes, Mark Laffey, Hugh Gusterson, and Raymond Duvall (Minneapolis: University of Minnesota Press, 1999), 327.

55. Jutta Weldes, Mark Laffey, Hugh Gusterson, and Raymond Duvall, "Introduction: Constructing Insecurity," in *Cultures of Insecurity*,18; Ole Wæver, "Identity, Communities and Foreign Policy: Discourse Analysis as Foreign Policy Theory," in *European Integration and National Identity: The Challenge of the Nordic States*, ed. L. Hansen and O. Wæver (London and New York: Routledge, 2002), 20–49.

56. Weldes et al., "Introduction: Constructing Insecurity," 19. See also Sharp, *Condensing the Cold War*. This emphasis on the extended state is indebted to Antonio Gramsci.

57. Gusterson, *Nuclear Rites*, 6.

58. There is a voluminous literature on this issue. For different theoretical approaches, see David Campbell, *Writing Security: United States Foreign Policy and the Politics of Identity*, 2nd ed. (Minneapolis, MN: University of Minnesota Press, 1998); Peter J. Katzenstein, ed., *The Culture of National Security: Norms and Identity in World Politics* (New York: Columbia University Press, 1996); Yosef Lapid and Friedrich Kratochwil, eds., *The Return of Culture and Identity in IR Theory* (Boulder, CO: Lynne Rienner Publishers, 1996); Iver B. Neumann, *The Uses of the Other: 'The East' in European Identity Formation* (Minneapolis: University of Minnesota Press, 1999); and Weldes et al., *Cultures of Insecurity*.

59. Lapid and Kratochwil, *Return of Culture and Identity in IR Theory*, 8.

60. Robert D. English, *Russia and the Idea of the West* (New York: Columbia University Press, 2000), 6; see also Ilya Prizel, *National Identity and Foreign Policy: Nationalism and Leadership in Poland, Russia and Ukraine* (Cambridge: Cambridge University Press, 1998).

61. Richard K. Ashley, "The Geopolitics of Geopolitical Space: Toward a Critical Social Theory of International Politics," *Alternatives* 12 (1987): 403–34, 303; Campbell, *Writing Security*, 217; Keith Krause and Michael C. Williams, "From Strategy to Security: Foundations of Critical Security Studies," in *Critical Security Studies*, ed. Krause and Williams, 48.

62. Weldes et al., "Introduction: Constructing Insecurity," 5. See also Donald Mitchell, "There's No Such Thing as Culture: Towards a Reconceptualisation of the Idea of Culture in Geography," *Transactions of the Institute of British Geographers* 19 (1995): 102–16.

63. Milan Kundera, "The Tragedy of Central Europe," *New York Review of Books*, April 26, 1984, 35.

64. Claus Offe, *Varieties of Transition* (London: Polity Press, 1996), 28.

65. For in-depth critiques of such uses of identity, see Rogers Brubaker and Frederick Cooper, "Beyond 'Identity,'" *Theory and Society* 29 (2000): 1–47; Campbell, *Writing Security*, chapter 8; Merje Kuus and John Agnew, "Theorizing the State Geographically," in *The Handbook of Political Geography*, ed. K. Cox, J. Robinson, and M. Low (Thousand Oaks, CA: Sage Publications, 2007).

66. William E. Connolly, *Identity/Difference: Democratic Negotiations of Political Paradox*, exp. ed. (Ithaca, NY: Cornell University Press, 2002), xiv.

See also Diez, "Europe's Others and the Return of Geopolitics"; Lene Hansen and Ole Wæver, eds. *European Integration and National Identity: The Challenge of the Nordic States* (London and New York: Routledge, 2002); Iver B. Neumann, "European Identity, EU Expansion, and the Integration/Exclusion Nexus," *Alternatives* 23 (1998): 397–416; Weldes et al., "Introduction: Constructing Insecurity,".

67. Dalby, "Critical Geopolitics: Discourse, Difference, and Dissent," 274; see also Agnew and Corbridge, *Mastering Space*, 87.

68. David Campbell, *Politics without Principle: Sovereignty, Ethics, and the Narratives of the Gulf War* (Boulder, CO: Lynne Rienner, 1993), 27.

69. Ole Wæver, "Securitization and Desecuritization," in *On Security*, ed. Ronnie D. Lipschutz (New York: Columbia University Press, 1995), 46–86; Krause and Williams, "From Strategy to Security."

70. Kuklick, *Blind Oracles*, 2.

71. Buzan, Wæver, and de Wilde, *Security: A New Framework for Analysis*, 31.

72. Carol Cohn, "Sex and Death in the Rational World of Defense Intellectuals," *Signs: Journal of Women in Culture and Society* 12 (1987): 687–718; Gusterson, *Nuclear Rites*; Gusterson, *People of the Bomb*; and Fred Kaplan, *The Wizards of Armaggedon* (New York: Simon and Schuster, 1983).

73. Gusterson, "Missing the End of the Cold War in International Security."

74. Sharp, *Condensing the Cold War*, 10.

75. Geopolitical reasoning is sometimes discussed in terms of formal, practical and popular geopolitics. Formal geopolitics is constructed though academic discourse; this is how geopolitics is traditionally understood. Practical geopolitics involves political rhetoric and commentary and draws from both academic research and commonsense narratives about places. Popular geopolitics is articulated through popular media and the arts. The distinction among the three types is problematic because all three rely on popular beliefs about the character of places. For the three types of geopolitical reasoning, see Gearóid Ó Tuathail, "Problematizing Geopolitics: Survey, Statesmanship and Strategy," *Transactions of the Institute of British Geographers* 19 (1994): 259–72.

76. Ó Tuathail and Agnew, "Geopolitics and Discourse," 193. On pundits, see Hugh Gusterson and Catherine Besteman, "Introduction," in *Why America's Top Pundits Are Wrong: Anthropologists Talk Back*, ed. Catherine Besteman and Hugh Gusterson (Berkeley, CA: University of California Press, 2005), 1–23.

77. Ó Tuathail and Agnew, "Geopolitics and Discourse," 195.

78. This empirical investigation is based on a systematic analysis of foreign policy texts. It draws from both primary and secondary sources. The primary material includes such political programs as national security concepts, as well as speeches and interviews by such key foreign policy officials as presidents and ministers of foreign affairs. I read all major speeches from the 1990s that were available on the Web sites of the ministerial and presidential offices. The secondary sources include various working papers and research reports available on the Web sites of national research institutes as

well as articles in such regional English-language media as *Transitions Online* (http://www.tol.cz), *The Prague Post* (http://www.praguepost.com), *The Budapest Sun* (http://www.budapestsun.com), *The Baltic Times* (http://www.baltictimes.com) and *The Warsaw Voice* (http://www.warsaw voice.pl). Many of these are usually not used in Western research although they are available in English. This approach enables me to highlight similar modes of analysis in security debates in Central Europe. While no two texts are completely identical, many of the metaphors are similar and are used repeatedly.

79. Barbara Falk, *The Dilemmas of Dissidence in East-Central Europe* (Budapest: Central European University Press, 2003); Merje Kuus, "Intellectuals and Geopolitics: The 'Cultural Politicians' of Central Europe," *Geoforum* 37 (2007): 241–51 Anatol Lieven, *The Baltic Revolution: Estonia, Latvia and Lithuania and the Path to Independence*, rev. ed. (New Haven, CT: Yale University Press, 1993).

80. The phrase is borrowed from Iver B. Neumann, "Forgetting the Central Europe of the 1980s," in *Central Europe: Core or Periphery?* ed. Christopher Lord (Copenhagen: Copenhagen Business School, 2003), 207–18.

81. Neumann, *Uses of the Other*; Neumann, "Forgetting the Central Europe of the 1980s," 207.

82. Attila Melegh, *On the East-West Slope: Globalization, Nationalism, Racism and Discourses on Eastern Europe* (Budapest and New York: Central European University Press, 2006), 2.

83. Kundera, "The Tragedy of Central Europe."

84. Caroline Humphrey, "Does the Category of 'Postsocialism' Still Make Sense?" in *Postsocialism: Ideals, Ideologies, and Practices in Eurasia*, ed. Chris M. Hann (London: Routledge, 2002), 13; see also Gregory Feldman, "Culture, State, and Security in Europe: the Case of Citizenship and Integration Policy in Estonia," *American Ethnologist* 32 (2005): 680.

85. Clifford Geertz, "The Thick Description: Toward an Interpretive Theory of Culture," in *The Interpretation of Cultures: Selected Essays by Clifford Geertz*, ed. Clifford Geertz (New York: Basic Books, 1973), 26. I thank David Ley for pointing me to Geertz's work. See David Ley, "Between Europe and Asia: The Case of Missing Sequoias," *Ecumene* 2 (1995), 185.

86. Sayer, *Method in Social Science*, 249.

87. Ibid., 248.

88. Huntington, *Clash of Civilizations*, 162.

89. Mart Laar, *Eesti uus algus* [Estonia's New Beginning] (Tallinn: Tanapaev, 2002).

90. The quotes come from the *Economist*, "Europe's Magnetic Attraction: Survey of EU Enlargement," May 17, 2001; and "Mart Laar, Estonia's Punchy Prime Minister," February 22, 2001. See also "Trouble in Paradise," July 2, 1998. Ronald Asmus remarked in 2002 that "When you look at the size of the Baltic countries, they receive more high-level policy attention than almost any other country in the world—with the possible exception of Israel

or Cuba." *City Paper*, "Towards Better Security," Interview with Ronald Asmus. http://www.balticsww.com/news/features/better_security.htm 1998 (accessed September 15, 2002). Asmus served from 1997 to 2000 as the United States Deputy Assistant Secretary of State for European Affairs.

91. Primary data for my analysis of Estonia are derived chiefly from three sources: (1) major national newspapers; (2) political speeches and parliamentary transcripts; and (3) policy programs. My media analysis focuses on mainstream national Estonian-language newspapers because these set the tone of political debate. Opinions expressed in the Russian-language media usually do not reach the threshold of national relevance. Estonian-language sources like newspaper columns and parliamentary debates almost never refer to Russian-language media. My analysis of parliamentary transcripts concentrates on three sets of debates. The first are the question-and-answer sessions between parliamentarians and the foreign minister following the minister's biannual "Guidelines of Estonian Foreign Policy" speech to the parliament. The second are debates focusing explicitly on security, such as the discussions of the National Security Concept. The third set of debates includes various discussions of ethnic integration because these directly link security and national identity. In addition, I also draw from parliamentary debates on European integration and some other topics relevant to the investigation. Although these data do not offer a comprehensive picture of parliamentary debates, they allow me to make generalizations about the dynamics and parameters of these debates. As in the case of Central Europe as a whole, the analysis of Estonia generally focuses on the period leading up to accession. The key dynamics of political debate from the preaccession era, however, are still in place.

92. Janine Wedel, *Collision and Collusion: The Strange Case of Western Aid to Eastern Europe*, 2nd ed. (New York: Palgrave, 2001), 3.

Chapter 2

1. John Borneman and Nick Fowler, "Europeanization," *Annual Review of Anthropology* 26 (1997): 488.

2. The concept of Europe is securitized not only in Central Europe but also in the wider European integration discourse. That discourse frames integration as an urgent task, the alternative to which is fragmentation. See Ole Wæver, "European Security Identities," *Journal of Common Market Studies* 34 (1996): 123. My investigation focuses on Central Europe, where the alternative to integration is not "fragmentation" but a more clear-cut notion of threat from the East.

3. Iver B. Neumann, *The Uses of the Other: 'The East' in European Identity Formation* (Minneapolis: University of Minnesota Press, 1999), 207. Matti Bunzl notes that despite the abundance of studies on East-Central Europe, there is a dearth of studies on the Western reinvention of Eastern Europe

engendered by postsocialist transformations and EU enlargement. Matti Bunzl, "The Prague Experience: Gay Male Sex Tourism and the Neocolonial Invention of the Embodied Border," in *Altering States: Ethnographies of Transition in Eastern Europe and the Former Soviet Union*, ed. Daphne Berdahl, Matti Bunzl, and Martha Lampland (Ann Arbor: University of Michigan Press, 2000), 76.

4. John A. Agnew, "How Many Europes?: The European Union, Eastward Enlargement and Uneven Development," *European Urban and Regional Studies* 8 (2001): 29–38; Luiza Bialasiewicz and John O'Loughlin, "Re-ordering Europe's Eastern Frontier: Galician Identities and Political Cartographies on the Polish-Ukrainian Border," in *Boundaries and Place: European Borderlands in Geographical Context*, ed. David Kaplan and Jouni Häkli (Lanham, MD: Rowman and Littlefield, 2002), 217–38; Anssi Paasi, "Europe as a Social Process and Discourse: Considerations of Place, Boundaries and Identity," *European Urban and Regional Studies* 8 (2001): 7–28.

5. Edward Said, *Orientalism*, 2nd ed. (New York: Vintage Books, 1994); Maria Todorova, *Imagining the Balkans* (New York: Oxford University Press, 1997).

6. Neumann, *Uses of the Other*, 78. Historical development of the discourse of Eastern Europe is beyond the scope of this investigation. I touch on history only to link the current productions of Eastern Europe to older constructions of the East. For historical analyses, see Michael Heffernan, *The Meaning of Europe: Geography and Geopolitics* (London: Arnold, 1998); Neumann, *Uses of the Other*; William Pietz, "The 'Post-colonialism' of Cold War Discourse," *Social Text* 19/20 (1988): 55–75; Todorova, *Imagining the Balkans*; and Larry Wolff, *Inventing Eastern Europe: The Map of Civilization on the Mind of the Enlightenment* (Stanford, CA: Stanford University Press, 1994).

7. Konrad Adenauer, quoted in Neumann, *Uses of the Other*, 102; George Kennan, quoted in Ó Tuathail and Agnew, 200.

8. Pietz, "'Post-colonialism' of Cold War Discourse," 58.

9. On the geopolitical assumptions underpinning area studies in general, see John A. Agnew, *Geopolitics: Re-visioning World Politics* (London: Routledge, 1998); Timothy Mitchell, *Rule of Experts: Egypt, Techno-politics, Modernity* (Berkeley, CA: University of California Press, 2002), chapter 4; and Immanuel Wallerstein, "The Unintended Consequences of Cold War Area Studies," in *The Cold War and the University: Toward an Intellectual History of the Postwar Years*, ed. Noam Chomsky et al. (New York: The Free Press, 1997), 195–232.

10. Katherine Verdery, *What Was Socialism, And What Comes Next?* (Princeton, NJ: Princeton University Press, 1996), 16.

11. Hugh Gusterson, "Missing the End of the Cold War in International Security," in *Cultures of Insecurity: States, Communities, and the Production of Danger*, ed. Jutta Weldes, Mark Laffey, Hugh Gusterson, and Raymond Duvall (Minneapolis: University of Minnesota Press, 1999), 327.

12. Philip G. Roeder, "The Revolution of 1989: Postcommunism and the Social Sciences," *Slavic Review* 58 (1999): 743.

13. György Csepeli, Antal örkény, and Kim Lane Scheppele. "Acquired Immune Deficiency Syndrome in Social Science in Eastern Europe." *Social Research* 63 (1996): 486–510, 487.

14. John Lewis Gaddis, "International Relations Theory and the End of the Cold War," *International Security* 17 (1992): 18, quoted in Archie Brown, "Gorbachev and the End of the Cold War," in *Ending the Cold War: Interpretations, Causation, and the Study of International Relations*, ed. Richard K. Herrmann and Richard Ned Lebow (New York: Palgrave MacMillan, 2004), 31. This critical work is voluminous and cannot be summarized here, but see Lebow and Risse-Kappen, eds., *International Relations Theory and the End of the Cold War*.

15. Michael Burawoy, "The End of Sovietology and the Renaissance of Modernization Theory," *Contemporary Sociology* 21 (1992): 774–85.

16. Ibid.

17. David Slater, "Geopolitical Imaginations across the North-South Divide: Issues of Difference, Development and Power," *Political Geography* 16 (1997): 643–44.

18. Alain Finkielkraut, "L'humanité perdue—Essai sur le XXème siècle" [Lost Mankind—Essay about the XXth Century] (Paris: Seuil, 1996), 139; quoted in Olivier Danjoux, *Reframing Citizenship in the Baltic Republics*, Lund Political Studies 122 (Lund: Department of Political Science, 2002), 59.

19. Csepeli, Örkény and Scheppele, "Acquired Immune Deficiency Syndrome."

20. Ibid., 487. As the expertise that "sold" focused on immediate economic opportunities, the humanities were further marginalized within transitology.

21. Janine Wedel, *Collision and Collusion: The Strange Case of Western Aid to Eastern Europe*, 2nd ed. (New York: Palgrave, 2001), 18.

22. Ibid., 6.

23. Danjoux, Reframing Citizenship, 51; Lazlo Kurti, "Homecoming: Affairs of Anthropologists in and of Eastern Europe," *Anthropology Today* 12 (1996): 11–15.

24. Michael Harloe, Ivan Szelenyi, and Gregory Andrusz, eds., *Cities after Socialism: Urban and Regional Change and Conflict in Post-Socialist Societies* (Oxford and Cambridge, MA: Blackwell, 1996), 3; see also Adrian Smith, "Imagining Geographies of the 'New Europe': Geo-economic Power and the New European Architecture of Integration," *Political Geography* 21 (2002): 647–70.

25. Quoted in Robert M. Hayden, *Blueprints for a House Divided: The Constitutional Logic of Yugoslav Conflicts* (Ann Arbor: University of Michigan Press, 1999), 6.

26. Wedel, *Collision and Collusion*, 39–40. A high Polish official suggested as early as 1992 that the main benefit derived from the "Marriott Brigade" was not the expertise they provided, but the hard currency they contributed to the local economy. Wedel, *Collision and Collusion*, 59.

27. *City Paper*, "Selling Estonia," Part 1 (1998): 4.
28. Valerie Bunce, "Lessons of the First Postsocialist Decade," *East European Politics and Societies* 13 (1999): 236–43; Michael Burawoy and Katherine Verdery, eds., *Uncertain Transition: Ethnographies of Change in the Postsocialist World* (Lanham, MD, Rowman and Littlefield Publishers, 1999); Gernot Grabher and David Stark, eds., *Restructuring Networks in Post-Socialism: Legacies, Linkages and Localities* (Oxford: Oxford University Press, 1996); Chris Hann, ed., *Postsocialism: Ideals, Ideologies and Practices in Eurasia* (London: Routledge, 2002); Michael D. Kennedy, *Cultural Formations of Postcommunism: Emancipation, Transition, Nation, and War* (Minneapolis: University of Minnesota Press, 2002); John Pickles and Adrian Smith, eds., *Theorising Transition: the Political Economy of Post-Communist Transformations* (London: Routledge, 1998); and David Stark and Laszlo Bruszt, *Post-Socialist Pathways: Transforming Politics and Property in Eastern Europe* (Cambridge: Cambridge University Press, 1997).
29. József Böröcz, "The Fox and the Raven: The European Union and Hungary Renegotiate the Margins of 'Europe,'" *Comparative Studies in Society and History* 4 (2000): 847–875.
30. BBC News, "Chirac Sparks 'New Europe' Ire," February 19, 2003.
31. Andrew Michta, "East European Area Studies and Security Studies: A New Approach," *NewsNet: News of the American Association for the Advancement of Slavic Studies* 43 (2003): 1–3.
32. Adam Krzeminski, "First Kant, Now Habermas: A Polish Perspective on 'Core Europe,'" in *Old Europe, New Europe, Core Europe: Transatlantic Relations after the Iraq War*, ed. Daniel Levy, Max Pensky and John Torpey (London: Verso, 2005), 147.
33. Andrzej Stasiuk, "Wild, Cunning, Exotic: The East Will Completely Shake Up Europe," *Süddeutsche Zeitung*, June 20, 2003. Reprinted in *Old Europe, New Europe, Core Europe: Transatlantic Relations After the Iraq War*, ed. Daniel Levy, Max Pensky, and John Torpey (London: Verso, 2005), 103–04.
34. Heffernan, *Meaning of Europe*, 185.
35. *Economist*, "Westward, Look, the Land Is Bright," October 24, 2002.
36. Lieven, *The Baltic Revolution*, 381; Rogers Brubaker points out a similar oscillation; see Rogers Brubaker, "Myths and Misconceptions in the Study of Nationalism," in *The State of the Nation: Ernest Gellner and the Theory of Nationalism*, ed. J. Hall (Cambridge: Cambridge University Press, 1998), 272–306.
37. For a more in-depth discussion, see Mitja Velikonja, *Eurosis: A Critique of New Eurocentrism*, Ljubljana, Mirovni Institut, 2005, e-book, http://mediawatch.mirovni-institut.si/eng/mw17.htm (accessed June 13, 2006).
38. Milan Kundera, "The Tragedy of Central Europe," *New York Review of Books*, April 26, 1984, 33.
39. *Economist*, "Europe's Magnetic Attraction," 1.
40. Frank Schimmelfennig, "International Socialization in the New Europe: Rational Action in an Institutional Environment," *European Journal of International Relations* 6 (2000): 109–39, 110–111.

41. Andrew H. Dawson and Rick Fawn, "The Changing Geopolitics of Eastern Europe: An Introduction," *Geopolitics* 6 (2001): 3.

42. Kathrin Hörschelmann, "Breaking Ground—Marginality and Resistance in (Post) Unification Germany," *Political Geography* 20 (2001): 986. For other exposés of such tropes, see Böröcz, "The Fox and the Raven"; Stephen F. Cohen, *Failed Crusade: America and the Tragedy of Post-Communist Russia* (New York: W. W. Norton, 2001); and Wedel, *Collision and Collusion*.

43. Cohen, *Failed Crusade*; Grabher and Stark, *Restructuring Networks in Post-Socialism*.

44. Schimmelfennig, "International Socialization," 111.

45. For a prominent example, see Juan J. Linz and Alfred Stepan, *Problems of Democratic Transition and Consolidation: Southern Europe, South America and Post-Communist Europe* (Baltimore, MD and London: Johns Hopkins University Press, 1996).

46. Neumann, *Uses of the Other*, 110; emphasis in original.

47. Ole Wæver, "The EU as Security Actor: Reflections from a Pessimistic Constructivist on Post-Sovereign Security Orders," in *International Relations Theory and the Politics of European Integration: Power, Security and Community*, ed. Morten Kelstrup and Michael C. Williams (London and New York: Routledge, 2000), 263.

48. For an analysis of these tropes in colonialist writings, see Dipesh Chakrabarti, *Provincializing Europe: Postcolonial Thought and Historical Difference* (Princeton, NJ: Princeton University Press, 2000).

49. Attila Melegh, *On the East-West Slope: Globalization, Nationalism, Racism and Discourses on Eastern Europe* (Budapest and New York: Central European University Press, 2006), 45.

50. Velikonja, *Eurosis*, 7.

51. Brubaker, "Myths and Misconceptions," 284.

52. Lieven, "Against Russophobia"; Neumann, *Uses of the Other*.

53. Brubaker, "Myths and Misconceptions," 281. There is a vast literature on this topic. For further critiques of the return-of-the-repressed view, see David Campbell, *National Deconstruction: Violence, Ethnicity and Justice in Bosnia* (Minneapolis: University of Minnesota Press, 1998); Hayden, *Blueprints for a House Divided*; and Todorova, *Imagining the Balkans*.

54. Jacques Rupnik, borrowing a phrase from the novelist William Faulkner, quoted in Krishan Kumar, *1989: Revolutionary Ideas and Ideals* (Minneapolis: University of Minnesota Press, 2001), 194; see also 12–13.

55. Magda Boguszakova, Ivan Gabal, Endre Hann, Piotr Starzynski, and Eva Taracova, "Public Attitudes in Four Central European Countries," in *Perceptions of Security: Public Opinion and Expert Assessments in Europe's New Democracies*, ed. R. Smoke (New York: Manchester University Press, 1996), 48. Boguzsakova and her colleagues interestingly note that this point is made specifically for the benefit of Western audiences. For the sake of consistency and readability, I generally use full names in running text only when quoting a well-known scholar or public figure. In most other times, the identity of the speaker is given in the note.

56. Frank Cataluccio, "Introduction: In Search of Lost Europe," in Bronislaw Geremek, *The Common Roots of Europe* (London: Polity Press, 1996), 2.

57. *Economist*, "Europe's Magnetic Attraction,".5.

58. According to Frank Schimmelfennig, NATO accepts only states "in which internalization [of Western norms] is advanced." Frank Schimmelfennig, "International Socialization," 110–11. This framework of "transition" to Western or European norms in part explains why the EU and NATO enlargements are frequently folded together as the "eastern enlargement of Europe." See Celeste A. Wallander, "NATO's Price: Shape Up or Ship Out," *Foreign Affairs* 81 (2002): 2–8.

59. Brubaker, "Myths and Misconceptions," 282.

60. Raimo Väyrynen, "The Security of the Baltic Countries: Co-operation and Defection," in *Stability and Security in the Baltic Sea Region. Russian, Nordic and European Aspects*, ed. Olav Knudsen (London and Portland, OR: Frank Cass, 1999), 216, emphasis added. See also Walter C. Clemens Jr., *The Baltic Transformed: Complexity Theory and European Security* (Lanham, MD: Rowman and Littlefield, 2001); Christian Haerpfer, Cezary Milosinski, and Claire Wallace, "Old and New Security Issues in Post-Communist Eastern Europe: Results of an 11 Nation Study," *Europe-Asia Studies* 51 (1999): 989–1011; Linz and Stepan, *Problems of Democratic Transition and Consolidation*.

61. Danjoux notes that significantly more Western research on identity and security has been devoted to Estonia and Latvia than to Lithuania. The former two have sizeable Russian-speaking populations that offer "convenient societal cleavages, especially marketable after the conflict in the former Yugoslavia," while the latter does not. Danjoux, *Reframing Citizenship in the Baltic Republics*, 59. A similar fascination with conflict is discernible in the Baltic Sea region. Christopher Browning and Pertti Joenniemi highlight the key role of security concerns in fueling regional cooperation, and ask whether regional cooperation can outlive concerns about security. Christopher Browning and Pertti Joenniemi, "Regionality beyond Security? The Baltic Sea Region after Enlargement," *Cooperation and Conflict* 39 (2004): 233–53. For critiques of viewing ethnic tensions in spectacular terms, see Rogers Brubaker, *Nationalism Reframed: Nationhood and the National Question in the New Europe* (Cambridge: Cambridge University Press, 1996); and David Laitin, *Identity in Formation: The Russian-Speaking Populations in the Near Abroad* (Ithaca, NY: Cornell University Press, 1998).

62. John O'Loughlin, "Ordering the 'Crush Zone': Geopolitical Games in Post-Cold War Eastern Europe," in *Geopolitics and Globalization: The Changing World Political Map*, ed. Nurit Kliot and David Newman (London: Frank Cass, 2001), 52. See also James F. Brown, *The Grooves of Change: Eastern Europe at the Turn of the Millennium* (Durham, NC: Duke University Press, 2001).

63. I will return to this issue in chapter 4. Michael Johns, "'Do as I Say, Not as I Do': The European Union, Eastern Europe and Minority Rights," *East European Politics and Societies* 17 (2003): 682–99; and Ronald Linden, ed., *Norms and Nannies: The Impact of International Organizations on the Central and East European States* (Lanham, MD: Rowman and Littlefield, 2002).

64. Pami Aalto and Eiki Berg, "Spatial Practices and Time in Estonia: From Post-Soviet Geopolitics to European Governance," *Space & Polity* 6 (2002): 267. See also Inga Pavlovaite, "Being European by Joining Europe: Accession and Identity Politics in Lithuania," *Cambridge Review of International Affairs* 16 (2003): 239–55.

65. Heather Rae, *State Identities and the Homogenisation of Peoples* (Cambridge: Cambridge University Press, 2002), 294. See also Elena Jurado, "Complying with European Standards of Minority Rights Education: Estonia's Relations with the European Union, OSCE and Council of Europe," *Journal of Baltic Studies* 34 (2003): 399–431; and Linz and Stepan, *Problems of Democratic Transition and Consolidation*. NATO enlargement in 2004 was justified in substantial part by invoking such incentives in realms ranging from civil-military relations to minority rights; see Wallander, "NATO's Price: Shape Up or Ship Out," 3.

66. David Laitin pointed out that in terms of their political culture, the EU's new member states are closer to the original six EEC members than the post-six entrants. The distinction between old and new is breaking down. David D. Laitin, "Culture and National Identity: 'The East' and European Integration," *West European Politics* 25 (2002): 55–80.

67. Agnew, "How Many Europes?" 29–38.

68. Charles Ingrao, "Understanding Ethnic Conflict in Central Europe: An Historical Perspective," Nationalities Papers 27 (1999): 291–318. Slavoj Zizek makes the same point about southeastern Europe—the Balkans always lie beyond the southern border of any particular state. Slavoj Žižek, *The Metastases of Enjoyment* (London: Verso, 1994). See also Lene Hansen, "Slovenian Identity: State Building on the Balkan Border," Alternatives 21 (1996): 473–95; Sami Moisio, "EU Eligibility, Central Europe and the Invention of Applicant State Narrative," *Geopolitics* 7 (2002): 89–116; Neumann, *Uses of the Other*; Patrick H. Patterson, "On the Edge of Reason: The Boundaries of Balkanism in Slovenian, Austrian, and Italian Discourse," *Slavic Review* 62 (2003): 110–41; and Todorova, *Imagining the Balkans*.

69. Wedel, *Collision and Collusion*,19.

70. Melegh, *On the East-West Slope*; see also note 68 above.

71. Kundera, "Tragedy of Central Europe," 33.

72. Ibid.

73. Janusz Stefanovicz, "Poland," in *Perceptions of Security: Public Opinion and Expert Assessments in Europe's New Democracies*, ed. R. Smoke (New York: Manchester University Press, 1996), 128.

74. Ronald D. Asmus, *Opening NATO's Door: How the Alliance Remade Itself for a New Era* (New York: Columbia University Press, 2002), 229.

75. Rotfeld, "Borderless Europe and Global Security."

76. Milica Bakic-Hayden, "Nesting Orientalisms: The Case of Former Yugoslavia," *Slavic Review* 54 (1995): 917–31.

77. Tomasz Zarycki, "Uses of Russia: The Role of Russia is the Modern Polish National Identity," *East European Politics and Societies* 18 (2004): 595–627, 600.

78. Melegh, *On the East-West Slope*, 5.
79. Milica Bakic-Hayden and Robert M. Hayden, "Orientalist Variations on the Theme 'Balkans': Symbolic Geography of Recent Yugoslav Cultural Politics," *Slavic Review* 51 (1992): 1–15; Hayden, *Blueprints for a House Divided*; Patterson, "On the Edge of Reason."
80. Moisio, "EU Eligibility."
81. Merje Kuus, "Toward Co-operative Security? International Integration and the Construction of Security in Estonia," *Millennium: Journal of International Studies* 31 (2002): 297–317; Grazina Miniotaite, "The Baltic States: in Search of Security and Identity," in *Almost NATO: Partners and Players in Central and Eastern European Security*, ed. Charles Krupnick (Lanham, MD: Rowman and Littlefield, 2002), 261–96. Elizabeth Dunn observes such East-West "topography of taste" even on the production and marketing of pork products. She reports that the production and availability of pork products in Poland is described not just in terms of expense (leaner products are more expensive) but also in terms of distance from Europe. Sausages thus become progressively less sophisticated (and cheaper) as one moves eastward from Western Europe through Poland to Ukraine. West Europeans are described as discerning customers, Poles are cast as a bit less so, and Russians are dismissed as unsophisticated consumers who do not care what they put in their mouths as long as it is cheap. This small vignette illustrates the commonsense character of the East-West slope even among actors who find themselves on that slope. Elizabeth C. Dunn, "Standards and Person-Making in East-Central Europe," in *Global Assemblages: Technology, Politics, and Ethics as Anthropological Problems*, ed. Aihwa Ong and Stephen Collier (Oxford: Blackwell Publishing, 2005), 182
82. Moisio, "EU Eligibility"; Krupnick, *Almost NATO*; Neumann, *Uses of the Other*; Smoke, *Perceptions of Security*.
83. Quoted in Iver B. Neumann, "European Identity, EU Expansion, and the Integration/Exclusion Nexus," *Alternatives* 23 (1998): 5.
84. *Gazeta Polska*, quoted in Zarycki, "Uses of Russia," 608.
85. Catherine Perron, "Local Political Elites Perceptions of the EU," in *The Road to the European Union*, Vol. 1: *The Czech and Slovak Republics*, ed. Jacques Rupnick and Jan Zielonka (Manchester and New York: Manchester University Press, 2003), 205. See also Peter Bugge, "Home at Last? Czech View of Joining the European Union, " in *Margins in European Integration*, ed. N. Parker and B. Armstrong (New York: St. Martin's Press, 2002), 203–29.
86. Quoted in Perron, "Local Political Elites," 205. The allusions to Mongols and Asians also indicate the strong racist connotations of the concept of Europe in Central Europe. For other studies that highlight such racialized narratives of Europe, see Merje Feldman, "European Integration and the Discourse of National Identity in Estonia," *National Identities* 3 (2001): 5–21; and Zarycki, "Uses of Russia."
87. Timothy Garton Ash, quoted in Cataluccio, "Introduction," 6. Garton Ash himself has been instrumental in the making of the concept of Central Europe.

88. Timothy Garton Ash, *History of the Present: Essays, Sketches and Dispatches from Europe in the 1990s* (London: Penguin Books, 1999), 387; Moisio, "EU Eligibility"; Neumann, *Uses of the Other*, 158.

89. Neumann, "Forgetting the Central Europe of the 1980s," 207. The discourse of Central Europe presents the region not simply as a part of Europe but indeed as an exemplary part of what Europe is supposed to be—Europe not tainted by Western consumerism, still authentic and pure.

90. Todorova, *Imagining the Balkans*, 160. A number of authors have noted the failure of Central Europe as a region-building tool because of the lack of a regional identity or interest. Central Europe does not work in the region; it works in the West.

91. Patterson, "On the Edge of Reason," 128.

92. Neumann, *Uses of the Other*, 144.

93. See Zarycki, "Uses of Russia," 602.

94. Merje Kuus, "Europe's Eastern Enlargement and the Re-inscription of Otherness in East-Central Europe," *Progress in Human Geography* 28 (2004): 472–89; Miniotaite, "The Baltic States"; Gabriel Popescu, "Diaspora Geopolitics: Romanian-Americans and NATO Expansion," *Geopolitics* 10 (2005): 455–81.

95. Perry Anderson, "The Europe to Come," *London Review of Books*, January 25, 1996, 21; quoted in Talal Asad, "Muslims and European Identity: Can Europe Represent Islam?" in *The Idea of Europe: from Antiquity to the European Union*, ed. Anthony Pagden (Cambridge and New York: Woodrow Wilson Center Press and Cambridge University Press, 2002), 209–27, 219.

96. Bakic-Hayden, "Nesting Orientalisms," 9.

97. Garton Ash, *History of the Present*, 384.

98. Péter Esterházy, "How Big Is the European Dwarf?" *Süddeutsche Zeitung*, June 11, 2003. Reprinted in *Old Europe, New Europe, Core Europe: Transatlantic Relations After the Iraq War*, ed. D. Levy, M. Pensky and J. Torpey (London: Verso, 2005), 74–9, 75.

99. Hayden White, "The Discourse of Europe and the Search for a European Identity," in *Europe and the Other and Europe as the Other*, ed. Bo Stråth (Brussels: P.I.E.–Peter Lang, 2000), 74. For an attempt to conceptualize the inscription of Europeanness through postcolonial theory, see Merje Kuus, "Europe's Eastern Enlargement."

100. This observation applies to some extent to the concept of Europe as well. Europe too is conceived spatially not as a territory but as an amalgam of zones and circles of Europeanness.

101. Melegh, *On the East-West Slope*, 97; Bahar Rumelili, "Constructing Identity and Relating to Difference," *Review of International Studies* 30 (2004): 27–47.

Chapter 3

1. Samuel Huntington, "The Clash of Civilizations?" *Foreign Affairs* 72 (1993): 25.

2. Gearóid O'Tuathail, *Critical Geopolitics: The Politics of Writing Global Space* (Minneapolis: University of Minnesota Press, 1996), 244.

3. Marju Lauristin, "Contexts of Transition," in *Return to the Western World: Cultural and Political Perspectives on the Estonian Post-Communist Transition*, ed. Marju Lauristin, Peeter Vihalemm, Karl Erik Rosengren, and Lennart Weibull (Tartu: Tartu University Press, 1997), 29.

4. Bronislaw Geremek, address on the occasion of the Protocols to the North Atlantic Treaty on the Accession of Poland, the Czech Republic, and Hungary, delivered in Brussels, December 16, 1997; quoted in Rebecca Moore, "Europe 'Whole and Free': NATO's Political Mission in the 21st Century," NATO–EAPC Research Fellowship Final Report (Brussels: NATO Office of Information and Press, 2003), 63.

5. *Economist*, "Europe's Magnetic Attraction," 8.

6. The phrase is borrowed from Przemyslav Grudzinski and Peter van Ham, *A Critical Approach to European Security* (London: Pinter, 1999), 201.

7. Ibid., 9. Huntington articulates his argument chiefly in his article "The Clash of Civilizations?" and its book-length version; see Samuel Huntington, *The Clash of Civilizations and the Remaking of the World Order* (New York: Simon and Schuster, 1996).

8. Huntington, *The Clash of Civilizations and the Remaking of the World Order*, 7.

9. Ibid., 43.

10. Huntington, "The Clash of Civilizations?" 25.

11. Huntington, *Clash of Civilizations and the Remaking of the World Order*, 128.

12. For an informative summary of both realist and constructivist critiques of Huntington, see Hugh Gusterson, *People of the Bomb: Portraits of America's Nuclear Complex* (Minneapolis: University of Minnesota Press, 2004), chapter 7.

13. Huntington, *Clash of Civilizations and the Remaking of the World Order*, 158.

14. Ibid., 161.

15. NATO enlargement is the subject of a large body of work, mostly in security studies and international relations theory. It tends to revolve around questions of efficacy—that is, whether NATO is an effective peacemaking tool and how strongly it has impacted on the applicant and member states. This scholarship tends to assume rather than interrogate a more liberal and socially oriented NATO that facilitates democracy and freedom in its member states and beyond. For informative overviews of this literature, see Karin M. Fierke and Antje Wiener, "Constructing Institutional Interests: EU and NATO Enlargement," *Journal of European Public Policy* 6 (1999): 721–42; and Moore, "Europe 'Whole and Free.'" For an insider's account of the diplomatic and political process of NATO enlargement, see Ronald D. Asmus, *Opening NATO's Door: How the Alliance Remade Itself for a New Era* (New York: Columbia University Press, 2002). For an insightful analysis of the (George W.) Bush administration's rhetoric on NATO enlargement, see Edward Rhodes, "The Good, the Bad, and the Righteous: Understanding the Bush Vision of a New NATO Partnership." *Millennium: Journal of International Studies* 33 (2004): 123–143.

16. Michael C. Williams and Iver B. Neumann, "From Alliance to Security Community: NATO, Russia, and the Power of Identity," *Millennium: Journal of International Studies* 29 (2000): 368.

17. Ibid., 361.

18. Kathryn Sikkink and Martha Finnemore, "International Norm Dynamics and Political Change," *International Organization* 52 (1998): 895, cited in Moore, "Europe 'Whole and Free,'" 45.

19. Grudzinski and van Ham, *Critical Approach to European Security*, 94.

20. There is a voluminous literature on the transformation of NATO in the post-Cold War era. See Williams and Neumann, "From Alliance to Security Community," 357–387; and Grudzinski and van Ham, *A Critical Approach to European Security*.

21. NATO, *Study of Enlargement* (Brussels: NATO, 1994); quoted in Williams and Neumann, "From Alliance to Security Community," 372.

22. The term comes from Grudzinski and van Ham, *Critical Approach to European Security*, 11.

23. Ibid., 156.

24. Quoted in Charles Krupnick and Carol Atkinson, "Slovakia and Security and the Center of Europe," in *Almost NATO: Partners and Players in Central and Eastern European Security*, ed. Charles Krupnick (Lanham, MD: Rowman and Littlefield, 2002), 70.

25. This point was repeated in both the member and the applicant states of NATO. See Moore, "Europe 'Whole and Free,'" 46.

26. U.S. State Department, "Powell Welcomes Seven New East European Members to NATO," press release, March 29, 2004, http://www.usembassy .it/file2004_03/alia/a4032901.htm (accessed September 13, 2005).

27. Giuliano Amato and Judy Batt, *The Long-term Implications of EU Enlargement: The Nature of the New Border* (Florence: European University Institute in Florence, 1999); Heather Grabbe, "The Sharp Edges of Europe: Extending Schengen Eastwards," *International Affairs* 76 (2000): 519–36; Grudzinski and van Ham, *Critical Approach to European Security*,150; and Walker, "The Subject of Security," 71.

28. Christopher Browning and Pertti Joenniemi, "The European Union's Two Dimensions: The Northern and the Eastern," *Security Dialogue* 34 (2003): 463–78; Browning and Joenniemi, "Regionality Beyond Security?"; Zielonka, *Europe as Empire*.

29. Giorgio Agamben, "Security and Terror," *Theory & Event* 5 (2002); Barry Buzan, Ole Wæver, and Jaape de Wilde, *Security: A New Framework for Analysis* (Boulder, CO: Lynne Rienner, 1998), 25; Jutta Weldes, Mark Laffey, Hugh Gusterson, and Raymond Duvall, eds., *Cultures of Insecurity: States, Communities, and the Production of Danger* (Minneapolis: University of Minnesota Press, 1999).

30. Buzan, Wæver, and de Wilde, *Security: A New Framework*, 23.

31. Moreover, broadening security to the realm of identity may also reinforce rather than undermine the power of the state. Ole Wæver points out that the

nation-state is a key part of the very concept of security; other definitions of the term work by comparing these "other" types of security to national security. Writings on broadened security agendas abound with such expressions as "not only but also" or "in addition to." They tend to apply security to more spheres of social life and thereby replicate the model of a sovereign state in a new mantle. Wæver, "European Security Identities," 104. See also Krause and Williams, "From Strategy to Security," 48.

32. Williams and Neumann, "From Alliance to Security Community," 385.

33. For a critique, see Christopher Browning, "The Region-Building Approach Revisited: the Continued Othering of Russia in Discourses of Region-Building in the European North," *Geopolitics* 8 (2003): 45–71.

34. Maria Todorova, "Isn't Central Europe Dead?" in *Central Europe: Core or Periphery?* ed. Christopher Lord (Copenhagen: Copenhagen Business School, 2003), 219–31.

35. The term comes from Timothy Garton Ash, *History of the Present: Essays, Sketches and Dispatches from Europe in the 1990s* (London: Penguin Books, 1999), 198. See also Stefano Guzzini, "'Self-fulfilling Geopolitics'? Or: The Social Production of Foreign Policy Expertise in Europe" (paper presented at the joint convention of the Central Eastern European International Studies Association and the International Studies Association, Budapest, Hungary, June 26–28, 2003).

36. Edward Rhodes, personal communication, December 2000.

37. Magda Boguszakova, Ivan Gabal, Endre Hann, Piotr Starzynski, and Eva Taracova, "Public Attitudes in Four Central European Countries," in *Perceptions of Security: Public Opinion and Expert Assessments in Europe's New Democracies*, ed. R. Smoke (New York: Manchester University Press, 1996), 34; emphasis added.

38. Ibid., 25; emphasis in original.

39. Ibid., 38.

40. Only 24 percent of the populations in these four states are afraid of Russia. For comparison, 21 percent believe that Germany is a potential security threat, and 21 percent have this opinion of the United States. The question asked was, "Do you think [Russia, Germany, the United States] poses a threat ("big threat" + "some threat") to peace and security in this society?' The data thus do not indicate what specific aspect of a country was considered threatening. See Christian Haerpfer, Cezary Milosinski, and Claire Wallace, "Old and New Security Issues in Post-Communist Eastern Europe: Results of an 11 Nation Study," *Europe-Asia Studies* 51 (1999): 989–1011.

41. Popular attitudes toward NATO are mixed and unstable. Results of surveys depend a great deal on when the surveys are carried out and what questions are used. Questions range from the more specific inquiries about voting intentions in the event of a referendum on NATO accession to more general questions about "support for" accession or "opinion of" or "confidence in" NATO as an institution, to the even more vague question of "strengthening links between" Central European countries and NATO It is fair to say that

over half the electorate—often 70 to 80 percent—expresses "support" for NATO accession, but the data allow no more specific claims. There are also considerable fluctuations over time. For example, support for NATO accession declined by 30 percent in Poland between 1996 and 1998. Zlatko Šabic and Ljubica Jelušic, "Slovenia and NATO Enlargement: Twists, Turns and Endless Frustrations," in *Almost NATO: Partners and Players in Central and Eastern European Security*, ed. Charles Krupnick (Lanham, MD: Rowman and Littlefield, 2002), 100. The United States Information Agency (USIA), which has regularly surveyed Central Europeans' attitudes toward NATO since the early 1990s, found that support for NATO accession is "shallow" and has generally declined since 1995. The agency noted that even if Central European populations support NATO accession, they are not keen to assume the responsibilities of membership. Large majorities across the region "favor social over military spending," according to USIA. Haerpfer et al., "Old and New Security Issues," 1009. See also BBC News, "Newcomers' Joy at NATO Invitation"; Christo Domozetov, *Public Perceptions of Euro-Atlantic Partnership: Issues of Security and Military. The case of Bulgaria* (NATO–EAPC Institutional Research Fellowship 1988–2000; Brussels: NATO Office of Information and Press. http://www.nato.int (accessed August 12, 2004); Paul Goble, "Divided on Security," *Baltic Times*, September 10, 1998; Krupnick, ed., *Almost NATO*; Smoke, *Perceptions of Security*. Furthermore, it is sometimes difficult to discern what a particular poll number really shows. In Estonia, for example, the government claimed at the turn of the decade that 65 percent of Estonians supported NATO membership. Yet the poll on which that claim was based indicated that 20 percent of Estonia's population strongly supported NATO membership. The 65 percent figure is correct only if "Estonian" means "ethnic Estonians," and "supports" means the sum of those who "strongly support" NATO membership and those who "support rather than oppose." Merje Kuus, "Toward Co-operative Security? International Integration and the Construction of Security in Estonia," *Millennium: Journal of International Studies* 31 (2002): 297–317.

42. Egdunas Racius, "Lithuania's New Cold War," *Baltic Times*, July 8, 2004.
43. Ian Taylor, "New Europe Gets Shock Lesson in Realpolitik," *Guardian*, April 28, 2003. Taylor is quoting Alexander Smolar, head of a Warsaw think-tank and a former aide to the prime minister.
44. Tomasz Zarycki, "Uses of Russia: The Role of Russia is the Modern Polish National Identity," *East European Politics and Societies* 18 (2004): 614.
45. Michael Tarm, "Alliance Bound," *City Paper's Baltic Worldwide*, 4. www.balticsww.com/alliance.htm (accessed 13 November 2002); also see Smoke, Perceptions of Security,
46. Smoke, *Perceptions of Security*, 44.
47. Quoted in Birkavs, Valdis. Interview in *City Paper* 36 (August–September 1998), www.balticsww.com/natoquotes.htm (accessed February 20, 2005).
48. Stefanovicz, "Poland," in Smoke, *Perceptions of Security*, 113.
49. Smoke, Perceptions of Security, chapters 8–12.

50. Quoted in Martin Smith, "The NATO Factor: A Spanner in the Works of EU and WEU Enlargement?" in *Back to Europe: Central and Eastern Europe and the European Union*, ed. Karen Henderson (London: UCL Press, 1999), 62.

51. Václav Havel, quoted in Haerpfer et al., "Old and New Security Issues," 989.

52. In the early 1990s, when NATO was still identified as a military defense alliance, neutrality was an option that was actually considered across Central Europe. Several Central European states were also proponents of a stronger Commission on Security and Cooperation in Europe (CSCE; later OSCE). See Olav F. Knudsen, ed., *Stability and Security in the Baltic Sea Region. Russian, Nordic and European Aspects* (London and Portland, OR: Frank Cass, 1999); Krupnick, ed., *Almost NATO*; and Smoke, ed., *Perceptions of Security*.

53. Arpad Göncz, Address at the meeting of the North Atlantic Council (NAC), Brussels, September 16, 1996.

54. Toomas Hendrik Ilves, address to Riigikogu, December 5, 1996. Tallinn: Estonian Ministry of Foreign Affairs. http://www.vm.ee/eng/pressreleases/speeches/1996/9612min.html (accessed June 2, 1999).

55. Václav Havel, "Quo Vadis, NATO?" *Washington Post*, May 19, 2002; Václav Klaus, address delivered on the occasion of the fifth anniversary of the Czech Republic's membership in NATO, Prague Castle, March 12, 2004.

56. Georgi Parvanov, "Bulgaria's New Role in the Region after Its Accession to NATO and as a Potential EU Member" (lecture at the National Palace of Culture, Sophia, May 12, 2004), http://www.president.bg (accessed July 16, 2004).

57. Aleksander Kwasniewski, "President of Poland's Interview for 'A Newshour' with Jim Lehrer," WETA, PBS, NPR, July 18, 2002.

58. Valdis Birkavs, interview with *City Paper* 36 (August–September 1998).

59. Toomas Hendrik Ilves, "The Road to European Integration: EU and NATO" (remarks made at the second annual Stockholm Conference on Baltic Sea Security and Co-operation, Stockholm, November 6, 1997).

60. Larry L. Watts, "Romania and NATO: The National-Regional Security Nexus," in *Almost NATO: Partners and Players in Central and Eastern European Security*, ed. Charles Krupnick (Lanham, MD: Rowman and Littlefield, 2002), 183.

61. Jacques Rupnik, "Eastern Europe: The International Context," *Journal of Democracy* 11 (2000): 122

62. All examples of the activities of the ATA-affiliated NGOs were obtained from the national associations' Web sites. All were accessed through the ATA Web site (http://www.atasec.org/index.html) in October 2005. I do not give specific Web site addresses for every claim because my analysis is based on analyzing the activities of all Central European affiliates over several years. The specific events are easy to find through the ATA Web site.

63. Latvian Transatlantic Organisation, "Civil Society Initiative in Security Policy Making," 2004, http://www.lato.lv/html/en/activities/projects/26232.html (accessed 18 October 18, 2005).

64. Pavla Kozakova, "Essays Earn Trio Trip to NATO," *Prague Post*, October 30, 2002.

65. Sten A. Hankevitz, "Leedu noored teevad Bushi auks peo," *Eesti Päevaleht*, November 22, 2002.

66. Ibid.

67. Latvian Transatlantic Organisation, *Baltic Manifest*, 2002, Riga: Latvian Transatlantic Organization, http://www.lato.lv (accessed October 15, 2005).

68. Eiki Berg, "Local Resistance, National Identity and Global Swings in Post-Soviet Estonia," *Europe-Asia Studies* 54 (2002): 109–22.

69. Šabic and Jelušic, "Slovenia and NATO Enlargement."

70. Andrew Stroehlein, "Land Corridor Brings Clearer Roles," *Central Europe Review* 31, April 26,1999, http://www.ce-review.org (accessed June 13, 2005). See also the contributions to Krupnick, ed., *Almost NATO*.

71. Havel, "Quo Vadis, NATO?"

72. Ibid.

73. Viivi Luik, Elmo Nüganen, Jüri Arrak, Jüri Englebrecht, Hirvo Surva, and Andrus Kivirähk, "Eestlaseks jääda saab vaid eurooplasena" [Only as Europeans Can We Remain Estonians], *Postimees*, August 8, 2003.

74. Lennart Meri, "750 Years of Lübeck," speech given at conference in Tallinn, May 16, 1998.

75. On the narrative of return, see Mikko Lagerspetz, "Postsocialism as a Return: Notes on a Discursive Strategy." *East European Politics and Societies* 13 (1999): 377–90.

76. Mare Haab, "Estonia," in *Bordering Russia: Theory and Prospects for Europe's Baltic Rim*, ed. Hans Mouritzen (Aldershot: Ashgate, 1998),109–29; Peeter Vares, "Estonia and Russia: Interethnic Relations and Regional Security," in *Stability and Security in the Baltic Sea Region. Russian, Nordic and European Aspects*, ed. Olav F. Knudsen (London and Portland, OR: Frank Cass, 1999).

77. Of the four scenarios—labeled "Big Bang," "Southern Finland," "Gateway," and "Cordon Sanitaire"—only the last posited an exclusively Western orientation. That scenario, however, was premised on the worsening of relations between the West and Russia. "Big Bang" and "Gateway" assumed a growing transit trade between the West and Russia, while "Southern Finland" posited a strong Finnish dominance. Eesti Tulevikuuuringute Instituut, *Eesti Tulevikustsenaariumid*. Tallinn: Eesti Tulevikuuuringute Insituut, 1997.

78. Marika Kirch, ed., *Changing Identities in Estonia: Sociological Facts and Commentaries*, Tallinn: Estonian Science Foundation, 1994; quoted in David Laitin, "National Revival and Competitive Assimilation in Estonia," *Post-Soviet Affairs* 12 (1996): 25–39, 25.

79. Marju Lauristin, one of the four editors of the book, is a widely admired public intellectual. From the late 1980s to the late 1990s, she was also a major politician.

80. Huntington, Samuel P. *Tsivilisatsioonide kokkupõrge ja maailmakorra ümberkujundamine*, translated by Mart Trummal. [The Clash of Civilizations and the Remaking of the World Order.] Tartu: Fontese Kirjastus, 1999.

81. *Eesti Päevaleht*, November 27, 1999, 17–18.

82. Jüri Saar, "Tsivilisatsioonide kokkup'rke teooria retseptsioonist Eestis," *Akadeemia* 10 (1998): 1512–18.

83. Mart Laar, "L'engagement européen de l'Estonie" (lecture delivered at the French Institute of International Affairs in Paris, April 10, 2000).

84. Luik et al., "Eestlaseks jääda saab vaid eurooplasena."

85. Marika Kirch, "Eesti Identiteet ja Euroopa liit" [Estonian Identity and the European Union], in *Mõtteline Eesti: valik esseid Euroopa Liidust* [Imagined Estonia: A selection of essays on the European Union], ed. Marek Tamm, and Märt Väljataga (Tallinn: Kirjastus Varrak, 2003), 156.

86. Eiki Berg, *Eesti tähendused, piirid ja kontekstid* [Estonia's Meanings, Borders, and Contexts] (Tartu: Tartu Ülikooli Kirjastus, 2002).

87. Andrei Hvostov, "Soometumise saladus," *Eesti Päevaleht*, November 30, 1999. Hvostov is among the more critical voices in Estonian foreign policy analysis, yet he too explicitly endorses Huntington's theory.

88. For examples of the ways in which education and population policy are defined as matters of national security and civilizational identity, see Kaido Jaanson, "EL ja Eesti rahvuslik identiteet" [Prof. Kaido Jaansoni peaettekande teesid akadeemilisel nõukogul 19. Veebruaril 1998] (Tallinn: Office of the President, 1998); Kalev Katus, "Rahvastiku areng," in *Eesti 21. sajandil: arengustrateegiad, visioonid, valikud*, ed. Ahto Oja (Tallinn: Estonian Academy of Sciences Press, 1999), 42–6.

89. Quoted in Merje Feldman, "European Integration and the Discourse of National Identity in Estonia," *National Identities* 3 (2001).

90. Rein Ruutsoo, "Introduction: Estonia on the Border of Two Civilizations," *Nationalities Papers* 23 (1995): 13–15.

91. Rein Ruutsoo, "Discursive Conflict and Estonian Post-Communist Nation-Building," in *The Challenge of the Russian Minority. Emerging Multicultural Democracy in Estonia*, ed. Marju Lauristin and Mati Heidmets (Tartu: Tartu University Press, 2002), 38.

92. Quoted in David J. Smith, *Estonia: Independence and European Integration* (London and New York: Routledge, 2001), 147.

93. Estonian Ministry of Foreign Affairs, Guidelines of the National Defence Policy of Estonia (Tallinn: Ministry of Foreign Affairs, 1996), http://www.vm.ee/eng/nato/def.policy.html (accessed March 14, 2001).

94. Toomas Hendrik Ilves, quoted in Piret Pernik, "Eesti identiteet välispoliitilises diskursuses 1990–1999," [Estonian Identity in the Foreign Policy Discourse 1990–1999] *Bakalaureusetöö* (Tallinn: Eesti Humanitaarinstituut, 2000), 78.

95. Estonian Ministry of Foreign Affairs, *National Security Concept of the Republic of Estonia* (Tallinn: Ministry of Foreign Affairs, 2001), 8.

96. Estonian Ministry of Foreign Affairs, *National Security Concept of the Republic of Estonia* (Tallinn: Ministry of Foreign Affairs, 2004).

97. See Eesti Vabariigi Riigikogu, *Riigikogu toimetatud stenogramm*, January 18 and 25, and March 6, 2001 (Tallinn: Riigikogu, 2001).

98. Erik Noreen, "Verbal Politics of Estonian Policy-Makers: Reframing Security and Identity," in *Threat Politics: New Perspectives on Security, Risk and Crisis Management*, ed. Johan Eriksson (Aldershot, UK: Ashgate, 2002), 84–99.

99. Rein Taagepera, "Europa into Estonia, Estonia into Europa," *Global Estonian* (Summer 1999): 24–27.

100. Peeter Kaldre, "Milline kolmas tee?" [What third way?], *Postimees*, February 15, 2001. The numerous articles by Marko Mihkelson and Mart Helme, both prominent commentators, offer similar examples.

101. Igor Gräzin, "Julgeolek ja elujäämine kõigepealt," *Postimees*, March 23, 1996.

102. Enn Soosaar, "Venemaa on Venemaa on Venemaa" [Russia is Russia is Russia], *Eesti Ekspress*, August 5, 2003.

103. Lennart Meri, European of the Year acceptance speech, *Global Estonian* 1 (Summer 1999): 6–11, 10.

104. Haab, "Estonia," 118. Haab makes this comment in the context of all the Baltic states. Such shifts are not endogenous to Estonia, of course. In the mid-1990s, the Clinton administration also started advocating Baltic membership in NATO. The issue for me is not what "caused" the Baltic states to pursue membership in NATO, but the parameters of debate on this issue.

105. *Eesti Päevaleht*, "Uuring: õpilased on riigikaitseõpetuse suhtes positiivselt meelestatud" [Study: Students Have Positive Attitudes toward Teaching State Defence], January 16. 2003. I am skeptical of the accuracy of these numbers, but there are no poll data to contest them.

106. Enn Soosaar, "Eesti teel Euroopasse: vahekokkuvõte" [Estonia's road to Europe: report from the midway], *Looming* 11 (1997): 1514.

107. Mart Laar, *Estonia: Little Country That Could* (London: Centre for Research into Post-Communist Economies, 2002).

108. Siim Kallas, "Kelle poolt on Eesti?" [Whom Does Estonia Support?], *Postimees*, February 11, 2003, http://www.postmees.ee (accessed March 16, 2003); Siim Kallas, "Peame m'tlema 85 aastat ette!" [We Must Think 85 Years in Advance!], *Postimees*, February 25, 2003, http://www.postimees.ee (accessed March 16, 2003).

109. Kallas, "Kelle poolt on Eesti?"

110. Siim Kallas, "Vaata raevus kaugemale" [Look Further in Anger], *Eesti Päevaleht*, October 30, 2002; Kallas, "Peame mõtlema 85 aastat ette!"; Kallas, "Kelle poolt on Eesti?"

111. Mart Helme, "Eesti teevalik Euroopa ja USA veskikivide vahel" [Estonia's Path between the Millstones of Europe and the United States], *Eesti Päevaleht*, September 28, 2002.

112. *Eesti Päevaleht*, "Vaher: paljukardetud oht idast ei ole kadunud" [Vaher: the Much-feared Threat from the East Has Not Disappeared], December 22, 2003.

113. *Eesti Päevaleht*, "Ilves loodab korrigeerida euroliidu välispoliitikat" [Ilves is hoping to adjust EU's foreign policy], July 23, 2004.

114. 1998 data from Goble, "Divided on Security"; see also Noreen, "Verbal Politics of Estonian Policy-Makers." Yet according to a poll from January

2000, 80 percent of ethnic Estonians consider Russia a threat to Estonia's independence. Antti Oolo, "Venemaa-hirm tuleneb ajaloost" [The Fear of Russia Stems from History], *Eesti Päevaleht*, March 20, 2000.

115. Pami Aalto, "Revisiting the Security-Identity Puzzle in Russo-Estonian Relations," *Journal of Peace Research* 40 (2003): 578; Erik Noreen and Roxanna Sjöstedt, "Estonian Identity Formations and Threat Framing in the Post-Cold War Era," *Journal of Peace Research* 41 (2004): 733–50.

116. Aalto, "Revisiting the Security-Identity Puzzle."

117. See Indrek Neivelt, "Unustatud Venemaa" [Forgotten Russia], Eesti Päevaleht, November 6, 2002; Jüri Mõis, "Euroopalik rahvuspoliitika on salliv" [[European Nationality Policy is Tolerant], *Eesti Päevaleht*, April 29, 1999; Mihhail Bronstein, "Idapoliiitika on tundeline teema" [Eastern Policy is a Sensitive Topic]. *Postimees*, July 5, 2002.

118. The move toward a revised Russian policy was controversial, however. Foreign Minister Kristiina Ojuland was depicted as naïve and inconsistent, and her foreign policy was accused of "lacking stamina."

119. Jaan Kaplinski, "Euroopa piir ja piirivalvurid" [Europe's Border and Border-Guards], *Eesti Ekspress*, October 2, 2003. Kaplinski's move of contrasting Eastern Orthodoxy with Western Christianity appears odd at first, given that Orthodoxy is a part of Christianity. However, the arguments that Kaplinski criticizes treat the two branches of Christianity as fundamentally different. Kaplinski counters that false dichotomy by pointing out that neither Eastern nor Western Christianity existed five thousand years ago.

120. See Sirje Kiin, Koik sõltub kultuurist [All Depends on Culture], Tallinn: Online, 2003. See also Toomas Hendrik Ilves, "The Double Enlargement and the Great Wall of Europe," in *Estonian Foreign Policy Yearbook* 2003, ed. A. Kasekamp (Tallinn, Estonian Foreign Policy Institute, 2003), 181–200. Similar shifts have been noted elsewhere in Central Europe. See Egle Rindzevicitute, "'Nation' and 'Europe': Re-approaching the Debates about Lithuanian National Identity," *Journal of Baltic Studies* 24 (2003): 74–91.

121. A key site of such mockery is the weekly *Eesti Ekspress*.

122. *Eesti Ekspress*, "Eestimaa aastal 2050: õnnelik riik" [Estonia in Year 2050: a Happy State], February 25, 1999. The Vikings traded with, as well as raided, the territories of today's Russia late in the first millennium AD. The object of the satire here is not the civilizational rhetoric per se. The satire rather counters the dogmatized status of the civilizational thesis in Estonia. The critics do not necessarily object to Huntington's argument as such; they object to its uncritical use in Estonia. I will re-visit the critical voices in chapter 4.

123. Aalto, "Revisiting the Security-Identity Puzzle in Russo-Estonian Relations," 575.

124. Jaan Kaplinski, "Kultuur ja kuldpuur [Culture and the Golden Cage]," *Sõnumileht*, September 5, 1998.

Chapter 4

1. Steven L. Burg, "The Nationalist Appeal and the Remaking of Eastern Europe," in *The National Idea in Eastern Europe: The Politics of Ethnic and Civic Community*, ed. Gerasimos Augustinos (Lexington, MA and Toronto: D.C. Heath and Company, 1996), 143–44.

2. Sami Moisio, "Competing Geographies of Sovereignty, Regionality and Globalisation: The Politics of EU Resistance in Finland 1991–1994," *Geopolitics* 11 (2006).

3. Vladimir Tismaneanu, "Discomforts of Victory: Democracy, Liberal Values and Nationalism in Post-Communist Europe," *West European Politics* 25 (2002): 84

4. The literature on Central European Euroscepticism is voluminous. Most of it focuses on categorizing and analyzing party-based contestation of EU accession. Some see Central European Euroscepticism as a part of Europe-wide trends while others view it in terms of the specific circumstances of Central Europe. See Jack Bielasiak, "Determinants of Public Opinion Differences on EU Accession in Poland," *Europe-Asia Studies* 54 (2002): 1241–66; Peter Bugge, "Czech Perceptions of EU Membership: Havel vs. Klaus," in *The Road to the European Union*, Vol. 1: *The Czech and Slovak Republics*, ed. Jacques Rupnick and Jan. Zielonka (Manchester and New York: Manchester University Press, 2003), 180–98; Rachel A. Cichowski, "Western Dreams, Eastern Realities: Support for the European Union in Central and Eastern Europe," *Comparative Political Studies* 33 (2000): 1243–78; Aleš Debeljak, "European Forms of Belonging," *East European Politics and Societies* 17 (2003): 151–65; Robert Harmsen and Menno Spiering, "Introduction: Euroscepticism and the Evolution of European Political Debate," in *Euroscepticism: Party Politics, National Identity and European Integration*, ed. Robert Harmsen and Menno Spiering, (Amsterdam and New York: Rodopi, 2004), 13–36; Petr Kopecki and Cas Mudde, "Two Sides of Euroscepticism: Party Positions on European Integration in East Central Europe," *European Union Politics* 3 (2002): 297–326; Markéta Rulikova, "The Influence of Pre-Accession Status on Euroscepticism in EU Candidate Countries," *Perspectives on European Politics and Society*.5 (2004): 29–60; Jacques Rupnick and Jan Zielonka, eds., *The Road to the European Union*, Vol. 1: *The Czech and Slovak Republics* (Manchester and New York: Manchester University Press, 2003); and Paul Taggart and Aleks Szczerbiak, *Opposing Europe? The Comparative Party Politics of Euroskepticism* (Oxford: Oxford University Press, 2005).

5. Michael Heffernan, *The Meaning of Europe: Geography and Geopolitics* (London: Arnold, 1998). Verena Stolcke argues that today's neo-right parties are not just simple neofascism. They represent cultural fundamentalism— the narrative according to which cultures are equal in merit but fundamentally incompatible and therefore every culture should be contained in its own territory. Verena Stolcke, "Talking Culture: New Boundaries, New Rhetorics

of Exclusion in Europe," *Current Anthropology* 63 (1995): 1–20; see also Douglas Holmes, *Integral Europe: Fast-capitalism, Multiculturalism, Neofascism* (Princeton, NJ: Princeton University Press, 2000).

6. Simone Weil, *The Need for Roots: Prelude to a Declaration of Duties toward Mankind* (New York: Ark, 1987), quoted in Liisa Malkki, "National Geographic: The Rooting of Peoples and the Territorialization of National Identity among Scholars and Refugees," *Cultural Anthropology* 7 (1992): 24.

7. John A. Agnew, "The Territorial Trap: The Geographical Assumptions of International Relations Theory," *Review of International Political Economy*, vol.1, 1994, 53–80; see also Gregory Feldman, "Culture, State, and Security in Europe: the Case of Citizenship and Integration Policy in Estonia," *American Ethnologist* 32 (2005): 680; Malkki, "National Geographic"; and Robert B. J. Walker, "Europe Is Not Where It Is Supposed to Be," in *International Relations Theory and the Politics of European Integration: Power, Security and Community*, ed. M. Kelstrup and M.C. Williams (London and New York: Routledge, 2000), 14–32.

8. Feldman, "Culture, State, and Security in Europe," 680.

9. John. A. Agnew, "Territoriality and Political Identity in Europe," in *Europe Without Borders: Remapping Territory, Citizenship, and Identity in a Transnational Age*, ed. Mabel Berezin and Martin A. Schain (New York: Columbia University Press, 2003), 219–20. This notion feeds into sociomedical conceptions of the state, the nation, and Europe. For further analysis, see Mika Luoma-Aho, "Body of Europe and Malignant Nationalism: A Pathology of the Balkans in European Security Discourse," *Geopolitics* 7 (2002): 117–42.

10. Feldman, "Culture, State, and Security in Europe"; and Robert M. Hayden, *Blueprints for a House Divided: The Constitutional Logic of Yugoslav Conflicts* (Ann Arbor: University of Michigan Press, 1999).

11. There is a large literature on the diffusion of European legal and political norms in the context of EU enlargement. Most of this literature views the Europeanization of Central Europe in terms of rule transfer and analyzes the mechanisms and effectiveness of the process. My question in this chapter is not how European norms are promoted and implemented or the way in which Central European states are socialized into the EU in the process of accession. I rather seek to understand the cultural and territorial logic of explanation that underpins particular practices of state socialization or norms transfer. For informative examples of the Europeanization literature, see Jeffery T. Checkel, "Norms, Institutions, and National Identity in Contemporary Europe," *International Studies Quarterly* 43 (1999): 83–114; Kevin Featherstone, "Introduction: in the Name of 'Europe,'" in *The Politics of Europeanization*, ed. Kevin Featherstone and Claudio M. Radaelli (Oxford: Oxford University Press, 2003); Karin M. Fierke and Antje Wiener, "Constructing Institutional Interests: EU and NATO Enlargement," *Journal of European Public Policy* 6 (1999); Ronald Linden, ed., *Norms and Nannies: The Impact of International Organizations on the Central and East European*

States (Lanham, MD: Rowman and Littlefield, 2002; Frank Schimmelfennig, *The EU, NATO and the Integration of Europe: Rules and Rhetoric* (Cambridge: Cambridge University Press, 2003); and Frank Schimmelfennig and Ulrich Sedelmeier, "Introduction: Conceptualizing the Europeanization of Central and Eastern Europe," in *The Europeanization of Central and Eastern Europe*, ed. Frank Schimmelfennig and Ulrich Sedelmeier (Ithaca, NY: Cornell University Press, 2005), 1–28.

12. *Economist*, "Snoring While a Superstate Emerges?" May 10, 2003.

13. Elizabeth C. Dunn, "Standards and Person-Making in East-Central Europe," in *Global Assemblages: Technology, Politics, and Ethics as Anthropological Problems*, ed. Aihwa Ong and Stephen Collier (Oxford: Blackwell Publishing, 2005).

14. Aart Jan Riekhoff, "The Transformation of East-Central European Security: Domestic Politics, International Constraints, and Opportunities for Policy-makers," *Perspectives*, Institute of International Relations Prague, Czech Republic, 21 (Winter 2003/2004): 55–70.

15. Václav Havel, "Who Threatens our Identity?" *Project Syndicate*, April 2001.

16. Vaira Vike-Freiberga, "Larger Europe—a Stronger Europe," address given at Leiden University, the Netherlands, January 18, 2005.

17. Across Central Europe, Euroscepticism is most prevalent among the elderly, the unskilled, and rural populations. These groups, already under economic and social stress from postsocialist transformations, fear further changes, rising prices, and further decline of rural life. The disillusionment is not just over EU standards but also over the slow pace of integration—which many people in Central Europe perceived as the EU's lack of commitment to the region. Aleks Szczerbiak, "Polish Euroscepticism in the Run-up to EU Accession," in *Euroscepticism: Party Politics, National Identity and European Integration*, ed. R. Harmsen and M. Spiering (Amsterdam and New York: Rodopi, 2004), 253. See also Sean Hanley, "From Neo-Liberalism to National Interests: Ideology, Strategy, and Party Development in the Euroscepticism of the Czech Right," *East European Politics and Societies* 18 (2004): 539; Richard Rose, "Indifference, Distrust, and Skepticism," *Transitions Online*, March 1, 2002. http://www.tol.cz (accessed September 15, 2002).

18. The equivalent number for the EU 15 is 42 percent. European Commission, *Candidate Countries Eurobarometer* (Brussels: European Commission, Public Opinon Analysis Sector, 2004), 1, http://ec.europa.eu/public_opinion/cceb_en.htm (accessed February 15, 2005), full joint report, C83.

19. Ibid., C47. The equivalent numbers for EU 15 were 40 percent in the fall of 2003 and 41 percent in the spring of 2004.

20. Another key Euroskeptic argument originates in center-right pro-business circles, which oppose the regulatory powers of the EU. In this argument, the EU is a stagnant geriatric entity that would hold down the more dynamic Central European states, the national cultures of which are more libertarian and pro-market. The argument is in part cultural, as the pro-business legislation of Central Europe is presented as a part of the countries' national

identity. I leave this argument out of the present analysis, because it does not securitize territorially and culturally defined nations to nearly the same extent that arguments about citizenship and minority rights do. For analyses of the libertarian variety of Euroscepticism, see Hanley, "From Neo-Liberalism to National Interests"; Nicole Lindstrom, "From Permissive Consensus to Contentious Politics: Varieties of Euroskepticism in Croatia and Slovenia," paper presented at the Cornell Mellon-Sawyer Seminar, April 9, 2002.

21. Quoted in Feldman, "Culture, State, and Security in Europe," 679.

22. Bielasiak, "Determinants of Public Opinion Differences on EU Accession in Poland," 1254; Debeljak, "European Forms of Belonging," 154; Krzysztof Jasiewicz, "Reluctantly European?" *Transitions Online*, March 1, 2002. http://www.tol.cz (accessed September 15, 2002); Jennifer Möll, "Who's Afraid of the Big Bad Wolf?" *Baltic Times*, November 20, 2003.

23. *EU Business*, "New Polish PM Wants Bigger Role, 'Moral Sovereignty' in EU," July 19, 2006. http://www.eubusiness.com/East_Europe/060719131330 .6e71mfws (accessed August 23, 2006).

24. The document passed after fifty-nine of the 101 MPs present supported it. These fifty-nine members represented only slightly more than a third of the 150-member legislature. Olga Gyárfášová, "Slovakia Heads for the EU: What Was Accomplished and What Lies Ahead?" *Az Európai Tanulmányok* (Európa 2002) 4 (2003); Petr Robejsek, "Parallel Paths East and West," *Transitions Online*, March 1, 2002, http://www.tol.cz (accessed September 15, 2002).

25. European Commission. Communication from the Commission: Countering Racism, Xenophobia and Anti-Semitism in the Candidate Countries (Brussels: European Commission, May 26, 1999), http://ec.europa.eu/comm/external _relations/human_rights/doc/com99_256_en.pdf (accessed September 15, 2006). The document does not list the relevant numbers for the remaining four central European states—Poland, The Czech Republic, Hungary, and Slovenia. According to other studies available through the European Commussion, minority populations account for less than 10 percent of the population in these four countries. See European Commission, *Support from the European Commission for Measures to Promote and Safeguard Regional or Minority Languages and Cultures* (Brussels: European Commission, 2004), http://ec .europa.eu/education/policies/lang/languages/langmin/euromosaic/index_en .html (accessed September 15, 2006).

26. There is a burgeoning research on the EU's impact on these laws. For recent work, see Nida M. Gelazis, "The Effects of EU Conditionality on Citizenship Policies and the Protection of National Minorities in the Baltic States," in *The Road to the European Union*, Vol. 2: *Estonia, Latvia, Lithuania*, ed. V. Pettai and J. Zielonka (Manchester and New York: Manchester University Press, 2003), 46–74; Johns, "'Do as I Say, Not as I Do'"; Jurado, "Complying with European Standards of Minority Rights Education"; Judith G. Kelley, *Ethnic Politics in Europe: The Power of Norms and Incentives* (Princeton, NJ

and Oxford: Princeton University Press, 2004); Rae, *State Identities and the Homogenisation of Peoples*; Lynn M. Tesser, "The Geopolitics of Tolerance: Minority Rights under EU Expansion in East-Central Europe," *East European Politics and Societies* 17 (2003): 483–532.

27. Feldman, "Culture, State, and Security in Europe," especially note 17, 690.

28. Rae, *State Identities and the Homogenisation of Peoples*, 267.

29. Quoted in Sharon Fisher, "Tottering in the Aftermath of Elections," *Transition*, March 29, 1995, 20–5; and Tesser, "Geopolitics of Tolerance," 517.

30. Tesser, "Geopolitics of Tolerance," 493.

31. Johns, "'Do as I Say, Not as I Do,'" 684. Russia comes into play in an insidious manner. The efforts of the EU, NATO, and individual Western states to improve relations with Russia further reinforce the emphasis on sovereignty in Central Europe. Thus, the West's cooperative rhetoric vis-à-vis Russia has fueled evocations of Trianon, Munich, or Yalta in Central Europe. During the summit meeting between Russia and the United States in Helsinki in 1997, Andrzej Karkoszka, the Polish deputy defense minister, stated that "the smell of Yalta is always with us," given the "curious willingness" of the West to accommodate "the unjustified desires" of Russia; quoted in Grudzinski and van Ham, *A Critical Approach to European Security*, 64.

32. Jüri Adams, "Riigikogu toimetatud stenogramm" [Edited Parliamentary Transcript], November 18, 1998.

33. Erkki Bahovski, "Baltlased EL kandidaatriikidest skeptilisimad" [Balts Most Skeptical Among the Candidate States], *Postimees*, November 8, 2000.

34. Ibid.

35. *EU Observer*, "Tight Race in Estonian Referendum Poll," July 11, 2003. Polling data vary considerably depending on the questions asked. Most polls measure the responder's opinion of the EU, support for EU accession, or intention to vote for accession at a referendum. Eurobarometer polls ask whether accession is "a good thing" for the country under consideration. In Estonia, the percentage of those who considered EU accession "a good thing" fluctuated between 29 percent and 38 percent between 2000 and 2004, while the average in the new member states fluctuated between 58 percent and 64 percent (European Commission, *Candidate Countries Eurobarometer*).

36. BBC News, "Estonia's Euro Vision," September 10, 2003; EU Observer, "Tight race in Estonian referendum poll," July 11, 2003; and Paavo Palk, "Euroopa Liidu toetajaid on rohkem kui vastalisi" [European Union has More Supporters than Opponents], *Eesti Päevaleht EPL*, March 8, 2000.

37. Referendum data from *City Paper*, "EU referendum News," September 2003, http:/:www.balticsww.com/EU: Baltics Say Yes.html (accessed December 18, 2003).

38. Graeme P. Herd and Joan Löfgren, "Societal Security, the Baltic States and EU Integration," *Cooperation and Conflict* 36 (2001): 273–96.

39. Andres Tarand, "Eesti iseseisvus ja euroliit," [Estonia's Independence and the Eurounion] *Postimees*, January 26, 2001, emphasis added.

40. *Luup*, "Lennart Meri: Eurooopa Uniooni on vaja riigi püsimiseks (Eesti presidendi aastalõpuintervjuu)" [Lennart Meri: European Union Is Necessary for the Survival of the State (The end-of-the-year interview with the Estonia President)], December 22, 1997.

41. *Constitution of the Republic of Estonia*, Tallinn: Estonian Ministry of Foreign Affairs, Chapter 1. See also Rain Maruste, "Eesti enne euro-otsust" [Estonian Before the Euro-decision], *Postimees*, June 12, 2001.

42. Liia Hänni, "Jah, härra justiitsminister!" ["Yes, Mister Justice Minister!"], *Postimees*, January 22, 2002.

43. *Eesti Euroskepsise pesa*, http://www.euroskepsis.ee (accessed August 22, 2006).

44. Erkki Bahovski, "Sovereignty in the European Union: Case Studies Relating to Estonia," in *The Estonian Foreign Policy Yearbook 2005*, ed. A. Kasekamp (Tallinn: Estonian Foreign Policy Institute, 2005), 126.

45. Põhiseaduse juriidilise ekspertiisi komisjon, *Aruanne*, Pt. 2.17, *Võimalik liitumine Euroopa Liiduga ja selle õiguslik tähendus Eesti riigiõiguse seisukohalt* [Possible Accession to the European Union and its Legal Impact to Estonian Constitutional Law] (Tallinn: Estonian Ministry of Justice, 1998), 3, http://www.euroskepsis.ee/ps/ps-euro.htm (accessed August 22, 2006). For a more in-depth analysis of the discursive bundling of ethnicity and sovereignty, see Merje Kuus, "Sovereignty for Security? The Discourse of Sovereignty in Estonia," *Political Geography* 21 (2002): 393–412.

46. *Constitution of the Republic of Estonia*, Preamble.

47. Rein Ruutsoo, "Eesti kodakondsuspoliitika ja rahvusriigi kujunemise piirjooned" [The Contours of Estonian Citizenship Policy and the Development of the Nation-State], in *Vene küsimus ja Eesti valikud* [The Russian Question and Estonia's Choices], ed. Mati Heidmets (Tallinn: Tallinn Pedagogical University, 1998), 139–202.

48. The ambiguous relationship between politically and culturally defined communities is central to the operation of nationalism. "The people" is imagined both as existing in an already constituted state and also as an entity that preexists the state. The state is consequently framed not only as a political but also as an organic cultural community. Together, the state and the nation constitute "the people's two bodies." Bernard Yack, "Popular Sovereignty and Nationalism," *Political Theory* 29 (2001): 519.

49. See Estonian Ministry of Foreign Affairs, *2000 Population and Housing Census: Citizenship, Nationality, Mother Tongue and Command of Foreign Languages* (Tallinn: Ministry of Foreign Affairs, September 27, 2002).

50. Klara Hallik, "Rahvuspoliitilised seisukohad parteiprogrammides ja valimisplatvormides" [Ethnopolitical Positions in Party Programs and Election Platforms], in *Vene küsimus ja Eesti valikud [The Russian Question and Estonia's Choices]*, ed. Mati Heidmets (Tallinn: Tallinn Pedagogical University, 1998), 95; Ruutsoo, "Eesti kodakondsuspoliitika ja rahvusriigi kujunemise piirjooned," 175.

51. Mart Kivimäe, "Euroskeptitsismi ajaloost Eesti kultuuris 20 sajandil," [On Euroskepticism in the Estonian Cultural History of the 20th Century] in

Eesti Euroopa Liidu lävepakul [Estonia at Europe's Threshold], ed. Rein Ruutsoo and Aksel Kirch (Tallinn: Teaduste Akadeemia Kirjastus, 1998).

52. Jaak Sarapuu, *Eesti algõpetus 2: õpik põhikoolile* [Primer in Estonian History 2: Textbook for Primary and Middle Schools], quoted in Eiki Berg, *Eesti tähendused, piirid ja kontekstid* [Estonia's Meanings, Borders, and Contexts] (Tartu: Tartu University Press, 2002), 170. Berg points to an overtly racist description of Estonians as "white" and physically strong in other textbooks. He also notes that the production as well as the adoption of textbooks is quite decentralized. Although the Ministry of Education must approve textbooks for classroom use, authors have considerable flexibility in presenting the material and teachers have considerable freedom in selecting textbooks for classroom use. For Berg, this fact shows that the tropes used in textbooks are not imposed on their authors by the government. I would add here that it also indicates the popular acceptance of these tropes.

53. See Merje Feldman, "European Integration and the Discourse of National Identity in Estonia," *National Identities* 3 (2001): 5–21, for a more in-depth discussion of the narrative of rootedness. See also Eiki Berg and Saima Oras, "Writing Post-Soviet Estonia on to the World Map," *Political Geography* 19 (2000): 601–25; Graham Smith, "Nation-building and Political Discourses of Identity Politics in the Baltic States," in *Nation-Building in the Post-Soviet Borderlands: The Politics of National Identities*, ed. Graham Smith et al. (New York and Cambridge: Cambridge University Press, 1998), 93–118; Tim Unwin, "Place, Territory, and National Identity in Estonia," in *Nested Identities: Nationalism, Territory and Scale*, ed. Guntram H. Herb and David H. Kaplan (Lanham, MD: Rowman and Littlefield Publishers, 1999), 151–73.

54. United Nations Development Programme (UNDP), *Eesti Inimarengu Aruanne* (Tallinn: UNDP, 1998), 47.

55. For informative overviews and detailed statistical data, see *Return to the Western World: Cultural and Political Perspectives on the Estonian Post-Communist Transition*, ed. Marju Lauristin, Peeter Vihalemm, Karl Erik Rosengren, and Lennart Weibull (Tartu: Tartu University Press, 1997); Lieven, *Baltic Revolution*; Toivo U. Raun, *Estonia and the Estonians*, 2nd ed. (Stanford, CA: Hoover Institution Press, 1994); Aleksei Semjonov, "Estonia: Nation-Building and Integration—Political and Legal Aspects," in *National Integration and Violent Conflict in Post-Soviet Societies*, ed. P. Kolstø (Lanham, MD: Rowman and Littlefield, 2002), 105–57; Rein Taagepera, *Estonia: Return to Independence* (Boulder, CO: Westview Press, 1993); and Raivo Vetik and Riina Kionka, "Estonia and the Estonians," in *The Nationalities Question in the Post-Soviet States*, ed. Graham Smith (London: Longman, 1995), 155–80.

56. Jaan Kaplinski, "Eesti kui usuasi" [Estonia as a Religion], *Eesti Ekspress*, May 13, 1999. Kaplinski is a prominent poet and a major social critic—a dissident in the Soviet and the re-independent Estonia alike. Other consistently critical voices include Barbi Pilvre, Andrei Hvostov, Rein Taagepera, and Tõnu Õnnepalu, among others. The following point by Olev Remsu, a writer,

is representative of the liberal minority. To ensure the survival of the Estonian nation, Remsu writes, Estonia has no other choice but to change its conception of the nation. The remedy against globalization is regionalization, not the glorification of one's nation. Olev Remsu, "Kohanev Eesti" [Adjusting Estonia], *Eesti Ekspress*, July 9, 2002. Such positions lie at the liberal end of the political mainstream and are uncommon in public debates.

57. For an informative analyses of the restitutionist logic of Estonia's citizenship and migration legislation, see Feldman, "Culture, State, and Security in Europe"; Vello Pettai, "Emerging Ethnic Democracy in Estonia and Latvia," in *Managing Diversity in Plural Societies: Minorities, Migration and Nation-Building in Post-Communist Europe*, ed. M. Opalski (Ottawa: Forum Eastern Europe, 1998), 15–32.

58. Gregory Feldman, "Neoliberal Nationalism: Ethnic Integration and Estonia's Accession to the European Union," in *Crossing European Boundaries: Beyond Conventional Geographical Categories*, ed. Helen Kopnina, Christina Moutsov, and Jaro Stacul (London and New York: Berghahn Press, 2005), 46.

59. Citizenship and Migration Board, *Määratlemata kodakondsusega isikute arvu muutumine, 1992–2000* [Change in the Numbers of Persons with Undetermined Citizenship 1992–2000] (Tallinn: Citizenship and Migration Board, 2000. Document obtained by request from the Citizenship and Migration Board, November 5, 2000). Similar data are provided by the Estonian census. Estonian Ministry of Foreign Affairs, *2000 Population and Housing Census: Citizenship, Nationality, Mother Tongue and Command of Foreign Languages* (Tallinn: Ministry of Foreign Affairs, 2002). That same year, Katrin Saks, the minister of ethnic affairs, said in a newspaper article around the time of the census that stateless persons made up approximately 17 percent of Estonia's population—compared to 12.4 percent in the data published by the Citizenship and Migration Board. Katrin Saks, "Üks riik, mitu kultuuri" [One State, Several Cultures], *Eesti Päevaleht*, March 2, 2000. I use conservative estimates here but I also note the estimate offered by the minister to illustrate the statistical confusion that is part of the integration process. The difference can be explained in part but not in full by considering that Estonia also had about 30,000–40,000 illegal residents at the time, most of whom were Russian speakers who had not obtained a residency permit from the Estonian state.

60. Data given for 2000 are census data from the Ministry of Foreign Affairs, contained in the *2000 Population and Housing Census*. Data for 2003 are taken from the Estonian Citizenship and Migration Board's *Yearbook 2003* (Tallinn, 2003).

61. European minority rights conventions leave the definition of national minority to the signatory states. See Feldman, "Culture, State, and Security in Europe."

62. The Russian-speaking minority also includes Russian-speaking citizens of Estonia, many of whom are fluent in Estonian, as well as citizens of Russia,

many of whom took Russian citizenship in the 1990s primarily because they gave up hope of attaining Estonian citizenship. Since Estonia does not allow dual citizenship for naturalized persons, Russian citizens do not qualify for Estonian citizenship.

63. *The Integration of Non-Estonians into Estonian Society: The Bases of the Estonian State Integration Policy* (Tallinn: Non-Estonians Integration Foundation, 1999).

64. Aleksander Astrov. "Aga sellepärast, et on po&#8230" [Just Because . . .]. *Eesti Päevaleht* 20 October 2005. The symbol string po&#8230 is used in the Estonian-language media to denote a Russian curse word that one would normally not find in the mainstream media. Astrov considers the practice offensive to Russian-speakers.

65. The title of the position was translated into English as Minister for Ethnic Affairs throughout the 1990s, although the Estonian term was Minister for Population [*Rahvastikuminister*]. The minister's portfolio included not only matters of ethnic integration but also Estonia's population decline. As of summer 2006, the official English-language name for the office is Office of the Minister for Population and Ethnic Affairs.

66. Estonian Ministry of Ethnic Affairs, *State Programme 'Integration in Estonian Society 2000–2007'* (Tallinn: Ministry of Ethnic Affairs, 2000), 17. Phare (Poland and Hungary: Assistance for Reconstructing their Economies) is an EU aid program. In the 1990s, it was the principal program through which the EU channeled aid to the applicant and candidate states.

67. Quoted in Feldman, "Culture, State, and Security in Europe," 680.

68. Gregory Feldman, "Essential Crises: A Performative Approach to Migrants, Minorities and the European Nation-state," *Anthropological Quarterly* 78 (2005): 231–46.

69. Kuus "Sovereignty for Security?"

70. See Feldman, "Culture, State, and Security in Europe."

71. For extensive data on public opinion, see Marju Lauristin and Mati Heidmets, eds., *The Challenge of the Russian Minority: Emerging Multicultural Democracy in Estonia* (Tartu: Tartu University Press, 2002). See also Lauristin et al., *Return to the Western World*.

72. Iris Pettai, "Eestlased pole võõraste tulekuks valmis" [Estonians are not Ready for the Arrival of Strangers], *Eesti Päevaleht*, August 9, 2005.

73. On polls from the late 1990s see Goble, "Divided on Security." For Western accounts that emphasize Estonia's pragmatism, see Danjoux, *Reframing Citizenship in the Baltic Republics*; and Lieven, *Baltic Revolution*.

74. Heidmets, *Vene küsimus ja Eesti valikud*; Lauristin and Heidmets, eds., *The Challenge of the Russian Minority*.

75. Jurado, "Complying with European Standards of Minority Rights Education," 422; Erik Noreen and Roxanna Sjöstedt, "Estonian Identity Formations and Threat Framing in the Post-Cold War Era," *Journal of Peace Research* 41 (2004).

76. Katrin Saks, "Üks riik, mitu kultuuri."

77. The quote is from Lieven *Baltic Revolution*, 304. Lieven discusses the Latvian context in this particular instance, but such discontent with the closed nature of identity debates is discernible among Estonian liberals as well. For a nuanced account of the enactments of identity in Estonia, see Robert Kaiser and Jelena Nikiforova. "Narratives and Enactments of Place and Identity in the Borderlands of Post-socialist Space: The Case of 'the Setos.'" *Ethnic and Racial Studies* 29 (2006): 928-958.

78. The concept of "Estonian cultural realm" is central to ethnic integration policy. For an analysis of the concept, see Feldman, "Culture, State, and Security in Europe."

79. Andrei Hvostov, "Valitsus kindlustab rahvusriigi alustalasid" [The Government is Securing the Pillars of the Nation-State], *Eesti Päevaleht*, December 14, 1997.

80. Ando Leps, *Riigikogu toimetatud stenogramm* [Edited Parliamentary Transcript], November 18, 1998.

81. *Presidendi Akadeemilise Nõukogu pöördumine Eesti avalikkuse poole* (Open Letter from the President's Academic Council to the Estonian Public, November 25, 1998). See also Rein Taagepera, "Eesti keele ja kultuuri väljavaated Euroopa Liidu ja arvuka muulaskonna tingimustes." Ettekande teesid Presidendi Akadeemilise Nõukogu istungiks, ["The Prospects of Estonian Language and Culture in the Context of the European Union and a Large Alien Population"] (thesis presented at the meeting of the President's Academic Council, April 23, 1998).

82. Eesti Vabariigi Riigikogu, *Riigikogu toimetamata stenogramm* [Unedited Parliamentary Transcript], October 25, 2001 (accessed July 8, 2002). The transcript misspells the representative's name, which is Doris Hertrampf.

83. Ibid., 11.

84. Feldman, "Essential Crises," 234.

85. Estonian Ministry of Ethnic Affairs, *State Programme 'Integration in Estonian Society 2000–2007.'*"

86. Party platforms in Estonia in the 1990s showed a strong ethnic self-defense orientation across all parties. The presence of Russian speakers in Estonia was seen as a major existential threat to the Estonian nation. Hallik, "Rahvuspoliitilised seisukohad parteiprogrammides ja valimisplatvormides" [Ethno-political Positions in Party Programs and Election Platforms].

87. Maaris Raudsepp, "Rahvusküsimus ajakirjanduse peeglis" [The Ethnic Question in the the Media] in *Vene küsimus ja Eesti valikud* [The Russian Question and Estonia's Choices], ed. Mati Heidmets (Tallinn: Tallinn Pedagogical University, 1998); and Enn Soosaar, "Eesti venelased teelahkmel," *Eesti Päevaleht*, November 15, 1999.

88. In 1995 the Ministry of Defense drew up a plan to establish an alternative form of service for non-citizen permanent residents—most of whom are Russian speakers—to train them to conduct rescue operations and provide them with Estonian- language courses. The proposal was stalled in the parliament because several MPs assessed it as leading to the potential formation of a trained fifth column. Haab, "Estonia."

89. Jüri Saar, "Tsivilisatsioonide kokkupõrke teooria retseptsioonist Eestis" [On the Reception of the Theory of Civilizational Clash in Estonia].

90. The phrase "Estonian mindset" is widely used in debates on ethnic integration. One of the foundational texts that placed the term in the public discouse is United Nations Development Programme, Integrating non-Estonians into Estonian Society: Setting the Course, (Tallinn: UNDP, 1997).

91. Andres Adamson and Sulev Valdmaa, Eesti ajalugu gümnaasiumile [Estonian History for Gymnasia] (Tallinn: Avita, 1999), 205; quoted in Berg, Eesti tähendused, 171. Berg notes that the textbook is approved for use in Estonian schools by the Ministry of Education, but the ministry does not accept liability for its content.

92. Tartu University Market Research Team, Estonia's Experiment—The Possibilities to Integrate Non-Citizens into the Estonian Society (Tallinn: Open Estonia Foundation, 1997).

93. Ibid.

94. Ibid., Chapter 7, 3.

95. Sirje Endre and Mart Laar, "Valitsus kõigutab rahvusriigi alustalasid," [Government is Shaking the Pillars of the Nation-State] Eesti Päevaleht, December 12, 1997.

96. Triin Vihalemm and Marju Lauristin, "Cultural Adjustment to the Changing Societal Environment: the Case of Russians in Estonia," in Return to the Western World: Cultural and Political Perspectives on the Estonian Post-Communist Transition, ed. Marju Lauristin, Peeter Vihalemm, Karl Erik Rosengren, and Lennart Weibull (Tartu: Tartu University Press, 1997), 280. A significant nuance here is that even though claims about the indigenous population seem to territorialize the state by rooting its legitimacy in the historic homeland, Estonian politics involves a pronounced nonterritorial aspect. There are an estimated 100,000 to 110,000 ethnic Estonian citizens living abroad, mostly in Sweden, Canada, and the United States. These individuals have actively shaped politics in Estonia, particularly since they account for approximately 8 percent of Estonia's electorate. Rein Ruutsoo, "Eesti kodakondsuspoliitika ja rahvusriigi kujunemise piirjooned," [The Contours of Estonian Citizenship Policy and the Development of the Nation-State] in Heidmets, Vene küsimus ja Eesti valikud, 188. The emphasis on territory thus works in tandem with ethnicity to selectively territorialize and deterritorialize the state. The rhetorical stress on territorial homeland is in conflict with the political reality of an extraterritorial electorate.

97. Merje Kuus, "European Integration in Identity Narratives in Estonia: A Quest for Security," Journal of Peace Research 39 (2002): 91–108. The criticism is usually directed against the EU, but NATO's "Russia-friendliness" is noted as well. According to MP Enn Tarto, NATO officials implied in 1998 that one condition of entry to NATO is to meet Russian demands regarding minority rights. "There is the thinking that when Russia no longer has demands on us, then we are ready for NATO accession. I have my own opinion. Russia's demands will never end." Enn Tarto's remarks to the parliament

in Eesti Vabariigi Riigikogu, *Riigikogu Toimetatud Stenogramm* [Edited Parliamentary Transcript], November 26, 1998 (Tallinn: Eesti Vabariigi Riigikogu, 1998). Euroskeptics also argue that the EU does not offer Estonia any meaningful military security against Russia, and they are generally more supportive of NATO accession. As Robert Lepikson, a prominent Euroskeptic, put it in one debate, "The European Union will not even squeak if Russia attacks Estonia." Siim Saidla, "Robert Lepikson seljatas Euroopa väitlusmeistrid" [Robert Lepikson Pinned European Debate Experts], *Eesti Päevaleht*, April 19, 2000.

98. Harri Tiido, "Kosovo õppetunnid maailma ja Eesti jaoks" [Lessons from Kosovo to Estonia and the Rest of the World], *Eesti Päevaleht*, June 12, 1999.

99. Mart Nutt, "Kui Läti murdub, asutakse Eesti kallale" [When Latvia Breaks, they will Get to Estonia], *Eesti Päevaleht*, June 20, 1996.

100. Mart Nutt, "Kas Euroopa Liit tagab julgeoleku?" [Will the European Union Ensure Security?] *Postimees*, September 15, 1998.

101. Thomas H. Ilves, Remarks to the parliament, *Riigikogu toimetatud stenogramm*, June 8, 2000.

102. Saidla, "Robert Lepikson seljatas Euroopa väitlusmeistrid."

103. Gregory Feldman, "Neoliberal Nationalism: Ethnic Integration and Estonia's Accession to the European Union," in *Crossing European Boundaries: Beyond Conventional Geographical Categories*, ed. Helen Kopnina, Christina Moutsov, and Jaro Stacul (London and New York: Berghahn Press, 2005), 49.

104. *City Paper*, "EU Referendum News," 2003, http/:www.balticsww.com/EU: Baltics Say Yes.html (accessed December 18, 2003).

105. Ibid.

106. Marko Mölder, "Teisenevast suveräänsusest" [On Metamorphosing Sovereignty], *Sirp*, September 17, 1999.

107. Rain Maruste, "Eesti enne euro-otsust" [Estonia Before the Euro-decision]. *Postimees*, June 12, 2001.

108. Marika Kirch, "Eestlaste otsus tulevasel euroreferendumil s'ltub Venemaast," [Estonians' Decision in the Future Euroreferendum will Depend on Russia] *Eesti Päevaleht*, March 28, 2000.

109. Feldman, "Culture, State, and Security in Europe"; Hayden, *Blueprints for a House Divided*.

Chapter 5

1. Zygmunt Bauman, "Intellectuals in East-Central Europe: Continuity and Change," *Eastern European Politics and Societies* 1 (1987): 162.

2. Lennart Meri, interview with *Le Figaro*, February 16, 1997.

3. Gearóid O'Tuathail, *Critical Geopolitics: The Politics of Writing Global Space* (Minneapolis: University of Minnesota Press, 1996).

4. Hans Morgenthau called diplomats the "brains of national power," but diplomats are only one group among many who participate in the conception,

legitimation, and implementation of foreign policy on a daily basis. Hans
Morgenthau, *Politics among Nations: The Struggle for Power and Peace*,
abridged ed (New York: McGraw-Hill, 1993), quoted in Rick Fawn,
"Symbolism in the Diplomacy of Czech President Vaclav Havel," *East
European Quarterly* 23 (1999): 13

5. Joanne Sharp, *Condensing the Cold War: Reader's Digest and American
Identity* (Minneapolis: University of Minnesota Press, 2000), 10. See also
Joanne Sharp, "Hegemony, Popular Culture and Geopolitics: The Reader's
Digest and the Construction of Danger," *Political Geography* 15 (1996): 557–70.

6. Gearóid Ó Tuathail and John Agnew, "Geopolitics and Discourse: Practical
Geopolitical Reasoning in American Foreign Policy," *Political Geography*.11
(1992): 193.

7. Milan Kundera, "The Tragedy of Central Europe," 35.

8. A historical and sociological analysis of Central European intellectual elites
is beyond the scope of this book. For further analysis of the historical devel-
opment and present-day sociology of the region's intellectuals, see *Between
Past and Future: The Revolutions of 1989 and Their Aftermath*, ed. Sorin
Antohi and Vladimir Tismaneanu (Budapest: CEU Press, 2000); Bauman,
"Intellectuals in East-Central Europe"; Andreás Bozóki, ed., *Intellectuals and
Politics in Central Europe* (Budapest: Central European University Press,
1999); Gil Eyal, Ivan Szelenyi, and Eleanor Townsley, *Making Capitalism
Without Capitalists: Class Formation and Elite Struggles in Post-Communist
Central Europe* (London and New York: Verso, 1998); Barbara Falk, *The
Dilemmas of Dissidence in East-Central Europe* (Budapest: Central European
University Press, 2003); Vladimir Tismaneanu, *Fantasies of Salvation:
Democracy, Nationalism, and Myth in Post-Communist Europe* (Princeton,
NJ: Princeton University Press, 1998); Anatol Lieven, *The Baltic Revolution:
Estonia, Latvia and Lithuania and the Path to Independence*, rev. ed. (New
Haven, CT: Yale University Press, 1993); and Katherine Verdery, *National
Ideology Under Socialism: Identity and Cultural Politics in Ceausescu's
Romania* (Berkeley and Los Angeles:: University of California Press, 1991).

9. Andreas Bozóki, "Introduction," in A. Bozóki, ed. *Intellectuals and Politics
in Central Europe*, 1–2.

10. Timothy Garton Ash, "Prague: Intellectuals & Politicians," *New York Review
of Books*, January 12, 1995.

11. Krishan Kumar, *1989: Revolutionary Ideas and Ideals* (Minneapolis:
University of Minnesota Press, 2001); Kundera, "The Tragedy of Central
Europe"; Lauristin et al., *Return to the Western World*.

12. Iver B. Neumann, *The Uses of the Other: 'The East' in European Identity
Formation* (Minneapolis: University of Minnesota Press, 1999).

13. Gil Eyal, *The Origins of Postcommunist Elites: From Prague Spring to the
Breakup of Czechoslovakia* (Minneapolis: University of Minnesota Press,
2003), xxii.

14. Katherine Verdery, *What Was Socialism, And What Comes Next?*
(Princeton, NJ: Princeton University Press, 1996), 106; see also Katherine
Verdery, *National Ideology under Socialism*, 15–17.

15. Verdery, *What Was Socialism*, 106.
16. Eyal, Szelenyi, and Townsley indeed argue that cultural capital was *the most important* source of political legitimacy in Central Europe in the 1990s. Eyal, Szelenyi, and Townsley, *Making Capitalism without Capitalists*, 6.
17. Lieven, *Baltic Revolution*; see also Timothy Garton Ash, *History of the Present: Essays, Sketches and Dispatches from Europe in the 1990s* (London: Penguin Books, 1999).
18. György Csepeli, Antal Örkény, and Kim Lane Scheppele, "Acquired Immune Deficiency Syndrome in Social Science in Eastern Europe." *Social Research* 63 (1996): 486–510, 487
19. Bauman, "Intellectuals in East-Central Europe"; Verdery, *National Ideology under Socialism*, 15–17.
20. Pierre Bourdieu, *Distinction: A Social Critique of the Judgement of Taste* (Cambridge, MA: Harvard University Press, 1984), 12–13.
21. Of the seventy-six individuals who served as foreign ministers of Central European states between the early 1990s and early 2005, and the thirty-seven individuals who served as heads of state during the same time period, my research assistant Chris Drake was able to access 75 biographical sketches out of the total of 113 on the Internet. Most are available through the official ministerial and presidential Web sites. Of these 75 individuals, 28—more than one-third—hold earned doctorates. All references to these individuals' educational and professional background come from their biographical sketches. As noted above, I deemphasize the significance of doctoral degrees in political science, economics, engineering, and the natural sciences because these fields are less directly relevant to the cultural framing of statecraft that interests me here. I concentrate on presidents and foreign ministers because they occupy the most important sites in foreign policy rhetoric in the countries in question.

    Intellectualism is only one of the idiosyncrasies of Central Europe's political elites compared to their Western counterparts. Their relatively young age is another important difference that receives much attention but little analysis. Individuals in their thirties holding high state positions are fairly common, and cabinet ministers in their twenties are not unheard-of even in 2007. In Timothy Garton Ash's first-hand account from NATO's Prague summit, he mentions the awkwardness with which American security intellectuals rubbed shoulders with beefy young men who looked like security guards but turned out to be high government officials from the accession states. See Timothy Garton Ash, "Love, Peace and NATO," *Guardian*, November 28, 2002.
22. The literature on Central Europe's foreign policy elites tends to focus on evaluating the opinions and ideological affinities of these elites. It asks whether individual elite members are "heroes" or "villains," "true" or only "superficial" reformers, "former Communists," "nationalists," "populists," and so on. See Fredo Arias-King, "The Centrality of Elites," *Democratizatsyia* 11 (Winter 2003), http://www.findarticles.com/p/articles/mi_qa3996/is_200301/ai_n9186590 (accessed May 18, 2005); and Anton Steen, *Between*

Past and Future: Elites, Democracy, and the State in Post-Communist Countries: A Comparison of Estonia, Latvia and Lithuania (Aldershot, UK: Ashgate, 1997), My concern here is not with the thoughts, ideological leanings, or management styles of Central Europe elites but rather with the role of one particular elite group—intellectuals—in the construction of a specific sphere, namely foreign policy.

23. Göncz has translated works by James Baldwin, William Faulkner, and Susan Sontag, among others. Meri has translated the works of Erich Maria Remarque, Graham Greene, and Aleksander Solzhenitsyn, among others.

24. Eyal, *Origins of Postcommunist Elites*; Lieven, *Baltic Revolution*.

25. This claim is based on reading numerous speeches and interviews by the intellectuals in question.

26. Fawn, "Symbolism in the Diplomacy of Vaclav Havel," 1; see also Tismaneanu, *Fantasies of Salvation*; and Garton Ash, *History of the Present*.

27. Aviezer Tucker, "The Politics of Conviction: the Rise and Fall of Czech Intellectual-Politicians," in *Intellectuals and Politics in Central Europe*, ed Andreás Bozóki (Budapest: Central European University Press, 1999).

28. Kalev Keskküla, "Diplomaadi vahearve" [Diplomat's Report], *Eesti Ekspress*, December 6, 2004. That same year, Joerüüt published a personal memoir of his diplomatic career. Excerpts from the book were published in *Looming*, Estonia's main literary journal, and won that journal's prize for creative work.

29. See Garton Ash, *History of the Present*; Lieven, *Baltic Revolution*; and Janine Wedel, *Collision and Collusion: The Strange Case of Western Aid to Eastern Europe*, 2nd ed. (New York: Palgrave, 2001).

30. Ian Traynor, "Hero of Czech Drama Bows out of World Stage," *Guardian*, February 6, 2003. Frank Zappa and Lou Reed are iconic figures in rock music. They were famous especially in the 1970s and the 1980s.

31. Lieven, *Baltic Revolution*, 273.

32. Quoted in Fawn, "Symbolism in the Diplomacy of Vaclav Havel," 13. In some cases, however, these figures are more popular abroad than in their own countries. This is the case with Havel, Meri, and Landsbergis, all of whom were accused of being too esoteric and moralistic—a kind of philosopher-king—at home.

33. See Merje Kuus, "'Those Goody-Goody Estonians': Toward Rethinking Security in the European Union Applicant States." *Environment and Planning D: Society and Space* 22 (2004): 191–207; Janine Wedel, "Tainted Transactions: Harvard, Chubais and Russia's Ruin," *National Interest* 59 (Spring 2000): 23–34.

34. *Economist*, "The Disappearing Czech Intellectual," August 21, 1999.

35. See Bozóki, ed., *Intellectuals and Politics in Central Europe*, especially Tucker, "The Politics of Conviction," on Havel.

36. Falk, *Dilemmas of Dissidence*, 356.

37. See Garton Ash, *History of the Present*; Ales Gaube, "Snubbing NATO", *Transitions Online*, December 13, 2002 http://www.tol.cz (accessed July 7, 2004); and Eyal, Szelenyi and Townsley, *Making Capitalism Without Capitalists*.

38. Martin Simecka, "The Havel Paradox," *Transitions Online*, March 21, 2003. http://www.told.cz (accessed May 20, 2005).

39. Lennart Meri, "Vabariigi Presidendi intervjuu prantsuse nädalalehele *La Vie*" [President of the Republic's interview with the French weekly *La Vie*], December 24, 1998.

40. This is mentioned in Meri's official biography as well as the numerous articles about him in the western media (e.g. Donald McNeil Jr. "Estonia's President: Un-Soviet and Un-Conventional" (*The New York Times*, April 7, 2001). The film does not appear among the official archive of the New York Film Festival films. I report the award here because it is a part of Meri's aura.

41. *Economist*. Obituary. "Lennart Meri," March 23, 2006.

42. *Pegasos: a literature related resource site*, Lennart Meri. http://www.kirjasto .sci.fi/lmeri.htm (accessed April 1, 2006).

43. Lieven, *Baltic Revolution*, 288.

44. *Economist*, "The Baltic Bobsleigh," February 5, 1998.

45. Lieven, *Baltic Revolution*, 288.

46. Lennart Meri, "Eesti ja Eurointegratsiooniprotsess" [Estonia and the Process of European Integration], speech delivered to the Paasikivi Society in Helsinki, Finland, September 3, 1997. Juho Paasikivi was instrumental in negotiating Finland's relationship with the Soviet Union throughout the first half of the twentieth century, and this is the context in which Meri invokes Paasikivi's diary.

47. Lieven, *Baltic Revolution*, 288.

48. *Economist*, "Baltic Bobsleigh"; Lieven, *Baltic Revolution*, 288.

49. Lennart Meri, *Riigimured* [Concerns of the State], in Speeches 1996–2001, ed. Toomas Kiho (Tartu: Ilmamaa, 2001), book jacket.

50. Ronald D. Asmus, *Opening NATO's Door: How the Alliance Remade Itself for a New Era* (New York: Columbia University Press, 2002), 237.

51. Lennart Meri, "Avasõna Europa Musicale kontserdil, München" (opening remarks at the Europa Musicale Concert in Munich, October 31, 1993).

52. Lennart Meri, "By the Will of Tacitus" (address given at the National Library, Tallinn, November 12, 1998).

53. Lennart Meri, "President Lennart Meri intervjuu kvartaliajakirjale *Politique Internationale*" [President Lennart Meri's interview with the quarterly *Politique Internationale*], January 31, 2000.

54. Lennart Meri, speech delivered at the dinner given in honor of Javier Solana, Secretary General of NATO, Tallinn, April 19, 1996 (Tallinn: Office of the President, 1996). The astronomer's name should be spelled Hoyle.

55. Lennart Meri, "Vabariigi Presidendi intervjuu prantsuse nädalalehele *La Vie*."

56. Lennart Meri, "Mis on Eesti" [What is Estonia], speech at St. Olaf University, Northfield, MN, April 6, 2000, in Lennart Meri, *Riigimured*, 179. "Mis on Eesti" Mis on Eesti [What is Estonia]. Speech at St. Olaf College, Northfield, Minnesota, April 6, 2000. In L. Meri, *Riigimured*.

57. Lennart Meri, *President Lennart Mere kõne Estonia kontserdisaalis* [President Lennart Meri's speech in Estonia Concert Hall], February 24, 1993 (Tallinn: Office of the President, 1993).

58. Lennart Meri, Julgeolek, julgeolek ja veelkord julgeolek" [Security, Security and Once Again Security] (remarks at the Institute for Strategic and International Studies, Washington, D.C., June 27, 1996).

59. Lennart Meri, *Vabariigi Presidendi intervjuu ajalehele Die Welt* [President of the Republic's interview with the German newspaper *Die Welt*] (Tallinn: Office of the President, January 21, 1995).

60. Kulle Raig, *Vikerkaare värvid, Lennart Meri elu sõprade pilgu läbi*, [Colors of the Rainbow: The Life of Lennart Meri through the Eyes of His Friends] (Tallinn: Varrak, 2003), 146.

61. Rein Veidemann, "Müütiline Meri" [Mythical Meri], *Eesti Päevaleht*, March 29, 1999, emphasis added.

62. Lennart Meri, interview with *Le Figaro*.

Chapter 6

1. Janine Wedel, *Collision and Collusion: The Strange Case of Western Aid to Eastern Europe*, 2nd ed. (New York: Palgrave, 2001), 3; emphasis in original.

2. Andrzej Stasiuk, "Wild, Cunning, Exotic: The East Will Completely Shake Up Europe," *Süddeutsche Zeitung*, June 20, 2003. Reprinted in *Old Europe, New Europe, Core Europe: Transatlantic Relations after the Iraq War*, edited by Daniel Levy, Max Pensky, and John Torpey (London: Verso, 2005), 104.

3. There is now a substantial interdisciplinary literature that highlights the agency of states and individuals in Central Europe vis-à-vis the so-called Western norms. See Lazlo Bruszt and David Stark, "Who Counts? Supranational Norms and Societal Needs," *East European Politics and Societies* 17 (2003): 74–82; Daphne Berdahl, Matti Bunzl and Martha Lampland, eds., *Altering States: Ethnographies of Transition in Eastern Europe and the Former Soviet Union* (Ann Arbor: University of Michigan Press, 2000); Michael Burawoy and Katherine Verdery, eds., *Uncertain Transition: Ethnographies of Change in the Postsocialist World* (Lanham, MD, Rowman and Littlefield Publishers, 1999); Elizabeth C. Dunn, *Privatizing Poland: Baby Food, Big Business, and the Remaking of Labor* (Ithaca, NY: Cornell University Press, 2005); Gernot Grabher and David Stark, eds., *Restructuring Networks in Post-Socialism: Legacies, Linkages and Localities* (Oxford: Oxford University Press, 1996); and John Pickles and Adrian Smith, eds., *Theorising Transition: the Political Economy of Post-Communist Transformations* (London: Routledge, 1998). However, most of this literature focuses on economic issues, especially privatization. It makes virtually no mention of foreign and security policy. For an exception, see Kuus, "'Those Goody-Goody Estonians.'"

4. Lieven, *Baltic Revolution*, xvi.

5. Dunn, *Privatizing Poland*; Wedel, *Collision and Collusion*.

6. Wedel, *Collision and Collusion*, 90. Wedel speaks of the Polish context, but her point is applicable throughout Central Europe.

7. An informant of Elizabeth Dunn, quoted in Dunn, *Privatizing Poland*, 51.

8. Dawson and Fawn, "Changing Geopolitics of Eastern Europe," 3.

9. Rebecca Moore, "Europe 'Whole and Free': NATO's Political Mission in the 21st Century," NATO–EAPC Research Fellowship Final Report (Brussels: NATO Office of Information and Press, 2003), 44.

10. Ibid.

11. See Ole Wæver, "The EU as Security Actor: Reflections from a Pessimistic Constructivist on Post-Sovereign Security Orders," in *International Relations Theory and the Politics of European Integration: Power, Security and Community*, ed. Morten Kelstrup and Michael C. Williams (London and New York: Routledge, 2000), 261.

12. The monitoring is discussed in greater detail in Chapter 4. See also Kelley, *Ethnic Politics in Europe*; and Rae, *State Identities and the Homogenisation of Peoples*.

13. The following vignette, offered by the Estonian journalist Kadri Liik, provides a good example of this kind of performance for Western colleagues and benefactors. Liik tells of an anonymous (liberal) Russian colleague who received many invitations in the early 1990s to speak about Russian views of security at Western seminars. After some time, the Russian journalist was apparently demoted from the so-called A-list. When he asked his Western colleagues why he was no longer invited, they said that "such pro-Western statements we can make ourselves as well. We need a different attitude from Russia . . ." Liik noted that pragmatic Russian analysts quickly figured out that attending Western seminars to play the Russian bear was good business. The average fee was $1,000 dollars per presentation, sometimes even more. For that kind of money, many speakers quickly started to oppose NATO. When circumstances changed, so did their positions. At the height of the Kosovo crisis in 1999, a BBC journalist told Liik that it was difficult to find a true NATO opponent—all the "bears" suddenly began to argue that NATO is a reality with which Russia must cope. The "bears" had realized that their good business was based on ambiguous relations between Russia and the West. If these relations become either too good or too bad, the seminars stop. Kadri Liik, "Analüüs: Venemaa, NATO ja meie kümne aasta lugu" [Analysis: Russia, NATO and the story of our decade], *Postimees*, February 6, 2000.

14. Tõnu Õnnepalu, *Border State* (Evanston, IL: Northwestern University Press, 2000), 20–1.

15. Turnover of personnel was especially high in the sphere of foreign and security policy, as persons associated with the former regime were often replaced by individuals with fewer "Eastern" and more "Western" connections. Derek Averre and Andrew Cottey, "Introduction: Thinking About Security in Postcommunist Europe," in *New Security Challenges in Postcommunist Europe*, ed. A. Cottey and D. Averre (Manchester: Manchester University Press, 2002).

16. See note 3, especially Kuus, "'Those Goody-Goody Estonians'"; Wedel, *Collision and Collusion*.

17. The research that appears in Western journals is only one part of Central European scholarship, but it makes the greatest impact in the West.

18. Local relationships and social patterns may not only block social transformations (as is commonly assumed), but also foster them. See Grabher and Stark, *Restructuring Networks in Post-Socialism*.

19. Wedel, *Collision and Collusion*, 25.

20. The 1990s witnessed a bifurcation of Eastern academics into those who travel abroad and speak in Western circles and those who stay at home and participate in intellectual debates there. These divisions created stratifications within the intelligentsia that do not have obvious parallels in the West, and Westerners often could not read the signals that these divisions conveyed. György Csepeli, Antal Örkény and Kim Lane Scheppele, "Acquired Immune Deficiency Syndrome in Social Science in Eastern Europe," 505.

21. Samuel P. Huntington, *The Clash of Civilizations and the Remaking of the World Order* (New York: Simon and Schuster, 1996),160.

22. Huntington, *Clash of Civilizations*, 158.

23. Mart Nutt, quoted in Gregory Feldman, *Many Nice People: Hegemony, State, and Empire in Estonia* (unpublished manuscript).

24. Asmus, *Opening NATO's Door*, 159. Ilves worked for Radio Free Europe for years before becoming involved in Estonian politics.

25. Lieven, *Baltic Revolution*, 420. Lieven points out that in the Baltic states at least, the diasporic groups tend to be more right-wing than the general populations.

26. Daphne Berdahl, "Introduction: An Anthropology of Postsocialism," in in *Altering States: Ethnographies of Transition in Eastern Europe and the Former Soviet Union*, ed. Daphne Berdahl, Matti Bunzl, and Martha Lampland (Ann Arbor: University of Michigan Press, 2000), 5.

27. Peter Van Ham, "The Baltic States and Europe: Identity and Institutions," in *Stability and Security in the Baltic Sea Region. Russian, Nordic and European Aspects*, ed. Olav Knudsen (London and Portland, OR: Frank Cass, 1999), 224; emphasis added.

28. *Economist*, "Trouble in Paradise."

29. *Economist*, "Toomas Ilves, Estonia's American-European."

30. *Economist*, "The Baltic Bobsleigh."

31. *Postimees*, "Laar on Euroopa 50 mõjukama liidri hulgas" [Laar is among the 50 most influential leaders in Europe], June 7, 2001.

32. Andres Tarand in an interview in 2000, quoted in Berg, *Eesti tähendused, piirid ja kontekstid* [Estonia's Meanings, Borders, and Contexts] (Tartu: Tartu University Press, 2002), 110.

33. Andrei Hvostov, "Kinderstube ja välispoliitika seosed" [The Links between Kinderstube and Foreign Policy], *Eesti Ekspress*, November 19, 2003.

34. Danjoux, *Reframing Citizenship in the Baltic Republics*, 50.

35. *City Paper*, "Selling Estonia," 7. The remark belongs to Scott Diel.

36. Andres Kasekamp, Toomas Riim, and Viljar Veebel, *Eesti koht ja valikud Euroopa ühises julgeoleku-ja kaitsepoliitikas* [Estonia's Place and Choices in

Europe's Common Foreign and Security Policy] (Tartu: Estonian Foreign Policy Institute, 2003). http://www.evi.ee (accessed July 5, 2004).

37. Toomas Hendrik Ilves, "Estonia as a Nordic Country," speech delivered at the Swedish Institute for International Relations, December 14, 1999, http://www.vm.ee/eng/pressreleases/speeches/1999/Ilves_stock1412.html; Toomas Hendrik Ilves and Kristiina Ojuland, "Main Guidelines of Estonia's Foreign Policy," address to the Riigikogu on behalf of the government of Estonia (Tallinn: Ministry of Foreign Affairs, June 13, 2002). http://www.vm.ee/eng/kat_140/2374.html (accessed January 11, 2001).

38. On the Estonian debate around the Estonia-Russian border dispute, see Eiki Berg, *Eesti tähendused, piirid ja kontekstid* [Estonia's meanings, borders, and contexts].

39. Quoted in Berg, 110.

40. Toomas Hendrik Ilves, "Eesti poliitika euroopastumine" [The Europeanization of Estonian Politics], *Luup*, 17 March 1997, http://www.postimees.ee/luup/97/06/sise2.htm (accessed February 2, 2001). See also Hannes Rumm, "Välisminister hajutab hirme," *Eesti Päevaleht*, March 20, 1997.

41. Andrei Hvostov, "Kübaratrikiga Euroopasse," *Eesti Ekspress*, February 8, 2001, http://www.ekspress.ee/arhiiv/2001/06/aosa/arvamus5.html (accessed July 3, 2002).

42. Marko Mihkelson, "Venemaa näitab tegelikku nägu," *Postimees*, April 14, 1998; Marko Mihkelson, "Venemaa isemeelne tee" [Russia's Stubborn Way], *Postimees*, December 10, 2003. Mihkelson is a leading expert on Russia.

43. Harri Tiido, "Eesmärgi püsivus olude muutumisel," *Eesti Päevaleht*, December 4, 2001.

44. Andres Kasekamp, "Euroopa ühine kaitsepoliitika ja meie" [Europe's Common Defense Policy and Us], *Postimees*, May 15, 2001.

45. Paul A. Goble, "Redefining Estonia's National Security," in *Estonian Foreign Policy Yearbook 2005*, ed. A. Kasekamp. (Tallinn: Estonian Foreign Policy Institute, 2005), 9–20. Goble is a long-time American observer of Baltic politics.

46. Aap Neljas, "Eesti julgeolekuriskide analüüs Eesti Julgeolekupoliitika Aluste Kontseptsioonis" [The Analysis of Estonia's Security Risks in the National Security Concept], paper presented at the First Estonian Social Science Conference, Tallinn, Estonia, November 25, 2000. Copy available from author.

47. Eesti Vabariigi Riigikogu. *Riigikogu toimetamata stenogramm* [Unedited Parliamentary Transcript], January 25, 2001 (accessed July 8, 2002); see also *Riigikogu toimetamata stenogramm* [Unedited Parliamentary Transcript], January 18 and March 6, 2001.

48. Eesti Vabariigi Riigikogu, *Riigikogu toimetamata stenogramm* [Unedited Parliamentary Transcript], October 25, 2001 (accessed July 8, 2002).

49. Erkki Bahovski, "Ilves ei usu suhete paranemist Venemaaga" [Ilves Does Not Believe in the Improvement of Relations with Russia], Ilves's interview with *Eesti Päevaleht*, *Eesti Päevaleht*, September 12, 2000.

50. Toomas Hendrik Ilves, "A Blueprint for Stability," Remarks by Toomas Hendrik Ilves at the Commission representation in Bonn, Germany,

February 19, 1997, http//www.vm.eng.pressreleases/speeches/1997/0218 bonn.html (accessed May 31, 2001).

51. I distinguish between Estonian and Western intellectuals of statecraft on the basis of their language skills. Members of the Estonian diaspora are thus defined as "Estonian" if they are fluent in the Estonian language. "Western" here encompasses Europe and North America. Although there are differences among the various Western countries policies toward the EU candidate states, the basic assumptions with which they approach the candidate states are similar. They are similar because they can be traced back to the broader othering conceptions of Eastern Europe.

52. Anneli Tarkmeel, "Eesti Kohalik Poliitiline Eliit," Bakalaureusetöö [Estonian Local Political Elite, bachelor's thesis], University of Tartu, Estonia, Department of Political Science, 1998.

53. On the Western side, the circle of Estonian specialists is also small, and that fact is well known to Estonians. The tightly woven networks mean that the Western ideas that are presented as cutting-edge come from very few Western sources.

54. Strobe Talbott, "A Baltic Home-coming," the Robert C. Frasure Memorial Lecture (Tallinn: Ministry of Foreign Affairs, January 24, 2000), http:// www.vm.ee/est/kat_140/825/html (accessed September 7, 2002).

55. Kadri Liik and Argo Ideon, "Eesti tormiline teekond: Moskva vangikongist NATO kaitsva vihmavarju alla" [Estonia's Stormy Journey from Moscow's Prison Cell to NATO's Protective Umbrella], *Postimees*, November 19, 2002.

56. Asmus, *Opening NATO's Door*, 235.

57. Mart Laar, *Eesti uus algus* [Estonia's New Beginning] (Tallinn: Tänapäev, 2000), 93.

58. Toomas Hendrik Ilves, "Kuidas vältida topelt ei-d?" [How to Avoid a Double "No"?], in Eesti Vabariigi Välisministeerium, *Teine tulemine: taasiseseisvunud Eesti välisesindused* [Second Coming: Foreign Representations of the Re-independent Estonia] (Tallinn: Eesti Vabariigi Välisministeerium, 2003), 13–18. It is possible that Estonian politicians exaggerate their closeness to Western dignitaries to boost their own image. My analysis errs on the side of caution and systematically under- rather than overestimates the personal contacts between Estonian and Western intellectuals of statecraft.

59. Remarks by Jüri Luik, Minister of Foreign Affairs of the Republic of Estonia, at the final conference in Paris for a stability pact in Europe (Tallinn: Ministry of Foreign Affairs, March 20, 1995), http://www.vm.ee/eng/pressreleases/ speeches/1995/9503221sp.html (accessed May 5, 1999).

60. Gregory Feldman, "Neoliberal Nationalism: Ethnic Integration and Estonia's Accession to the European Union," in *Crossing European Boundaries: Beyond Conventional Geographical Categories*, ed. Helen Kopnina, Christina Moutsov, and Jaro Stacul (London and New York: Berghahn Press, 2005), 49.

61. Ibid., 52.

62. Quoted in Gregory Feldman, "Culture, State, and Security in Europe: the Case of Citizenship and Integration Policy in Estonia," *American Ethnologist* 32 (2005): 679.

63. Asmus, *Opening NATO's Door*.

64. Apollo Raamatumaja. Product description of Mihkel Mutt, *Rahvusvaheline Mees* [International Man] (Tallinn: Eesti Päevalehe Kirjastus), http://www.apollo.ee (accessed August 20, 2006). Mutt is a prominent writer and public intellectual who worked in the foreign ministry in the early 1990s. The book is a fictional account of his experiences there. A key character in the plot is Rudolfo, a colorful figure whose prototype is Foreign Minister (later President) Lennart Meri.

Chapter 7

1. Michael Dillon, *Politics of Security: Towards a Political Philosophy of Continental Thought* (London and New York: Routledge, 1996), 16.

2. Václav Havel, "Beyond Revolutionary Disillusion," Project Syndicate, March 2006, http://www.project-syndicate.org/print_commentary/havel26/English (accessed July 18, 2006).

3. David Campbell, *Writing Security: United States Foreign Policy and the Politics of Identity*, 2nd ed. (Minneapolis: University of Minnesota Press, 1998). Prior to EU and NATO accession, the central premise of security debates was that Central European states were insecure because they were not EU and NATO members, and were therefore vulnerable to bullying from other states. Since the accession, the premise is that these states are insecure because they are EU and NATO members, and they are therefore vulnerable to terrorist plots against Western political and military institutions.

4. Michael Hardt and Antonio Negri, *Empire* (Cambridge, MA: Harvard University Press, 2000), 198.

5. Sandra Kalniete, "Latvia Empathizes with Iraq," *Baltic Times*, December 4, 2003. See also Siim Kallas, "Kelle poolt on Eesti?" [Whom Does Estonia Support?], *Postimees*, February 11, 2003, http://www.postimees.ee (accessed March 16, 2003).

6. This observation echoes Milan Kundera's claim that Central Europe is more authentically European than the western part of the continent because Central Europe has retained the moral and cultural values that have been commodified and lost in Western Europe. Given that Laar's statement appeared in his editorial in the *Wall Street Journal*, it was written explicitly for an American audience. Mart Laar, "New Europe Won't Keep Quiet Until All Europe is New," *Wall Street Journal*, February 19, 2003, emphasis added.

7. Michael J. Shapiro, *Violent Cartographies: Mapping Cultures of War* (Minneapolis: University of Minnesota Press, 1997), 16.

8. Such a conversion of difference into distance has been the mainstay of geopolitical discourses at least since the Age of Exploration. John A. Agnew,

Geopolitics: Re-visioning World Politics (London: Routledge, 1998); and Walter D. Mignolo, *Local Histories, Global Designs: Coloniality, Subaltern Knowledges, and Border Thinking* (Princeton, NJ: Princeton University Press, 2000).

9. Thomas Diez, "Europe's Others and the Return of Geopolitics," Cambridge Review of International Affairs 17 (2004): 331.

10. Most existing scholarship, especially in IR, looks primarily at EU policy and formal political statements by EU officials. For a good overview of this scholarship, see Bahar Rumelili, "Constructing Identity and Relating to Difference," Review of International Studies 30 (2004): 27–47.

11. Douglas Holmes, *Integral Europe: Fast-capitalism, Multiculturalism, Neofascism* (Princeton, NJ: Princeton University Press, 2000); and Verena Stolcke, "Talking Culture: New Boundaries, New Rhetorics of Exclusion in Europe," *Current Anthropology* 63 (1995): 1–20

12. Hannah Arendt, *Eichmann in Jerusalem: A Report on the Banality of Evil*, rev. ed. (New York: Viking, 1964), 288. See also Michael Billig, *Banal Nationalism* (Thousand Oaks, CA: Sage Publications, 1995); Derek Gregory, *The Colonial Present* (Oxford and Malden, MA: Blackwell, 2004); and Richard Ned Lebow, *The Tragic Vision of Politics: Ethics, Interests and Orders* (Cambridge: Cambridge University Press, 2003).

13. Militarization here refers to the multilayered sociopolitical dynamic through which militarism gains popular and elite acceptance. See Cynthia H. Enloe, *The Curious Feminist: Searching for Women in an Age of Empire* (Berkeley, CA: University of California Press, 2004), 219.

14. Giorgio Agamben, "Security and Terror," *Theory & Event* 5 (2002).

15. Noel Parker, "Integrated Europe and its 'Margins': Action and Reaction," in *Margins in European Integration*, ed. N. Parker and B. Armstrong (New York: St. Martin's Press, 2000), 1.

16. Etienne Balibar, "The Borders of Europe," in *Cosmopolitics: Thinking and Feeling Beyond the Nation*, ed. Bruce Robbins and Cheah Phen (Minneapolis: University of Minnesota Press, 1998). See also Mabel Berezin and Martin A. Schain, eds., *Europe without Borders: Remapping Territory, Citizenship, and Identity in a Transnational Age* (New York: Columbia University Press, 2003).

17. Ole Wæver, "Imperial Metaphors: Emerging European Analogies to Pre-Nation-State Imperial Systems," in *Geopolitics in Post-Wall Europe: Security, Territory and Identity*, ed. O. Tunander, P. Baev and V. I. Einagel (London: Sage, 1997), 80; and Hayden White, "The Discourse of Europe and the Search for a European Identity," in *Europe and the Other and Europe as the Other*, ed. Bo Stråth (Brussels: P.I.E.–Peter Lang, 2000).

18. Iver B. Neumann, *The Uses of the Other: 'The East' in European Identity Formation* (Minneapolis: University of Minnesota Press, 1999).

19. Wæver, "Imperial Metaphors"; Ole Wæver, "The EU as Security Actor: Reflections from a Pessimistic Constructivist on Post-Sovereign Security Orders," in *International Relations Theory and the Politics of European*

Integration: Power, Security and Community, ed. Morten Kelstrup and Michael C. Williams (London and New York: Routledge, 2000); and Jan Zielonka, *Europe as Empire: The Nature of the Enlarged European Union.* Oxford: Oxford University Press, 2006).

20. Wæver, "The EU as Security Actor."
21. Romano Prodi, "Sharing Stability and Prosperity," Speech Delivered at the Tempus MEDA Regional Conference, Bibliotheca Alexandrina, October 13, 2003; quoted in Raffaella A. Del Sarto and Tobias Schuhmacher, "From EMP to ENP: What's at Stake with the European Neighbourhood Policy towards the Southern Mediterranean?" *European Foreign Affairs Review* 10 (2005): 30.
22. Zielonka, Europe as Empire.
23. Stefan Elbe, "'We Good Europeans': Genealogical Reflections on the Idea of Europe." *Millennium: Journal of International Studies* 30 (2001): 259–83.
24. A review of the European Neighbourhood Policy is beyond the scope of this book, but see Roberto Aliboni, "The Geopolitical Implications of the European Neighbourhood Policy," *European Foreign Affairs Review* 10 (2005):1–16; Christopher Browning and Pertti Joenniemi, "The European Union's Two Dimensions: The Northern and the Eastern," *Security Dialogue* 34 (2003): 463–78; Del Sarto and Schumacher, "From EMP to ENP"; Diez, "Europe's Others and the Return of Geopolitics"; Karen E. Smith "The outsiders: the European neighbourhood policy" *International Affairs* 81 (2005): 757–73.
25. BBC News. "Poles Stick to Russia talks veto" November 23, 2006; http://news.bbc.co.uk (accessed November 23, 2006). Poland's decision was linked to Russia's embargo on Polish meat. Poland wanted a clear link between talks of the new agreement and lifting of the embargo.
26. Celeste A. Wallander, "NATO's Price: Shape Up or Ship Out," *Foreign Affairs* 81 (2002): 5.
27. Zielonka, Europe as Empire, 22.

Bibliography

I. Scholarly Books and Articles

Aalto, Pami. "Revisiting the Security-Identity Puzzle in Russo-Estonian Relations." *Journal of Peace Research* 40 (2003): 573–91.

Aalto, Pami, and Eiki Berg. "Spatial Practices and Time in Estonia: From Post-Soviet Geopolitics to European Governance." *Space & Polity* 6 (2002): 253–70.

Aalto, Pami, Simon Dalby, and Vilho Harle. "The Critical Geopolitics of Northern Europe: Identity Politics Unlimited." *Geopolitics* 8 (2003): 1–19.

Adamson, Andres, and Sulev Valdmaa. *Eesti ajalugu gümnaasiumile* [Estonian History for Gymnasiums]. Tallinn: Avita, 1999.

Agamben, Giorgio. "Security and Terror." *Theory & Event* 5 (2002). http://muse.jhu.edu/journals/theory_and_event/v005/5.4agamben.html (accessed January 3, 2006).

Agnew, John A. *Geopolitics: Re-visioning World Politics*. London: Routledge, 1998.

———. "How Many Europes?: The European Union, Eastward Enlargement and Uneven Development." *European Urban and Regional Studies* 8 (2001): 29–38.

———. "Regions on the Mind Does Not Equal Regions of the Mind." *Progress in Human Geography* 23 (1999): 91–96.

———. "The Territorial Trap: The Geographical Assumptions of International Relations Theory." *Review of International Political Economy* 1 (1994): 53–80.

———. "Territoriality and Political Identity in Europe." In *Europe Without Borders: Remapping Territory, Citizenship, and Identity in a Transnational Age*, edited by M. Berezin and M. A. Schain, 219–342. New York: Columbia University Press, 2003.

Agnew, John A., and Stuart Corbridge. Mastering Space: Hegemony, Territory and International Political Economy. New York: Routledge, 1995.

Aliboni, Roberto. "The Geopolitical Implications of the European Neighbourhood Policy." *European Foreign Affairs Review* 10 (2005): 1–16.

Amato, Giuliano, and Judy Batt. *The Long-term Implications of EU Enlargement: The Nature of the New Border*. Florence: European University Institute in Florence, 1999.

Antohi, Sorin, and Vladimir Tismaneanu, eds. *Between Past and Future: The Revolutions of 1989 and Their Aftermath*. Budapest: CEU Press, 2000.

Arendt, Hannah. *Eichmann in Jerusalem: A Report on the Banality of Evil*, rev.ed. New York: Viking Press, 1964.

Arias-King, Fredo. "The Centrality of Elites." *Democratizatsyia* 11 (Winter 2003), http://www.findarticles.com/p/articles/mi_qa3996/is_200301/ai_n9186590 (accessed May 18, 2005).

Asad, Talal. "Muslims and European Identity: Can Europe Represent Islam?" In *The Idea of Europe: from Antiquity to the European Union*, edited by Anthony Pagden, 209–227. Cambridge and New York: Woodrow Wilson Center Press and Cambridge University Press, 2002.

Ashley, Richard K. "The Geopolitics of Geopolitical Space: Toward a Critical Social Theory of International Politics." *Alternatives* 12 (1987): 403–434.

Asmus, Ronald D. *Opening NATO's Door: How the Alliance Remade Itself for a New Era*. New York: Columbia University Press, 2002.

Atkinson, David, and Klaus Dodds. "Introduction. Geopolitical Traditions: A Century of Geopolitical Thought". In *Geopolitical Traditions: A Century of Geopolitical Thought*, edited by David Atkinson and Klaus Dodds.: 1–24 London: Routledge, 2000.

Augustinos, Gerasimos, ed. *The National Idea in Eastern Europe: The Politics of Ethnic and Civic Community*. Lexington, MA and Toronto, ON: D.C. Heath and Company, 1996.

Averre, Derek, and Andrew Cottey. "Introduction: Thinking About Security in Postcommunist Europe." In *New Security Challenges in Postcommunist Europe*, edited by Derek Averre and Andrew Cottey, 1–25. Manchester, UK: Manchester University Press, 2002.

Bakic-Hayden, Milica. "Nesting Orientalisms: The Case of Former Yugoslavia." *Slavic Review* 54 (1995): 917–31.

Bakic-Hayden, Milica, and Robert M. Hayden. "Orientalist Variations on the Theme 'Balkans': Symbolic Geography of Recent Yugoslav Cultural Politics." *Slavic Review* 51 (1992): 1–15.

Balibar, Etienne. "The Borders of Europe." In *Cosmopolitics: Thinking and Feeling Beyond the Nation*, edited by B. Robbins and C. Phen, 216–29. Minneapolis: University of Minnesota Press, 1998.

Bauman, Zygmunt. "Intellectuals in East-Central Europe: Continuity and Change." *Eastern European Politics and Societies* 1 (1987): 162–86.

Berdahl, Daphne. "Introduction: An Anthropology of Postsocialism." In *Altering States: Ethnographies of Transition in Eastern Europe and the Former Soviet Union*, edited by D. Berdahl, M. Bunzl, and M. Lampland, 3–22. Ann Arbor: University of Michigan Press, 2000.

Berdahl, Daphne, Matti Bunzl, and Martha Lampland, eds. *Altering States: Ethnographies of Transition in Eastern Europe and the Former Soviet Union*. Ann Arbor: University of Michigan Press, 2000.

Berezin, Mabel, and Martin A. Schain, eds. Europe without Borders: Remapping Territory, Citizenship, and Identity in a Transnational Age. New York: Columbia University Press, 2005.

Berg, Eiki. *Eesti tähendused, piirid ja kontekstid* [Estonia's Meanings, Borders, and Contexts]. Tartu: Tartu University Press, 2002.

————. "Local Resistance, National Identity and Global Swings in Post-Soviet Estonia." *Europe-Asia Studies* 54 (2002): 109–22.

Berg, Eiki, and Saima Oras. "Writing Post-Soviet Estonia on to the World Map." *Political Geography* 19 (2000): 601–625.

Bialasiewicz, Luiza, and John O'Loughlin. "Re-ordering Europe's Eastern Frontier: Galician Identities and Political Cartographies on the Polish-Ukrainian Border." In *Boundaries and Place: European Borderlands in Geographical Context*, edited by D. Kaplan, and J. Häkli, 217–38. Lanham, MD: Rowman and Littlefield, 2002.

Bielasiak, Jack. "Determinants of Public Opinion Differences on EU Accession in Poland." *Europe-Asia Studies* 54 (2002): 1241–66.

Billig, Michael. *Banal Nationalism*. Thousand Oaks, CA: Sage Publications, 1995.

Boguszakova, Magda, Ivan Gabal, Endre Hann, Piotr Starzynski, and Eva Taracova. "Public Attitudes in Four Central European Countries." In *Perceptions of Security: Public Opinion and Expert Assessments in Europe's New Democracies*, edited by R. Smoke, 33–54. Manchester and New York: Manchester University Press, 1996.

Borneman, John, and Nick Fowler. "Europeanization." *Annual Review of Anthropology* 26 (1997): 487–514.

Böröcz, József. "The Fox and the Raven: The European Union and Hungary Renegotiate the Margins of 'Europe.'" *Comparative Studies in Society and History* 4 (2000): 847–875.

Bourdieu. Pierre. *Distinction: A Social Critique of the Judgement of Taste*. Cambridge, MA: Harvard University Press, 1984.

Bozóki, András, ed. *Intellectuals and Politics in Central Europe*. Budapest: Central European University Press, 1999.

————. "Introduction." In *Intellectuals and Politics in Central Europe*, edited by A. Bozóki, 1–15. Budapest: Central European University Press, 1999.

Brown, Archie. "Gorbachev and the End of the Cold War." In *Ending the Cold War: Interpretations, Causation, and the Study of International Relations*, edited by R.K. Herrmann and R. N. Lebow, 31–57. New York: Palgrave MacMillan, 2004.

Brown, James F. The Grooves of Change: Eastern Europe at the Turn of the Millennium. Durham, NC: Duke University Press, 2001.

Browning, Christopher. "The Internal/External Security Paradox and the Reconstruction of Boundaries in the Baltic: The Case of Kaliningrad." *Alternatives* 28 (2003): 454–581.

————. "The Region-Building Approach Revisited: The Continued Othering of Russia in Discourses of Region-Building in the European North." *Geopolitics* 8 (2003): 45–71.

Browning, Christopher, and Pertti Joenniemi. "The European Union's Two Dimensions: The Northern and the Eastern." *Security Dialogue* 34 (2003): 463–78.

————. "Regionality Beyond Security? The Baltic Sea Region after Enlargement." *Cooperation and Conflict* 39 (2004): 233–53.

Brubaker, Rogers. "Myths and Misconceptions in the Study of Nationalism." In *The State of the Nation: Ernest Gellner and the Theory of Nationalism*, edited by J. Hall, 272–306.Cambridge: Cambridge University Press, 1998.

———. *Nationalism Reframed: Nationhood and the National Question in the New Europe*. Cambridge: Cambridge University Press, 1996.

Brubaker, Rogers, and Frederick Cooper. "Beyond 'Identity.'" *Theory and Society* 29 (2000): 1–47.

Bruszt, Lazlo, and David Stark. "Who Counts? Supranational Norms and Societal Needs." *East European Politics and Societies* 17 (2003): 74–82.

Bugge, Peter. "Czech Perceptions of EU Membership: Havel vs. Klaus." In *The Road to the European Union*. Vol. 1, *The Czech and Slovak Republics*, edited by J. Rupnik and J. Zielonka, 180–98. Manchester and New York: Manchester University Press, 2003.

———. "Home at Last? Czech View of Joining the European Union." In *Margins in European Integration*, edited by N. Parker and B. Armstrong, 203–29. New York: St. Martin's Press, 2002.

Bunce, Valerie. "Lessons of the First Postsocialist Decade." *East European Politics and Societies* 13 (1999): 236–43.

Bunzl, Matti. "The Prague Experience: Gay Male Sex Tourism and the Neocolonial Invention of the Embodied Border." In *Altering States: Ethnographies of Transition in Eastern Europe and the Former Soviet Union*, edited by D. Berdahl, M. Bunzl, and M. Lampland, 70–95. Ann Arbor: University of Michigan Press, 2000.

Burawoy, Michael. "The End of Sovietology and the Renaissance of Modernization Theory." *Contemporary Sociology*, 21 (1992): 774–85.

Burawoy, Michael, and Katherine Verdery, eds. *Uncertain Transition: Ethnographies of Change in the Postsocialist World*. Lanham, MD: Rowman and Littlefield Publishers, 1999.

Burg, Steven L. "The Nationalist Appeal and the Remaking of Eastern Europe." In *The National Idea in Eastern Europe: The Politics of Ethnic and Civic Community*, edited by G. Augustinos, 143–44. Lexington, MA and Toronto, ON: D.C. Heath and Company, 1996.

Buzan, Barry, and Wæver, Ole. "EU-Europe: the European Union and its 'Near Abroad'". In *Regions and Powers: the Structure of International Security*, edited by B. Buzan and O. Wæver, 352–76. Cambridge and New York: Cambridge University Press, 2003.

Buzan, Barry, Ole Wæver, and Jaape de Wilde. *Security: A New Framework for Analysis*. Boulder, CO: Lynne Rienner, 1998.

Campbell, David. "Apartheid Geography: The Political Anthropology and Spatial Effects of International Diplomacy in Bosnia." *Political Geography* 18 (1999): 395–435.

———. *National Deconstruction: Violence, Ethnicity and Justice in Bosnia*. Minneapolis: University of Minnesota Press, 1998.

———. *Politics without Principle: Sovereignty, Ethics, and the Narratives of the Gulf War*. Boulder, CO: Lynne Rienner, 1993.

————. *Writing Security: United States Foreign Policy and the Politics of Identity*, Minneapolis: University of Minnesota Press, 2nd ed., 1998.

Cataluccio, Frank. "Introduction: In Search of Lost Europe." In Bronislaw Geremek *The Common Roots of Europe*: 1–16. London: Polity Press, 1996.

Chakrabarti, Dipesh. *Provincializing Europe: Postcolonial Thought and Historical Difference*. Princeton, NJ: Princeton University Press, 2000.

Checkel, Jeffery T. "Norms, Institutions, and National Identity in Contemporary Europe." *International Studies Quarterly* 43 (1999): 83–114.

Cichowski, Rachel A. "Western Dreams, Eastern Realities: Support for the European Union in Central and Eastern Europe." *Comparative Political Studies* 33 (2000):1243–78.

Clemens, Walter C., Jr. *The Baltic Transformed: Complexity Theory and European Security*. Lanham, MD: Rowman and Littlefield, 2001.

Cohn, Carol. "Sex and Death in the Rational World of Defense Intellectuals." *Signs: Journal of Women in Culture and Society* 12 (1987): 687–718.

Cohen, Stephen F. *Failed Crusade: America and the Tragedy of Post-Communist Russia*. New York: W. W. Norton, 2001.

Connolly, William E. *Identity/Difference: Democratic Negotiations of Political Paradox*. Ithaca, NY: Cornell University Press, 2002, exp. ed.

Csepeli, György, Antal örkény, and Kim Lane Scheppele. "Acquired Immune Deficiency Syndrome in Social Science in Eastern Europe." *Social Research* 63 (1996): 486–510.

Dalby, Simon. "Contesting an Essential Concept: Reading the Dilemmas in Contemporary Security Discourse." In *Critical Security Studies: Concepts and Cases*, edited by K. Krause, and M. C. Williams, 3–32. Minneapolis: University of Minnesota Press, 1997.

————. Creating the Second Cold War: The Discourse of Politics. New York: Guilford Press, 1990.

————. "Critical Geopolitics: Discourse, Difference, and Dissent." *Environment and Planning D: Society and Space* 9 (1991): 261–83.

————. *Environmental Security*. Minneapolis: University of Minnesota Press, 2002.

Danjoux, Olivier. *Reframing Citizenship in the Baltic Republics*. Lund: Lund University, Department of Political Science, 2002.

Dawisha, Karen. "The Social Science and Area Studies: Never the Twain Shall Meet?" *NewsNet* 43 (2003): 3–5.

Dawson, Andrew H., and Rick Fawn. "The Changing Geopolitics of Eastern Europe: An Introduction." *Geopolitics* 6 (2001): 1–5.

Debeljak, Aleš. "European Forms of Belonging." *East European Politics and Societies* 17 (2003): 151–65.

Del Sarto, Raffaella A., and Tobias Schuhmacher. "From EMP to ENP: What's at Stake with the European Neighbourhood Policy towards the Southern Mediterranean?" *European Foreign Affairs Review* 10 (2005): 17–38.

Diez, Thomas. "Europe's Others and the Return of Geopolitics." *Cambridge Review of International Affairs* 17 (2004): 319–35.

Dillon, Michael. *Politics of Security: Towards a Political Philosophy of Continental Thought.* London and New York: Routledge, 1996.

Dodds, Klaus, and David Atkinson, eds. *Geopolitical Traditions: A Century of Geopolitical Thought.* London: Routledge, 2000.

Dodds, Klaus, and James D. Sidaway. "Halford Mackinder and the 'Geographical Pivot of History': A Centennial Retrospective." *Geographical Journal* 170 (2004): 292–97.

Dunn, Elizabeth C. *Privatizing Poland: Baby Food, Big Business, and the Remaking of Labor.* Ithaca, NY: Cornell University Press, 2005.

———. "Standards and Person-Making in East-Central Europe." In *Global Assemblages: Technology, Politics, and Ethics as Anthropological Problems,* edited by Aihwa Ong and Stephen Collier, 173–93. Oxford: Blackwell Publishing, 2005.

Elbe, Stefan. "'We Good Europeans': Genealogical Reflections on the Idea of Europe." *Millennium: Journal of International Studies* 30 (2001): 259–83.

English, Robert D. *Russia and the Idea of the West.* New York: Columbia University Press, 2000.

Enloe, Cynthia H. *The Curious Feminist: Searching for Women in an Age of Empire.* Berkeley, CA: University of California Press, 2004.

Esterházy, Péter. "How Big Is the European Dwarf?" *Süddeutsche Zeitung,* June 11, 2003. Reprinted in *Old Europe, New Europe, Core Europe: Transatlantic Relations After the Iraq War,* edited by D. Levy, M. Pensky and J. Torpey, 74–79. London: Verso, 2005.

Eyal, Gil. *The Origins of Postcommunist Elites: From Prague Spring to the Breakup of Czechoslovakia.* Minneapolis: University of Minnesota Press, 2003.

Eyal, Gil, Ivan Szelenyi, and Eleanor Townsley. *Making Capitalism without Capitalists: Class Formation and Elite Struggles in Post-Communist Central Europe.* London and New York: Verso, 1998.

Falk, Barbara. *The Dilemmas of Dissidence in East-Central Europe.* Budapest: Central European University Press, 2003.

Fawn, Rick. "Symbolism in the Diplomacy of Czech President Vaclav Havel." *East European Quarterly* 23 (1999): 1–19.

Featherstone, Kevin. "Introduction: in the Name of 'Europe.'" In *The Politics of Europeanization,* edited by K. Featherstone and C. M. Radaelli, 3–26. Oxford: Oxford University Press, 2003.

Feldman, Gregory. "Culture, State, and Security in Europe: The Case of Citizenship and Integration Policy in Estonia." *American Ethnologist* 32 (2005): 676–94.

———. "Essential Crises: A Performative Approach to Migrants, Minorities and the European Nation-state." *Anthropological Quarterly* 78 (2005): 231–46.

———. "Estranged States: Diplomacy and Containment of National Minorities in Europe." *Anthropological Theory* 5 (2005): 219–45.

———. "Many Nice People: Hegemony, State, and Empire in Estonia." Unpublished manuscript, n.d..

———. "Neoliberal Nationalism: Ethnic Integration and Estonia's Accession to the European Union." In *Crossing European Boundaries: Beyond Conventional*

Geographical Categories, edited by H. Kopnina, C. Moutsov, and J. Stacul, 41–63. London and New York: Berghahn Press, 2005.

Feldman, Merje. "European Integration and the Discourse of National Identity in Estonia." *National Identities* 3 (2001): 5–21.

Fierke, Karin, M., and Antje Wiener. "Constructing Institutional Interests: EU and NATO Enlargement." Journal of European Public Policy 6 (1999): 721–42.

Finkielkraut, Alain. "L'humanité perdue—Essai sur le XXème siècle" [Lost Mankind—Essay about the XXth Century] (Paris: Seuil, 1996)

Finnemore, Martha, and Kathryn Sikkink. "International Norm Dynamics and Political Change." *International Organization* 52 (1998): 895.

Foucault, Michel. "Polemics, Politics, and Problemizations: An Interview with Michel Foucault." In *The Foucault Reader*, edited by M. Foucault, 101–20. New York: Pantheon Books, 1984.

Gaddis, John Lewis. "International Relations Theory and the End of the Cold War." *International Security* 17 (1992): 5–58.

Garton Ash, Timothy. *History of the Present: Essays, Sketches and Dispatches from Europe in the 1990s*. London: Penguin Books, 1999.

———. *The Uses of Adversity: Essays on the Fate of Central Europe*. New York: Random House, 1989.

Geertz, Clifford. *Local Knowledge: Further Essays in Interpretive Anthropology*. New York: Basic Books, 1983.

———. "The Thick Description: Toward an Interpretive Theory of Culture." In *The Interpretation of Cultures: Selected Essays by Clifford Geertz*, 3–30. New York: Basic Books, 1973.

Gelazis, Nida M. "The Effects of EU Conditionality on Citizenship Policies and the Protection of National Minorities in the Baltic States." In *The Road to the European Union*, Vol. 2, *Estonia, Latvia, Lithuania*, edited by V. Pettai and J. Zielonka, 46–74. Manchester and New York: Manchester University Press, 2003.

Grabbe, Heather. "The Sharp Edges of Europe: Extending Schengen Eastwards." *International Affairs* 76 (2000): 519–36.

Grabher, Gernot, and David Stark, eds. *Restructuring Networks in Post-Socialism: Legacies, Linkages and Localities*. Oxford: Oxford University Press, 1996.

Gray, Colin, and Geoffrey Sloan, eds. *Geography, Geopolitics and Strategy*. London: Frank Cass, 1999.

Gregory, Derek. *The Colonial Present*. Oxford and Malden, MA: Blackwell, 2004.

Grudzinski, Przemyslav, and Peter van Ham. *A Critical Approach to European Security*. London: Pinter, 1999.

Gusterson, Hugh. "Missing the End of the Cold War in International Security." In *Cultures of Insecurity: States, Communities, and the Production of Danger*, edited by Jutta Weldes, Mark Laffey, Hugh Gusterson, and Raymond Duvall Weldes et al, 319–45. Minneapolis: University of Minnesota Press, 1999.

———. *Nuclear Rites: A Weapons Laboratory and the End of the Cold War*. Berkeley, CA: University of California Press, 1996.

———. *People of the Bomb: Portraits of America's Nuclear Complex*. Minneapolis: University of Minnesota Press, 2004.

Gusterson, Hugh, and Catherine Besteman, Catherine. "Introduction." In *Why America's Top Pundits Are Wrong: Anthropologists Talk Back*, edited by C. Besteman and H. Gusterson, 1–23. Berkeley, CA: University of California Press, 2005.

Guzzini, Stefano. "'Self-fulfilling Geopolitics'?, Or: The Social Production of Foreign Policy Expertise in Europe." Paper presented at the joint convention of the Central Eastern European International Studies Association and the International Studies Association, Budapest, Hungary, June 26–28, 2003.

Gyárfášová, Olga. "Slovakia Heads for the EU: What was Accomplished and what lies Ahead?" *Az Európai Tanulmányok (Európa 2002)* 4 (2003): 1–12.

Haab, Mare. "Estonia." In *Bordering Russia: Theory and Prospects for Europe's Baltic Rim*, edited by H. Mouritzen, 109–29. Aldershot, UK: Ashgate, 1998.

Haerpfer, Christian, Cezary Milosinski, and Claire Wallace. "Old and New Security Issues in Post-Communist Eastern Europe: Results of an 11 Nation Study." *Europe-Asia Studies* 51 (1999): 989–1011.

Hallik, Klara. "Rahvuspoliitilised seisukohad parteiprogrammides ja valimis-platvormides" [Ethnopolitical Positions in Party Programs and Election Platforms]. In *Vene küsimus ja Eesti valikud* [The Russian Question and Estonia's Choices], edited by M. Heidmets, 77–100. Tallinn: Tallinn Pedagogical University, 1998.

Hanley, Sean. "From Neo-Liberalism to National Interests: Ideology, Strategy, and Party Development in the Euroscepticism of the Czech Right." *East European Politics and Societies* 18 (2004): 513–48.

Hann, Chris, ed. Postsocialism: Ideals, Ideologies and Practices in Eurasia. London: Routledge, 2002.

Hansen, Lene. "Slovenian Identity: State Building on the Balkan Border." *Alternatives* 21 (1996): 473–95.

Hansen, Lene, and Ole Wæver, eds. *European Integration and National Identity: The Challenge of the Nordic States*. London and New York: Routledge, 2002.

Hardt, Michael, and Antonio Negri. *Empire*. Cambridge, MA: Harvard University Press, 2000.

Harloe, Michael, Ivan Szelenyi, and Gregory Andrusz, eds. *Cities after Socialism: Urban and Regional Change and Conflict in Post-Socialist Societies*. Oxford and Cambridge, MA: Blackwell, 1996.

Harmsen, Robert, and Menno Spiering. "Introduction: Euroscepticism and the Evolution of European Political Debate." In *Euroscepticism: Party Politics, National Identity and European Integration*, edited by R. Harmsen and M. Spiering, 13–36. Amsterdam and New York: Rodopi, 2004.

Hayden, Robert M. *Blueprints for a House Divided: The Constitutional Logic of Yugoslav Conflicts*. Ann Arbor: University of Michigan Press, 1999.

Heffernan, Michael. *The Meaning of Europe: Geography and Geopolitics*. London: Arnold, 1998.

Heidmets, Mati, ed. *Vene küsimus ja Eesti valikud*. [The Russian Question and Estonia's Choices]. Tallinn: Tallinn Pedagogical University, 1998.

Herd, Graeme R., and Joan Lofgren. "'Societal Security', the Baltic States and EU Integration." *Cooperation and Conflict* 36 (2001): 273–96.

Herrmann, Richard K., and Richard Ned Lebow, eds. *Ending the Cold War: Interpretations, Causation, and the Study of International Relations*, New York: Palgrave MacMillan, 2004.

Holmes, Douglas. *Integral Europe: Fast-capitalism, Multiculturalism, Neofascism*. Princeton, NJ: Princeton University Press, 2000.

Hörschelmann, Kathrin. "Breaking Ground—Marginality and Resistance in (Post) Unification Germany." *Political Geography* 20 (2001): 981–1004.

Humphrey, Caroline. "Does the Category of 'Postsocialist' Still Make Sense?" In *Postsocialism: Ideals, Ideologies, and Practices in Eurasia*, edited by C. M. Hann, 12–15. London: Routledge, 2002.

Huntington, Samuel P. "The Clash of Civilizations?" *Foreign Affairs* 72 (1993): 22–49.

———. *The Clash of Civilizations and the Remaking of the World Order*. New York: Simon and Schuster, 1996.

———. *Tsivilisatsioonide kokkupõrge ja maailmakorra ümberkujundamine*, trans. Mart Trummal. [The Clash of Civilizations and the Remaking of the World Order.] Tartu: Fontese Kirjastus, 1999.

Hyndman, Jennifer. *Managing Displacement: Refugees and the Politics of Humanitarianism*. Minneapolis: University of Minnesota Press, 2000.

Ingrao, Charles. "Understanding Ethnic Conflict in Central Europe: An Historical Perspective." *Nationalities Papers* 27 (1999): 291–318.

Johns, Michael. "'Do as I Say, Not as I Do': The European Union, Eastern Europe and Minority Rights." *East European Politics and Societies* 17 (2003): 682–99.

Jurado, Elena. "Complying with European Standards of Minority Rights Education: Estonia's Relations with the European Union, OSCE and Council of Europe." *Journal of Baltic Studies* 34 (2003): 399–431.

Kaiser Robert, and Jelena Nikiforova. "Narratives and Enactments of Place and Identity in the Borderlands of Post-socialist Space: The Case of 'the Setos.'" *Ethnic and Racial Studies* 29 (2006): 928-958.

Kaplan, Fred. *The Wizards of Armaggedon*. New York: Simon and Schuster, 1983.

Kaplan, Robert D. *The Coming Anarchy: Shattering the Dreams of the Post Cold War*. New York: Random House, 2000.

Katzenstein, Peter J., ed. *The Culture of National Security: Norms and Identity in World Politics*. New York: Columbia University Press, 1996.

———. *A World of Regions: Asia and Europe in the American Imperium*. Ithaca, NY: Cornell University Press, 2005.

Kelley, Judith G. *Ethnic Politics in Europe: The Power of Norms and Incentives*. Princeton, NJ: Princeton University Press, 2004.

Kennedy, Michael D. *Cultural Formations of Postcommunism: Emancipation, Transition, Nation, and War*. Minneapolis: University of Minnesota Press, 2002.

Kirch, Marika, ed. *Changing Identities in Estonia: Sociological Facts and Commentaries*. Tallinn: Estonian Science Foundation, 1994.

Kivimäe, Mart. "Euroskeptitsismi ajaloost Eesti kultuuris 20 sajandil" [On Euroskepticism in the Estonian Cultural History of the 20th Century]. In *Eesti Euroopa Liidu lävepakul* [Estonia at Europe's Threshold], edited by R. Ruutsoo and A. Kirch, 112–137. Tallinn: Teaduste Akadeemia Kirjastus, 1998.

Knudsen, Olav F., ed. *Stability and Security in the Baltic Sea Region. Russian, Nordic and European Aspects.* London and Portland, OR: Frank Cass, 1999.

Kopecki, Petr, and Cas Mudde. "Two Sides of Euroscepticism: Party Positions on European Integration in East Central Europe." *European Union Politics* 3 (2002): 297–326.

Krause, Keith, and Michael C. Williams. "From Strategy to Security: Foundations of Critical Security Studies," in *Critical Security Studies: Concepts and Cases*, edited by K. Krause and M.C. Williams, 33–59. Minneapolis: University of Minnesota Press, 1997.

Krupnick, Charles, ed. *Almost NATO: Partners and Players in Central and Eastern European Security.* Lanham, MD: Rowman and Littlefield, 2002.

Krupnick, Charles, and Carol Atkinson. "Slovakia and Security and the Center of Europe." In *Almost NATO: Partners and Players in Central and Eastern European Security*, edited by C. Krupnick, 47–82. Lanham, MD: Rowman and Littlefield, 2002.

Krzeminski, Adam. "First Kant, Now Habermas: A Polish Perspective on 'Core Europe.'" In *Old Europe, New Europe, Core Europe: Transatlantic Relations After the Iraq War*, edited by D. Levy, M. Pensky, and J. Torpey, 146–52. London: Verso, 2005.

Kuklick, Bruce. *Blind Oracles: Intellectuals and War from Kennan to Kissinger.* Princeton, NJ: Princeton University Press, 2006.

Kumar, Krishan. *1989: Revolutionary Ideas and Ideals.* Minneapolis: University of Minnesota Press, 2001.

Kundera, Milan. "The Tragedy of Central Europe." *New York Review of Books*, April 26, 1984, 33–38.

Kurti, Lazlo. "Homecoming: Affairs of Anthropologists in and of Eastern Europe." *Anthropology Today* 12 (1996): 11–15.

Kuus, Merje. "European Integration in Identity Narratives in Estonia: A Quest for Security." *Journal of Peace Research* 39 (2002): 91–108.

———. "Europe's Eastern Enlargement and the Re-inscription of Otherness in East-Central Europe." *Progress in Human Geography* 28 (2004): 472–89.

———. "Intellectuals and Geopolitics: The 'Cultural Politicians' of Central Europe." *Geoforum* 37 (2007): 241–51.

———. "Love, Peace and NATO? Imperial Subject-Making in Central Europe." *Antipode* 2007 39 (2007): 269-290.

———. "Sovereignty for Security?: The Discourse of Sovereignty in Estonia." *Political Geography* 21 (2002): 393–412.

———. "'Those Goody-Goody Estonians': Toward Rethinking Security in the European Union Applicant States." *Environment and Planning D: Society and Space* 22 (2004): 191–207.

———. "Toward Co-operative Security? International Integration and the Construction of Security in Estonia." *Millennium: Journal of International Studies* 31 (2002): 297–317.

Kuus, Merje, and John Agnew. "Theorizing the State Geographically." In *The Handbook of Political Geography*, edited by K. Cox, J. Robinson, and M. Low. Thousand Oaks, CA: Sage Publications, 2007.

Laar, Mart. *Eesti uus algus.* [Estonia's New Beginning]. Tallinn: Tänapäev, 2002.

Lagerspetz, Mikko. "Postsocialism as a Return: Notes on a Discursive Strategy." *East European Politics and Societies* 13 (1999): 377–90.

Laitin, David D. "Culture and National Identity: 'The East' and European Integration." *West European Politics* 25 (2002): 55–80.

———. *Identity in Formation: The Russian-Speaking Populations in the Near Abroad.* Ithaca, NY: Cornell University Press, 1998.

———. "National Revival and Competitive Assimilation in Estonia." *Post-Soviet Affairs* 12 (1996): 25–39.

Lapid, Yosef, and Friedrich Kratochwil, eds. *The Return of Culture and Identity in IR Theory.* Boulder, CO: Lynne Rienner Publishers, 1996.

Lauristin, Marju. "Contexts of Transition." In *Return to the Western World: Cultural and Political Perspectives on the Estonian Post-Communist Transition,* edited by M. Lauristin, P. Vihalemm, K.-E. Rosengren, and L. Weibull, 25–40. Tartu: Tartu University Press 1997.

Lauristin, Marju, and Mati Heidmets, eds. *The Challenge of the Russian Minority. Emerging Multicultural Democracy in Estonia.* Tartu: Tartu University Press, 2002.

Lauristin, Marju, and Peeter Vihalemm. "Recent Historical Developments in Estonia: Three Stages of Transition." In *Return to the Western World: Cultural and Political Perspectives on the Estonian Post-Communist Transition,* edited by M. Lauristin et al., 73–126. Tartu: Tartu University Press, 1997.

Lauristin, Marju, Peeter Vihalemm, Karl Erik Rosengren, and Lennart Weibull, eds. *Return to the Western World: Cultural and Political Perspectives on the Estonian Post-Communist Transition.* Tartu: Tartu University Press, 1997.

Lebow, Richard Ned. *The Tragic Vision of Politics: Ethics, Interests and Orders.* Cambridge: Cambridge University Press, 2003.

Lebow, Richard Ned, and Thomas Risse-Kappen. "Introduction: International Relations Theory and the End of the Cold War." In *International Relations Theory and the End of the Cold War,* edited by Richard Ned Lebow and Thomas Risse-Kappen, 1–21. New York: Columbia University Press, 1995.

Lebow, Richard Ned, and Thomas Risse-Kappen, eds. *International Relations Theory and the End of the Cold War.* New York: Columbia University Press, 1995.

Lewis, Martin W., and Karen E. Wigen. *The Myth of Continents: A Critique of Metageography.* Berkeley, CA: University of California Press, 1997.

Ley, David. "Between Europe and Asia: The Case of Missing Sequoias." *Ecumene* 2 (1995): 185–210.

Lieven, Anatol. "Against Russophobia." *World Policy Journal* 17 (Winter 2000/2001). http://www.carnegieendowment.org/publications/index.cfm?fa=view&id=626) (accessed 8 March 2001).

———. *The Baltic Revolution: Estonia, Latvia and Lithuania and the Path to Independence,* rev. ed. New Haven, CT: Yale University Press, 1993.

Linden, Ronald, ed. *Norms and Nannies: The Impact of International Organizations on the Central and East European States.* Lanham, MD: Rowman and Littlefield, 2002.

Lindstrom, Nicole. "From Permissive Consensus to Contentious Politics: Varieties of Euroskepticism in Croatia and Slovenia." Paper presented at the Mellon-Sawyer Seminar Series, Cornell University, Ithaca, NY, April 9, 2002.

Linz, Juan J., and Alfred Stepan. Problems of Democratic Transition and Consolidation: Southern Europe, South America and Post-Communist Europe. Baltimore, MD: Johns Hopkins University Press, 1996.

Luoma-Aho, Mika. "Body of Europe and Malignant Nationalism: A Pathology of the Balkans in European Security Discourse." Geopolitics 7 (2002):117–142.

Malkki, Liisa. "National Geographic: The Rooting of Peoples and the Territorialization of National Identity among Scholars and Refugees." Cultural Anthropology 7 (1992): 24–44.

McColl, Robert W. "A Geographical Model for International Behaviour." In Pluralism and Political Geography, edited by N. Kliot and S. Waterman, 284–294. London: Croom Helm, 1983.

Melegh, Attila. On the East-West Slope: Globalization, Nationalism, Racism and Discourses on Eastern Europe. Budapest and New York: Central European University Press, 2006.

Michta, Andrew. "East European Area Studies and Security Studies: A New Approach." NewsNet: News of the American Association for the Advancement of Slavic Studies 43 (2003): 1–3.

Mignolo, Walter D. Local Histories, Global Designs: Coloniality, Subaltern Knowledges, and Border Thinking. Princeton, NJ: Princeton University Press, 2000.

Miniotaite, Grazina. "The Baltic States: in Search of Security and Identity." In Almost NATO: Partners and Players in Central and Eastern European Security, edited by C. Krupnick, 161–196. Lanham, MD: Rowman and Littlefield, 2002.

Mitchell, Donald. "There's No Such Thing as Culture: Towards a Reconceptualisation of the Idea of Culture in Geography." Transactions of the Institute of British Geographers 19 (1995): 102–16.

Mitchell, Timothy. Rule of Experts: Egypt, Techno-politics, Modernity. Berkeley, CA: University of California Press, 2002.

Moisio, Sami. "Competing Geographies of Sovereignty, Regionality and Globalisation: The Politics of EU Resistance in Finland 1991–1994," Geopolitics 11 (2006): 439–64.

———. "EU Eligibility, Central Europe and the Invention of Applicant State Narrative." Geopolitics 7 (2002): 89–116.

Moore, Rebecca. Europe 'Whole and Free': NATO's Political Mission in the 21st Century. NATO_EAPC Research Fellowship Final Report. Brussels: NATO Office of Information and Press, 2003 (http://www.nato.int).

Morgenthau, Hans. Politics Among Nations: The Struggle for Power and Peace, brief ed. New York: McGraw-Hill, 1993.

Neumann, Iver B. "European Identity, EU Expansion, and the Integration/Exclusion Nexus." Alternatives 23 (1998): 397–416.

———. "Forgetting the Central Europe of the 1980s." In Central Europe: Core or Periphery?, edited by C. Lord, 207–18. Copenhagen: Copenhagen Business School, 2003.

———. "Returning Practice to the Linguistic Turn: The Case of Diplomacy." *Millennium: Journal of International Studies* 31 (2002): 627–51.

———. *The Uses of the Other: 'The East' in European Identity Formation.* Minneapolis: University of Minnesota Press, 1999.

Newman, David. "Geopolitics Renaissant: Territory, Sovereignty and the World Political Map." *Geopolitics and International Boundaries* 1 (1998): 1–16.

Noreen, Erik. "Verbal Politics of Estonian Policy-Makers: Reframing Security and Identity." In *Threat Politics: New Perspectives on Security, Risk and Crisis Management,* edited by J. Eriksson, 84–99. Aldershot, UK: Ashgate, 2002.

Noreen, Erik, and Roxanna Sjöstedt. "Estonian Identity Formations and Threat Framing in the Post-Cold War Era." *Journal of Peace Research* 41 (2004): 733–50.

Offe, Claus. *Varieties of Transition.* London: Polity Press, 1996.

O'Loughlin, John. "Ordering the 'Crush Zone': Geopolitical Games in Post-Cold War Eastern Europe." In *Geopolitics at the End of the Twentieth Century: The Changing World Political Map,* edited by N. Kliot, and D. Newman., 34–56 London: Frank Cass, 2001.

Õnnepalu, Tõnu. *Border State.* Evanston, IL: Northwestern University Press, 2000.

Ó Tuathail, Gearóid. *Critical Geopolitics: The Politics of Writing Global Space.* Minneapolis: University of Minnesota Press, 1996.

———. "Displacing Geopolitics: Writing the Maps of Global Politics." *Environment and Planning D: Society and Space* 12 (1994): 525–46.

———. "Problematizing Geopolitics: Survey, Statesmanship and Strategy." *Transactions of the Institute of British Geographers* 19 (1994): 259–72.

Ó Tuathail, Gearóid, and John Agnew. "Geopolitics and Discourse: Practical Geopolitical Reasoning in American Foreign Policy." *Political Geography* 11 (1992): 190–204.

Paasi, Anssi. "Europe as a Social Process and Discourse: Considerations of Place, Boundaries and Identity." *European Urban and Regional Studies* 8 (2001): 7–28.

Parker, Geoffrey. *Geopolitics: Past, Present, and Future.* London: Pinter, 1998.

Parker, Noel. "Integrated Europe and its 'Margins': Action and Reaction." In *Margins in European Integration,* edited by N. Parker and B. Armstrong, 3–27. New York: St. Martin's Press, 2000.

Patterson, Patrick H. "On the Edge of Reason: The Boundaries of Balkanism in Slovenian, Austrian, and Italian Discourse." *Slavic Review* 62 (2003): 110–41.

Pavlovaite, Inga. "Being European by Joining Europe: Accession and Identity Politics in Lithuania." *Cambridge Review of International Affairs* 16 (2003): 239–55.

Perron, Catherine. "Local Political Elites Perceptions of the EU". In *The Road to the European Union,* Vol. 1, *The Czech and Slovak Republics,* edited by J. Rupnik and J. Zielonka, 199–219. Manchester and New York: Manchester University Press, 2003.

Pettai, Vello. "Emerging Ethnic Democracy in Estonia and Latvia." In *Managing Diversity in Plural Societies: Minorities, Migration and Nation-Building in Post-Communist Europe,* edited by M. Opalski, 15–32. Ottawa: Forum Eastern Europe, 1998.

Pickles, John, and Adrian Smith, eds. *Theorising Transition: the Political Economy of Post-Communist Transformations.* London: Routledge, 1998.

Pietz, William. "The 'Post-colonialism' of Cold War Discourse." *Social Text* 19/20 (1988): 55–75.

Popescu, Gabriel. "Diaspora Geopolitics: Romanian-Americans and NATO Expansion." *Geopolitics* 10 (2005): 455–81.

Prizel, Ilya. *National Identity and Foreign Policy: Nationalism and Leadership in Poland, Russia and Ukraine.* Cambridge: Cambridge University Press, 1998.

Rae, Heather. *State Identities and the Homogenisation of Peoples.* Cambridge: Cambridge University Press, 2002.

Raig, Kulle. *Vikerkaare värvid: Lennart Meri elu sõprade pilgu läbi* [Colors of the Rainbow: The Life of Lennart Meri in the Eyes of His Friends] Tallinn: Varrak, 2003.

Raudsepp, Maaris. "Rahvusküsimus ajakirjanduse peeglis" [The Ethnic Question in the the Media]. In *Vene küsimus ja Eesti valikud* [The Russian Question and Estonia's Choices], edited by M. Heidmets, 113–34. Tallinn: Tallinn Pedagogical University, 1998.

Raun, Toivo U. *Estonia and the Estonians,* 2nd ed. Stanford, CA: Hoover Institution Press, 1994.

Rhodes, Edward. "The Good, the Bad, and the Righteous: Understanding the Bush Vision of a New NATO Partnership." *Millennium: Journal of International Studies* 33 (2004): 123–43.

Rindzevicitute, Egle. "'Nation' and 'Europe': Re-approaching the Debates about Lithuanian National Identity." *Journal of Baltic Studies* 24 (2003): 74–91.

Riekhoff, Aart Jan. "The Transformation of East-Central European Security: Domestic Politics, International Constraints, and Opportunities for Policymakers." *Perspectives* 21 (Winter 2003/2004): 55–70.

Roeder, Philip. G. "The Revolution of 1989: Postcommunism and the Social Sciences." *Slavic Review* 58 (1999): 743–55.

Rulikova, Markéta. "The Influence of Pre-Accession Status on Euroscepticism in EU Candidate Countries." *Perspectives on European Politics and Society* 5 (2004): 29–60.

Rumelili, Bahar. "Constructing Identity and Relating to Difference: Understanding the EU's Mode of Differentiation," *Review of International Studies* 30 (2004): 27–47.

Rupnik, Jacques. "Eastern Europe: The International Context." *Journal of Democracy* 11 (2000):115–29.

Rupnik, Jacques, and Jan Zielonka, eds. *The Road to the European Union.* Vol. 1: *The Czech and Slovak Republics.* Manchester and New York: Manchester University Press, 2003.

Ruutsoo, Rein. "Discursive Conflict and Estonian Post-Communist Nation-Building." In. *The Challenge of the Russian Minority. Emerging Multicultural Democracy in Estonia,* edited by M. Lauristin and M. Heidmets, 31–54. Tartu: Tartu University Press, 2002.

———. "Eesti kodakondsuspoliitika ja rahvusriigi kujunemise piirjooned" [The Contours of Estonian Citizenship Policy and the Development of the Nation-State] In *Vene küsimus ja Eesti valikud.* [The Russian Question and Estonia's

Choices], edited by M. Heidmets, 139–202. Tallinn: Tallinn Pedagogical University, 1998.

———. "Introduction: Estonia on the Border of Two Civilizations." *Nationalities Papers* 23 (1995): 13–15.

Šabic, Zlatko, and Ljubica Jelušic. "Slovenia and NATO Enlargement: Twists, Turns, and Endless Frustrations." In *Almost NATO: Partners and Players in Central and Eastern European Security*, edited by C. Krupnick, 83–117. Lanham, MD: Rowman and Littlefield, 2002.

Said, Edward. *Orientalism*, 2nd ed. New York: Vintage Books, 1994.

Sayer, Andrew R. *Method in Social Science: A Realist Approach*, 2nd ed. London: Routledge, 1992.

Schimmelfennig, Frank. *The EU, NATO and the Integration of Europe: Rules and Rhetoric*. Cambridge: Cambridge University Press, 2003.

———. "International Socialization in the New Europe: Rational Action in an Institutional Environment." *European Journal of International Relations* 6 (2000): 109–39.

Schimmelfennig, Frank, and Ulrich Sedelmeier. "Introduction: Conceptualizing the Europeanization of Central and Eastern Europe." In *The Europeanization of Central and Eastern Europe*, edited by F. Schimmelfennig and U. Sedelmeier, 1–28. Ithaca, NY: Cornell University Press, 2005.

Semjonov, Aleksei. "Estonia: Nation-Building and Integration—Political and Legal Aspects." In *National Integration and Violent Conflict in Post-Soviet Societies*, edited by P. Kolstø, 105–57. Lanham, MD: Rowman and Littlefield, 2002.

Shapiro, Michael J. *Violent Cartographies: Mapping Cultures of War*. Minneapolis: University of Minnesota Press, 1997.

Sharp, Joanne. *Condensing the Cold War: Reader's Digest and American Identity*. Minneapolis: University of Minnesota Press, 2000.

———. "Hegemony, Popular Culture and Geopolitics: The *Reader's Digest* and the Construction of Danger." *Political Geography* 15 (1996): 557–70.

Slater, David. "Geopolitical Imaginations across the North-South Divide: Issues of Difference, Development and Power." *Political Geography* 16 (1997): 631–53.

Smith, Adrian. "Imagining Geographies of the 'New Europe': Geo-economic Power and the New European Architecture of Integration." *Political Geography* 21 (2002): 647–70.

Smith, David J. *Estonia: Independence and European Integration*. London and New York: Routledge, 2001.

Smith, Graham, ed. The Baltic States: The National Self-Determination of Estonia, Latvia and Lithuania. New York: St. Martin's Press, 1994.

———. "Nation-building and Political Discourses of Identity Politics in the Baltic States." In *Nation-Building in the Post-Soviet Borderlands: The Politics of National Identities*, edited by G. Smith et al., 93–118. New York and Cambridge: Cambridge University Press, 1998.

Smith, Karen E. "The outsiders: the European neighbourhood policy." *International Affairs* 81 (2005): 757–73.

Smith, Martin. "The NATO Factor: A Spanner in the Works of EU and WEU Enlargement?" In *Back to Europe: Central and Eastern Europe and the European Union*, edited by K. Henderson, 53–67. London: UCL Press, 1999.

Smoke, Richard, ed. Perceptions of Security: Public Opinion and Expert Assessments in Europe's New Democracies. New York: Manchester University Press, 1996.

Spykman, Nicholas. "Geography and Foreign Policy, I." *American Political Science Review* 32 (1938): 28–50.

Stark, David, and Laszlo Bruszt. *Post-Socialist Pathways: Transforming Politics and Property in Eastern Europe*. Cambridge: Cambridge University Press, 1997.

Starzynski, Piotr. "Poland." In *Perceptions of Security: Public Opinion and Expert Assessments in Europe's New Democracies*, edited by R. Smoke, 55–63. Manchester and New York: Manchester University Press, 1996.

Stasiuk, Andrzej. "Wild, Cunning, Exotic: The East Will Completely Shake Up Europe." *Süddeutsche Zeitung*, June 20, 2003. Reprinted in *Old Europe, New Europe, Core Europe: Transatlantic Relations After the Iraq War*, edited by Daniel Levy, Max Pensky, and John Torpey, 103–106. London: Verso, 2005.

Steen, Anton. Between Past and Future: Elites, Democracy, and the State in Post-Communist Countries: A Comparison of Estonia, Latvia and Lithuania. Aldershot, UK: Ashgate, 1997.

Stefanovicz, Janusz. "Poland." In *Perceptions of Security: Public Opinion and Expert Assessments in Europe's New Democracies*, edited by R. Smoke, 107–128. Manchester and New York: Manchester University Press, 1996.

Stolcke, Verena. "Talking Culture: New Boundaries, New Rhetorics of Exclusion in Europe." *Current Anthropology* 63 (1995): 1–20.

Szczerbiak, Aleks. "Polish Euroscepticism in the Run-up to EU Accession." In *Euroscepticism: Party Politics, National Identity and European Integration*, edited by R. Harmsen and M. Spiering, 247–68. Amsterdam and New York: Rodopi, 2004.

Taagepera, Rein. *Estonia: Return to Independence*. Boulder, CO: Westview Press, 1993.

Taggart, Paul, and Aleks Szczerbiak. *Opposing Europe? The Comparative Party Politics of Euroskepticism*. Oxford: Oxford University Press, 2005.

Tesser, Lynn M. "The Geopolitics of Tolerance: Minority Rights under EU Expansion in East-Central Europe." *East European Politics and Societies* 17 (2003): 483–532.

Tismaneanu, Vladimir. "Discomforts of Victory: Democracy, Liberal Values and Nationalism in Post-Communist Europe." *West European Politics* 25 (2002): 81–100.

———. *Fantasies of Salvation: Democracy, Nationalism, and Myth in Post-Communist Europe*. Princeton, NJ: Princeton University Press, 1998.

Todorova, Maria. *Imagining the Balkans*. New York: Oxford University Press, 1997.

———. "Isn't Central Europe Dead?". In *Central Europe: Core or Periphery?* edited by C. Lord, 219–31. Copenhagen: Copenhagen Business School, 2003.

Tucker, Aviezer. "The Politics of Conviction: The Rise and Fall of Czech Intellectual-Politicians." In *Intellectuals and Politics in Central Europe*, edited by A. Bozóki, 185–205. Budapest: Central European University Press, 1999.

Tunander, Ola. "Swedish *Geopolitics*: from Rudolf Kjellén to a Swedish 'Dual State'". *Geopolitics* 10 (2005): 546–66.

Tunander, Ola, Pavel Baev, and Victoria Ingrid Einagel, eds. *Geopolitics in Post-Wall Europe: Security, Territory and Identity*. Oslo: International Peace Research Institute, 1997.

Unwin, Tim. "Place, Territory, and National Identity in Estonia." In *Nested Identities: Nationalism, Territory and Scale*, edited by G. H. Herb, and D. H. Kaplan, 151–73. Lanham, MD: Rowman and Littlefield Publishers, 1999.

Van Ham, Peter. "The Baltic States and Europe: Identity and Institutions." In *Stability and Security in the Baltic Sea Region. Russian, Nordic and European Aspects*, edited by O. Knudsen, 223–38. London and Portland, OR: Frank Cass, 1999.

Vares, Peeter. "Estonia and Russia: Interethnic Relations and Regional Security." In *Stability and Security in the Baltic Sea Region. Russian, Nordic and European Aspects*, edited by O. Knudsen, 155–164. London and Portland, OR: Frank Cass, 1999.

Väyrynen, Raimo. "The Security of the Baltic Countries: Co-operation and Defection." In *Stability and Security in the Baltic Sea Region. Russian, Nordic and European Aspects*, edited by O. Knudsen, 204–22. London and Portland, OR: Frank Cass, 1999.

Velikonja, Mitja. *Eurosis: A Critique of New Eurocentrism*. Ljubljana: Mirovni Institut, 2005. Mediawatch e-book: http://mediawatch.mirovni-institut.si/eng/mw17.htm (accessed June 13, 2006).

Verdery, Katherine. *National Ideology under Socialism: Identity and Cultural Politics in Ceausescu's Romania*. Berkeley and Los Angeles: University of California Press, 1991.

———. "'The 'New' Eastern Europe in an Anthropology of Europe." *American Anthropologist* 99 (1997): 715–17.

———. "Post-Soviet Area Studies?" *NewsNet* 43 (2003): 7–8.

———. *What Was Socialism, and What Comes Next?* Princeton, NJ: Princeton University Press, 1996.

Vetik, Raivo. "Ethnic Conflict and Accommodation in Post-Communist Estonia." *Journal of Peace Research* 30 (2000): 271–80.

Vetik, Raivo, and Riina Kionka. "Estonia and the Estonians." In *The Nationalities Question in the Post-Soviet States*. edited by G. Smith, 155–180. London: Longman, 1995.

Vihalemm, Triin, and Marju Lauristin. "Cultural Adjustment to the Changing Societal Environment: the Case of Russians in Estonia." In *Return to the Western World: Cultural and Political Perspectives on the Estonian Post-Communist Transition*, edited by M. Lauristin et al., 279–97. Tartu: Tartu University Press, 1997.

Wæver, Ole. "The EU as Security Actor: Reflections from a Pessimistic Constructivist on Post-Sovereign Security Orders." In *International Relations Theory and the Politics of European Integration: Power, Security and Community*, edited M. Kelstrup and M. C. Williams, 250–94. London and New York: Routledge, 2000.

———. "European Security Identities." *Journal of Common Market Studies* 34 (1996): 103–132.

———. "Identity, Communities and Foreign Policy: Discourse Analysis as Foreign Policy Theory." In *European Integration and National Identity: The Challenge of the Nordic States*, edited by L. Hansen and O. Wæver, 20–49. London and New York: Routledge, 2002.

———. "Imperial Metaphors: Emerging European Analogies to Pre-Nation-State Imperial Systems." In *Geopolitics in Post-Wall Europe: Security, Territory and Identity*, edited by O. Tunander, P. Baev and V. I. Einagel, 59–93. London: Sage, 1997.

———. "Securitization and Desecuritization." In *On Security*, edited by R. D. Lipschutz, 46–86. New York: Columbia University Press, 1995.

Walker, Robert B. J. "Europe Is Not Where It Is Supposed to Be." In *International Relations Theory and the Politics of European Integration: Power, Security and Community*, edited by M. Kelstrup and M.C. Williams, 14–32. London and New York: Routledge, 2000.

———. "The Subject of Security." In *Critical Security Studies: Concepts and Cases*, edited by K. Krause and M. C. Williams, 61–81. Minneapolis: University of Minnesota Press, 1997.

Wallander, Celeste A. "NATO's Price: Shape Up or Ship Out," *Foreign Affairs* 81 (2002): 2–8.

Wallerstein, Immanuel. "The Unintended Consequences of Cold War Area Studies." In *The Cold War and the University: Toward an Intellectual History of the Postwar Years*, edited by N. Chomsky et al, 195–232. New York: The Free Press, 1997.

Watts, Larry L. "Romania and NATO: The National-Regional Security Nexus." In *Almost NATO: Partners and Players in Central and Eastern European Security*, edited by C. Krupnick, 157–98. Lanham, MD: Rowman and Littlefield, 2002.

Wedel, Janine. *Collision and Collusion: The Strange Case of Western Aid to Eastern Europe*, 2nd ed. New York: Palgrave, 2001.

———. "Tainted Transactions: Harvard, Chubais and Russia's Ruin." *The National Interest* 59 (Spring 2000): 23–34.

Weil, Simone. *The Need for Roots: Prelude to a Declaration of Duties toward Mankind*. New York: Ark, 1987[1952].

Weldes, Jutta, Mark Laffey, Hugh Gusterson, and Raymond Duvall, eds. *Cultures of Insecurity: States, Communities and the Production of Danger*. Minneapolis: University of Minnesota Press, 1999.

———. "Introduction: Constructing Insecurity." In *Cultures of Insecurity: States, Communities and the Production of Danger*, edited by J. Weldes, M. Laffey, H. Gusterson and R. Duvall, 1–33. Minneapolis: University of Minnesota Press, 1999.

Weldes, Jutta, and Diana Saco. "Making State Action Possible: The United States and the Discursive Construction of 'The Cuban Problem', 1960–1994". *Millennium: Journal of International Studies* 25 (1996): 361–95.

White, Hayden. *The Content of the Form: Narrative Discourse and Historical Representation.* Baltimore, MD: Johns Hopkins University Press, 1987.

———. "The Discourse of Europe and the Search for a European Identity." In *Europe and the Other and Europe as the Other*, edited by B.Stråth, 67–85. Brussels: P.I.E.–Peter Lang, 2000.

Williams, Michael C., and Iver B. Neumann. "From Alliance to Security Community: NATO, Russia, and the Power of Identity." *Millennium: Journal of International Studies* 29 (2000): 357–87.

Wolff, Larry. *Inventing Eastern Europe: The Map of Civilization on the Mind of the Enlightenment.* Stanford, CA: Stanford University Press, 1994.

Yack, Bernard. "Popular Sovereignty and Nationalism." *Political Theory* 29 (2001): 517–36.

Zarycki, Tomasz. "Uses of Russia: The Role of Russia in the Modern Polish National Identity." *East European Politics and Societies* 18 (2004): 595–627.

Zielonka, Jan. *Europe as Empire: The Nature of the Enlarged European Union.* Oxford: Oxford University Press, 2006.

⬚⬚ek, Slavoj. *The Metastases of Enjoyment.* London: Verso, 1994.

II. Speeches, Political Documents, News Media

Unless otherwise noted, newspaper articles from the Estonian media were accessed through the homepages of the newspapers, mostly between February 2000 and August 2006. All can be accessed by the date of publication. The most important homepages are: Eesti Ekspress (http://www.ekspress.ee); *Eesti Päevaleht* (http://www.epl.ee); *Postimees*: (http://www.postimees.ee). All articles from the daily Sõnumileht were accessed through http://www.sl.ee before July 2000, when the paper was merged Õhtuleht.

Beyond Estonia, the most important sources of media coverage are *Transitions Online* (http://www.tol.cz), *The Prague Post* (http://www.praguepost .com), and *The Baltic Times* (http://www.baltictimes.com). The articles from these sites were accessed between July 2004 and August 2006; all can be accessed by date of publication.

Unless otherwise noted, political speeches were accessed through the official websites of foreign ministries and presidential chancelleries. These can be accessed by date. The most important websites are: Estonian Ministry of Foreign Affairs (http://www.vm.ee); Office of the President of the Republic of Estonia: (http://www.president.ee).

Transcripts of Estonian parliamentary debates were accessed through the website of the Estonian parliament Riigikogu (http://www.riigikogu.ee). These were accessed between January 2000 and December 2006; all can be accessed by date.

Note on translations: All translations from Estonian-language sources were made by the author. When materials like official speeches were available in English, I tried to use the official English translation whenever possible.

Adams, Jüri. "Riigikogu toimetatud Stenogramm" [Edited Parliamentary Transcript], November 18, 1998.

Anderson, Perry. "The Europe to Come." *London Review of Books*, January 25, 1996.: 21–22.

Apollo Raamatumaja [Apollo Bookshop]. Product description of Mihkel Mutt, *Rahvusvaheline Mees* [International Man]. Tallinn: Eesti Päevalehe Kirjastus, 2006. http://www.apollo.ee (accessed August 20, 2006).

Astrov, Aleksander. "Aga sellepärast, et on po&#8230" [Just Because . . .]. *Eesti Päevaleht*, October 20, 2005.

Azula, Alfredo. "NATO Summit 2002 Ends." *Prague Post*, November 22, 2002.

Bahovski, Erkki. "Baltlased EL kandidaatriikidest skeptilisimad" [Balts Most Skeptical of All Candidate States]. *Postimees*, November 8, 2000.

———. "Ilves ei usu suhete paranemist Venemaaga" [Ilves Does Not Believe in the Improvement of Relations with Russia]. Interview with Foreign Minister Ilves. *Eesti Päevaleht*, September 12, 2000.

———. "Sovereignty in the European Union: Case Studies Relating to Estonia." In *The Estonian Foreign Policy Yearbook 2005*, edited by A. Kasekamp. 111–134. Tallinn: Estonian Foreign Policy Institute, 2005.

BBC Monitoring. "Roundup of West European Press Comment on the NATO Prague Summit," November 25, 2002, http://news.bbc.co.uk (accessed June 10, 2006).

BBC News. "Poles Stick to Russia talks veto" November 23, 2006. http://news.bbc.co.uk (accessed November 23, 2006).

BBC News. "Chirac Sparks 'New Europe' Ire," February 19, 2003. http://news.bbc.co.uk (accessed July 28, 2004).

———. "Estonia's Euro Vision," December 10, 2002. http://news.bbc.co.uk/2/hi/europe/2556449.stm (accessed December 27, 2002).

———. "Newcomers' Joy at NATO Invitation," November 22, 2002. http://news.bbc.co.uk/1/hi/not_in_website/syndication/monitoring/media_reports/2503211.stm (accessed June 5, 2006).

Birkavs, Valdis. Interview in *City Paper* 36 (August–September 1998). www.balticsww.com/natoquotes.htm (accessed February 20, 2005).

Bronstein, Mihhail. "Idapoliiitika on tundeline teema" [Eastern Policy is a Sensitive Topic]. *Postimees*, July 5, 2002.

City Paper. "EU Referendum News." September 2003. http/:www.balticsww.com/EU: Baltics Say Yes.html (accessed December 18, 2003).

———. "Selling Estonia." n.d. www.balticsww.com/selling.html (accessed January 11, 2001).

———. "Towards Better Security." n.d. Interview with Ronald Asmus. http://www.balticsww.com/news/features/better_security.htm (accessed January 11, 2001).

Domozetov, Christo. *Public Perceptions of Euro-Atlantic Partnership: Issues of Security and Military. The Case of Bulgaria* NATO–EAPC Institutional Research Fellowship 1988–2000. Brussels: NATO Office of Information and Press. http://www.nato.int (accessed August 12, 2004).

Economist. "The Baltic Bobsleigh." February 5, 1998.

———. "The Disappearing Czech Intellectual." August 21, 1999.

———. "Europe's Magnetic Attraction: Survey of EU Enlargement." May 17, 2001.

———. "Lennart Meri." Obituary, March 23, 2006.

———. "Mart Laar, Estonia's Punchy Prime Minister." February 22, 2001.

———. "Snoring While a Superstate Emerges?" May 10, 2003.

———. "Toomas Ilves, Estonia's American-European." October 29, 1998.

———. "Trouble in Paradise." July 2, 1998.

———. "Westward, Look, the Land Is Bright." October 24, 2002.

Eesti Ekspress. "Eestimaa aastal 2050: õnnelik riik" [Estonia in Year 2050: a Happy State]. February 25, 1999.

Eesti Euroskepsise pesa [The Nest of Estonian Euroskepticism]. n.d. www.euroskepsis.ee. (accessed August 22, 2006).

Eesti Päevaleht, November 27, 1999.

———. "Ilves loodab korrigerida euroliidu välispoliitikat" [Ilves is Hoping to Adjust EU's Foreign Policy], July 23, 2004.

———. "Uuring: õpilased on riigikaitseõpetuse suhtes positiivselt meelestatud" [Study: Students Have Positive Attitudes toward Teaching State Defence], January 16, 2003.

———. "Vaher: paljukardetud oht idast ei ole kadunud" [Vaher: The Much-Feared Threat from the East Has Not Disappeared], December 22, 2003.

Eesti Tulevikuuuringute Instituut. *Eesti Tulevikustsenaariumid* [Estonia's Future Scenarios]. Tallinn: Eesti Tulevikuuuringute Instituut, 1997.

Eesti Vabariigi Riigikogu. *Riigikogu Toimetamata Transcript* [Unedited Parliamentary Transcript], October 25, 2001.

———. *Riigikogu Toimetatud Transcript* [Edited Parliamentary Transcript], November 26, 1998. Tallinn: Eesti Vabariigi Riigikogu.

———. Riigikogu Toimetamata Transcript [Unedited Parliamentary Transcript], January, 18, January 25, and March 6, 2001 Tallinn: Riigikogu, 2001.

Endre, Sirje and Mart Laar. "Valitsus kõigutab rahvusriigi alustalasid" [Government is Shaking the Pillars of the Nation-State]. *Eesti Päevaleht*, December 12, 1997.

Estonian Citizenship and Migration Board. *Määratlemata kodakondusega isikute arvu muutumine, 1992–2000* [Change in the Numbers of Persons with Undetermined Citizenship 1992–2000]. Tallinn: Citizenship and Migration Board, 2000.

———. *Yearbook 2003*. Tallinn, Citizenship and Migration Board, 2003.

Estonian Ministry of Ethnic Affairs. *State Programme 'Integration in Estonian Society 2000–2007.'* Tallinn: Ministry of Ethnic Affairs, 2000.

Estonian Ministry of Foreign Affairs. *The 2000 Population and Housing Census: Citizenship, Nationality, Mother Tongue and Command of Foreign Languages.* Tallinn: Ministry of Foreign Affairs, 2002.

———. *Guidelines of the National Defence Policy of Estonia*. Tallinn: Ministry of Foreign Affairs, 1996. http://www.vm.ee/eng/nato/def.policy.html (accessed March 14, 2001).

————. *National Security Concept of the Republic of Estonia.* Tallinn: Ministry of Foreign Affairs, 2001.

————. *National Security Concept of the Republic of Estonia.* Tallinn: Ministry of Foreign Affairs, 2004.

EU Business. "New Polish PM Wants Bigger Role, 'Moral Sovereignty' in EU," July 19, 2006. http://www.eubusiness.com/East_Europe/060719131330.6e71mfws (accessed August 23, 2006).

EU Observer. "Tight Race in Estonian Referendum Poll," July 11, 2003.

European Commission. *Communication from the Commission: Countering Racism, Xenophobia and Anti-Semitism in the Candidate Countries.* Brussels: European Commission. May 26, 1999. COM(1000)256 final. http://ec.europa .eu/comm/external_relations/human_rights/doc/com99_256_en.pdf (accessed September 15, 2006).

————. *Euromed report 66.* October 14, 2003. http://ec.europa.eu/comm/ external_relations/euromed/publication/euromed_report66_en.pdf (accessed August 2, 2006).

————. *Support from the European Commission for measures to promote and safeguard regional or minority languages and cultures.* Brussels: European Commission, 2004. http://ec.europa.eu/education/policies/lang/languages/ langmin/euromosaic/index_en.html (accessed September 15, 2006)

————. *Candidate Countries Eurobarometer* 2004: 1. Brussels: European Commission, Public Opinon Analysis Sector, 2004. http://ec.europa.eu/ public_opinion/cceb_en.htm (accessed February 15, 2005).

Fisher, Sharon. "Tottering in the Aftermath of Elections." *Transition,* March 29, 1995, 20–25.

Fitchett, Joseph. "Meanwhile: Havel, a Class Act, Exists with Humor." *International Herald Tribune,* February 4, 2003.

Garton Ash, Timothy. "Love, Peace and NATO." *Guardian,* November 28, 2002.

————. "Prague: Intellectuals & Politicians," *New York Review,* January 12, 1995.

Gaube, Ales. "Snubbing NATO." *Transitions Online,* December 13, 2002. http://www.tol.cz (accessed July 7, 2004).

Geremek, Bronislaw. Address by Polish Foreign Minister Geremek on the Occasion of the Protocols to the North Atlantic Treaty on the Accession of Poland, the Czech Republic, and Hungary. Brussels, December 16, 1997.

Goble, Paul. "Divided on Security." *Baltic Times,* September 10, 1998.

Göncz, Arpad. Address by H.E. Mr. Arpad Göncz, President of the Republic of Hungary, at the North Atlantic Council, Brussels. Brussels: NATO, September 16, 1996. www.nato.int/docu/speech/1996/s960916b.htm (accessed March 6, 2005).

Gräzin, Igor. "Julgeolek ja elujäämine kõigepealt" [Security and Survival First]. *Postimees,* March 23, 1996.

Hamm, Jennifer. "City Locks Down for Summit Safety." *Prague Post,* November 20, 2002.

————. "Positive Reflection." *Prague Post,* November 27, 2002.

Hankevitz, Sten A. "Leedu noored teevad Bushi auks peo" [Lithuanian Youth Organize a Party to Honor Bush]. *Eesti Päevaleht*, November 22, 2002.

Hänni, Liia. "Jah, härra justiitsminister!" ["Yes, Mr. Justice Minister!"]. *Postimees*, January 22, 2002.

Havel, Václav. "Beyond Revolutionary Disillusion." *Project Syndicate*, March 2006. http://www.project-syndicate.org/print_commentary/havel26/English (accessed July 18, 2006).

———. "Europe: Twilight at Dawn." *Project Syndicate*, December 1996. http://www.project-syndicate.org/print_commentary/hav2/English (accessed July 18, 2006).

———. "Quo Vadis, NATO?" *Washington Post*, May 19, 2002. http://old.hrad.cz (accessed July 12, 2004).

———. "Redefining the West." *Project Syndicate*, October 2001. http://www.project-syndicate.org/print_commentary/havel22/English (accessed July 18, 2006).

———. "The Transformation of NATO". Opening speech at the Prague Conference, November 20, 2002.

———. "Who Threatens Our Identity?" *Project Syndicate*, April 2001. http://www.project-syndicate.org/print_commentary/havel20/English (accessed July 18, 2006).

Helme, Mart. "Eesti teevalik Euroopa ja USA veskikivide vahel" [Estonia's Path between the Millstones of Europe and the United States]. *Eesti Päevaleht*, September 28, 2002.

Hvostov, Andrei. "Kinderstube ja välispoliitika seosed" [The Links between the Nursery and Foreign Policy]. *Eesti Ekspress*, November 19, 2003.

———. "Kübaratrikiga Euroopasse" [To Europe with a Hat Trick]. *Eesti Ekspress*, February 8, 2001.

———. "Soometumise saladus" [The Secret of Finlandization]. *Eesti Päevaleht*, November 30, 1999.

———. "Valitsus kindlustab rahvusriigi alustalasid" [The Government is Securing the Pillars of the Nation-State]. *Eesti Päevaleht*, December 14, 1997.

Ilves, Toomas Hendrik. *Address to Riigikogu*. Tallinn: Estonian Ministry of Foreign Affairs, December 5, 1996. http://www.vm.ee/eng/pressreleases/speeches/1996/9612min.html (accessed January 11, 2001).

———. "A Blueprint for Stability." Remarks at the Commission Representation, Bonn, Germany, February 19, 1997. http//www.vm.eng.pressreleases/speeches/1997/0218bonn.html (accessed May 31, 2001).

———. "The Double Enlargement and the Great Wall of Europe." In *Estonian Foreign Policy Yearbook 2003*, edited by in A. Kasekamp, 9–20. Tallinn: The Estonian Foreign Policy Institute, 2003

———. "Eesti poliitika euroopastumine" [The Europeanization of Estonian Politics]. *Luup*, March 17, 1997. http://www.postimees.ee/luup/97/06/sise2.htm (accessed February 2, 2001).

———. *Estonia as a Nordic Country*. Speech delivered at the Swedish Institute for International Relations, December 14, 1999. http://www.vm.ee/eng/pressreleases/speeches/1999/Ilves_stock1412.html, (accessed January 11, 2001)

————. "Kuidas vältida topelt ei-d?" [How to Avoid a Double 'No']. In *Teine tulemine: taasiseseisvunud Eesti Välisesindused* [Second Coming: Foreign Representations of the Re-independent Estonia], edited by Eesti Vabariigi Välisministeerium, 13–18. Tallinn: Eesti Vabariigi Välisministeerium, 2003.

————. Remarks to the Parliament. *Riigikogu toimetatud Transcript*, June 8, 2000.

————. "The Road to European Integration: EU and NATO." Remarks at the second annual Stockholm Conference on Baltic Sea Security and Co-operation, Stockholm, Sweden, November 6, 1997.

Estonian Ministry of Ethnic Affairs. *The Integration of Non-Estonians into Estonian Society: The Bases of the Estonian State Integration Policy.* Tallinn: Non-Estonians Integration Foundation, 1999.

Jaanson, Kaido. *EL ja Eesti rahvuslik identiteet.* Prof. Kaido Jaansoni peaettekande teesid akadeemilisel nõukogul [The EU and Estonian National Identity. Thesis of the Keynote Speech by Professor Kaido Jaanson at the President's Academic Council]. Tallinn: Office of the President, February 19, 1998.

Jasiewicz, Krzysztof. "Reluctantly European?" *Transitions Online,* March 1, 2002. http://www.tol.cz (accessed September 15, 2002).

Kaldre, Peeter. "Milline kolmas tee?" [What Third Way?]. *Postimees,* February 15, 2001.

Kallas, Siim. "Vaata raevus kaugemale" [Look Further in Anger]. *Eesti Päevaleht,* October 30, 2002.

Kallas, Siim. "Kelle poolt on Eesti?" [Whom Does Estonia Support?]. *Postimees,* February 11, 2003.

————. "Peame mõtlema 85 aastat ette!" [We Must Think 85 Years in Advance!]. *Postimees,* February 25, 2003. http://www.postimees.ee (accessed March 16, 2003).

Kalniete, Sandra. "Latvia Empathizes with Iraq." *Baltic Times,* December 4, 2003.

Kaplinski, Jaan. "Eesti kui usuasi" [Estonia as a Religion]. *Eesti Ekspress,* May 13, 1999.

————. "Euroopa piir ja piirivalvurid" [Europe's Border and Border-Guards]. *Eesti Ekspress,* October 2, 2003.

————. "Kultuur ja kuldpuur" [Culture and a Golden Cage]. *Sõnumileht,* September 5, 1998.

Karpa, Kärt. "Suursaadik Kannike kuulas NATO otsust pisarsilmil" [Ambassador Kannike listened to NATO's decision with teary eyes]. *Eesti Päevaleht,* November 22, 2002.

Kasekamp, Andres. "Euroopa ühine kaitsepoliitika ja meie" [Europe's Common Defense Policy and Us], *Postimees,* May 15, 2001.

Kasekamp, Andres, Toomas Riim, and Viljar Veebel. *Eesti koht ja valikud Euroopa ühises julgeoleku-ja kaitsepoliitikas* [Estonia's Place and Choices in Europe's Common Foreign and Security Policy]. Tartu: Estonian Foreign Policy Institute, 2003, http://www.evi.ee (accessed July 5, 2004).

Katus, Kalev. "Rahvastiku areng" [Population Development]. In *Eesti 21. sajandil: arengustrateegiad, visioonid, valikud,* edited by Ahto Oja, 42–46. Tallinn: Estonian Academy of Sciences Press, 1999.

Keskküla, Kalev. "Diplomaadi vahearve" [Diplomat's Report]. *Eesti Ekspress*, December 6, 2004.

Kiin, Sirje. *Koik sõltub kultuurist* [All Depends on Culture]. Tallinn: Online, 2003.

Kirch, Marika. "Eesti Identiteet ja Euroopa liit" [Estonian Identity and the European Union]. In *Mõtteline Eesti: valik esseid Euroopa Liidust* [Imagined Estonia: A selection of essays on the European Union], edited by Marek Tamm and Märt Väljataga, 156. Tallinn: Kirjastus Varrak, 2003.

———. "Eestlaste otsus tulevasel euroreferendumil sõltub Venemaast" [Estonians' Decision on the Future Euroreferendum will Depend on Russia]. *EPL*, March 28, 2000.

Klaus, Václav. Address delivered on the occasion of the fifth anniversary of the Czech Republic's membership in NATO. Prague Castle, Czech Republic, March 12, 2004.

Kozakova, Pavla. "Essays Earn Trio Trip to NATO." *Prague Post*, October 30, 2002.

Kwasniewski, Aleksander. "President of Poland Interview for 'A Newshour with Jim Lehrer," WETA, PBS, NPR, Washington DC, Blair House, 18 July 2002,

Laar, Mart. *Eesti uus algus* [Estonia's New Beginning]. Tallinn: Tänapaev, 2002.

———. *Estonia: Little Country That Could.* London: Centre for Research into Post-Communist Economies, 2002.

———. "L'engagement européen de l'Estonie," lecture given at the French Institute of International Affairs in Paris, April 10, 2000, http://www.vm.ee/eng/pressreleases/speeches/2000/MLaar.htm. (accessed January 11, 2001).

———. "New Europe Won't Keep Quiet Until All Europe is New." *Wall Street Journal*, February 19, 2003.

Latvian Transatlantic Organisation. *Baltic Manifest*. Riga: Latvian Transatlantic Organisation. 2002. http://www.lato.lv (accessed October 15, 2005).

———. "Civil Society Initiative in Security Policy Making." 2004. http://www.lato.lv/html/en/activities/projects/26232.html (accessed 18 October 18, 2005).

LeBor, Adam. "The Other Big Brother in Prague." *Budapest Sun* November 28, 2002, http://www.budapestsun.com (accessed November 1, 2004).

Leps, Ando. *Riigikogu toimetatud stenogramm* [Edited Parliamentary Transcript], November 18, 1998.

Liik, Kadri. "Analüüs: Venemaa, NATO ja meie kümne aasta lugu" [Analysis: Russia, NATO and the Story of Our Decade]. *Postimees*, February 6, 2000.

Liik, Kadri, and Ideon, Argo. "Eesti tormiline teekond: Moskva vangikongist NATO kaitsva vihmavarju alla" [Estonia's Stormy Journey: From Moscow's Prison Cell to NATO's Protective Umbrella]. *Postimees*, November 19, 2002.

Luik, Jüri. Remarks at the Final Conference for a Pact of Stability in Europe, March 20, 1995, in Paris. Tallinn: Ministry of Foreign Affairs, 1995. http://www.vm.ee/eng/pressreleases/speeches/1995/9503221sp.html (accessed May 5, 1999).

Luik, Viivi, Elmo Nüganen, Jüri Arrak, Jüri Englebrecht, Hirvo Surva, and Andrus Kivirähk. "Eestlaseks jääda saab vaid eurooplasena" [Only as Europeans can we Remain Estonians]. *Postimees*, August 8, 2003.

Luup. "Lennart Meri: Euroopa Uniooni on vaja riigi püsimiseks" [Lennart Meri: European Union is Necessary for the Continuation of the State], December 22, 1997.

Maruste, Rain. "Eesti enne euro-otsust" [Estonia Before the Euro-decision]. *Postimees*, June 12, 2001.

McNeil, Donald G. Jr. "Estonia's President: Un-Soviet and Un-Conventional". The New York Times April 7, 2001

Meri, Lennart. "750 Years of Lübeck." Speech given to the Conference "750 Years of Lübeck," held at the Estonian National Library, Tallinn, May 16, 1998. Tallinn: Estonian National Library.

———. *Avasõna Europa Musicale kontserdil, München* [Opening Remarks at the *Europa Musicale* Concert, Munich], October 31, 1993.

———. "By the Will of Tacitus." Address delivered at the National Library, Tallinn. Tallinn: Office of the President, November 12, 1998.

———. "Culture Is Politics, Politics Is Culture." Speech in Estonia Concert Hall, February 24, 1994.

———. "Eesti ja Eurointegratsiooniprotsess" [Estonia and the Process of European Integration]. Speech given to the Paasikivi Society in Helsinki, Finland, September 3, 1997.

———. Interview with the French daily *Le Figaro*, February 16, 1997.

———. "Julgeolek, julgeolek ja veelkord julgeolek" [Security, Security and Once Again Security]. Remarks at the Institute for Strategic and International Studies, Washington, D.C., June 27, 1996. Tallinn: Office of the President, 1996.

———. "Lennart Meri European of the Year Acceptance Speech." *Global Estonian* 1 (Summer 1999): 6–11.

———. "Mis on Eesti" Mis on Eesti [What is Estonia]. Speech at St. Olaf College, Northfield, Minnesota, April 6, 2000. In L. Meri, *Riigimured* [*Concerns of the State*]. Speeches 1996–2001, edited by Toomas Kiho, 176–181. Tartu: Ilmamaa, 2001.

———. "President Lennart Meri intervjuu kvartaliajakirjale *Politique Internationale*" [President Lennart Meri's Interview with the quarterly *Politique Internationale*]. Tallinn: Office of the President, January 31, 2000.

———. *President Lennart Mere kõne Estonia kontserdisaalis* [President Lennart Meri's speech in Estonia Concert Hall], February 24, 1993. Tallinn: Office of the President, 1993.

———. *Riigimured* [Concerns of the State]. Speeches 1996–2001, edited by Toomas Kiho. Tartu: Ilmamaa, 2001.

———. Speech given at a dinner in honor of Javier Solana, Secretary General of NATO, Tallinn, April 19, 1996.

———. "Vabariigi Presidendi intervjuu ajalehele *Die Welt*" [President of the Republic's Interview with the German Newspaper *Die Welt*]. Tallinn: Office of the President, January 21, 1995.

———.. "Vabariigi Presidendi intervjuu prantsuse nädalalehele *La Vie*" [President of the Republic's Interview with the French weekly *La Vie*], December 24, 1998.

Mihkelson, Marko. Venemaa isemeelne tee [Russia's Stubborn Way]. *Postimees,* December 10, 2003.

———. "Venemaa näitab tegelikku nägu" [Russia is Showing its Real Face]. *Postimees,* April 14, 1998.

Mõis, Jüri. "Euroopalik rahvuspoliitika on salliv" [European Nationality Policy is Tolerant]. *Eesti Päevaleht,* April 29, 1999.

Mölder, Marko. "Teisenevast suveräänsusest" [On Metamorphosing Sovereignty]. *Sirp,* September 17, 1999.

Möll, Jennifer. "Who's Afraid of the Big Bad Wolf?"*Baltic Times,* November 20, 2003.

Neivelt, Indrek. "Unustatud Venemaa" [Forgotten Russia]. *Eesti Päevaleht,* November 6, 2002.

Neljas, Aap. "Eesti julgeolekuriskide analüüs Eesti Julgeolekupoliitika Aluste Kontseptsioonis" [The Analysis of Estonia's Security Risks in the National Security Concept]. Paper presented at the First Estonian Social Science Conference, Tallinn, Estonia, November 25, 2000.

North Atlantic Treaty Organization (NATO). *Study of Enlargement.* Brussels: NATO, 1994.

Nutt, Mart. "Kas Euroopa Liit tagab julgeoleku?" [Will the European Union Guarantee Security?]. *Postimees,* September 15, 1998.

———. "Kui Läti murdub, asutakse Eesti kallale" [When Latvia Breaks, they will get to Estonia]. *Eesti Päevaleht,* June 20, 1996.

Ojuland, Kristiina. "Main Guidelines of Estonia's Foreign Policy." Address to the *Riigikogu* on behalf of the Government of Estonia. Tallinn: Ministry of Foreign Affairs, June 13, 2002. http://www.vm.ee/eng/kat_140/2374.html (accessed July 4, 2002).

Oolo, Antti. "Venemaa-hirm tuleneb ajaloost" [Fear of Russia Stems from History]. *Eesti Päevaleht* March 20, 2000.

Palk, Paavo. "Euroopa Liidu toetajaid on rohkem kui vastalisi" [European Union has More Supporters than Opponents]. *Eesti Päevaleht.* March 8, 2000.

Parvanov, Georgi. "Bulgaria's New Role in the Region After its Accession to NATO and as a Potential EU Member." Lecture at the National Palace of Culture, Sophia. Sophia: Office of the President of Bulgaria, May 12, 2004. http://www.president.bg (accessed July 16, 2004).

Pegasos. "Lennart Meri." *Pegasos: a literature related resource site.* http://www .kirjasto.sci.fi/lmeri.htm (Accessed April 15, 2005).

Pernik, Piret. "Eesti identiteet välispoliitilises diskursuses 1990–1999" [Estonian Identity in the Foreign Policy Discourse 1990–1999]. Unpublished Bachelor of Arts thesis. Tallinn: Eesti Humanitaarinstituut, 2000.

Pettai, Iris, "Eestlased pole võõraste tulekuks valmis" [Estonians are not Ready for the Arrival of Strangers]. *Eesti Päevaleht,* August 9, 2005.

Põhiseaduse juriidilise ekspertiisi komisjon, *Aruanne,* Pt. 2.17, *Võimalik liitumine Euroopa Liiduga ja selle õiguslik tähendus Eesti riigiõiguse seisukohalt.* [Report: Possible Accession to the European Union and Its Legal Meaning from the Point of Estonian Constitutional Law]. Tallinn: Estonian Ministry of Justice, 1998. http://www.euroskepsis.ee/ps/ps-euro.htm (accessed August 2, 2006).

Postimees. "Laar on Euroopa 50 mõjukama liidri hulgas" [Laar is Among the 50 Most Influential Leaders in Europe], June 7, 2001.

Presidendi Akadeemilise Nõukogu pöördumine Eesti avalikkuse poole [President of the Academic Council's Letter to the Estonian Public]. Tallinn: Office of the President, November 25, 1998.

Prodi, Romano. "Sharing Stability and Prosperity," Speech Delivered at the Tempus Meda Regional Conference, Bibliotheca Alexandrina. October 13, 2003.

Racius, Egdunas. "Lithuania's New Cold War." *Baltic Times*, July 8, 2004.

Remsu, Olev. "Kohanev Eesti" [Adjusting Estonia]. *Eesti Ekspress*, July 9, 2002.

Robejsek, Petr. "Parallel Paths East and West." *Transitions Online*, March 1, 2002.

Rose, Richard. "Indifference, Distrust, and Skepticism." *Transitions Online*, March 1, 2002. http://www.tol.cz (accessed September 15, 2002).

Rotfeld, Adam Daniel. "Borderless Europe and Global Security." Address at the Ron Brown Fellowship Programme Alumni Conference in Kraków, Poland, September 26–28, 2003.

Rumm, Hannes. "Välisminister hajutab hirme" [Foreign Minister is Diffusing Fears]. *Eesti Päevaleht*, March 29, 1997.

Saar, Jüri. "Tsivilisatsioonide kokkupõrke teooria retseptsioonist Eestis" [On the Reception of the Theory of Civilizational Clash in Estonia]. *Akadeemia* 10 (1998): 1512–18.

Saidla, Siim. "Robert Lepikson seljatas Euroopa väitlusmeistrid" [Robert Lepikson Pinned European Debate Experts]. *Eesti Päevaleht*, April 19, 2000.

Saks, Katrin. "Üks riik, mitu kultuuri" [One State, Several Cultures]. *Eesti Päevaleht*, March 2, 2000.

Sarapuu, Jaak. *Eesti ajaloo algõpetus 2: õpik põhikoolile* [Primer in Estonian History 2: Textbook for Primary and Middle Schools]. Quoted in Eiki Berg, *Eesti tähendused, piirid ja kontekstid* [Estonia's Meanings, Borders, and Contexts], 170. Tartu: Tartu University Press, 2002.

Schiller, Ben. "International Students Gather for Summit Simulation." *Prague Post*, November 27, 2002.

———. "NATO Draws Arms Industry." *Prague Post*, November 6, 2002.

Simecka, Martin. "The Havel Paradox." *Transitions Online*, March 21, 2003. http://www.told.cz (accessed May 20, 2005)

Soosaar, Enn. "Eesti teel Euroopasse: vahekokkuvõte" [Estonia's Road to Europe: Report from the Midway]. *Looming* 11 (1997): 1510–19.

———. "Eesti venelased teelahkmel" [Estonia's Russians at the Fork on the Road]. *Eesti Päevaleht*, November 15, 1999.

———. "Venemaa on Venemaaa on Venemaa" [Russia is Russia is Russia]. *Eesti Ekspress*, August 5, 2003.

Spritzer, Dinah. "Praguers Wary of Terrorist Attacks." *Prague Post*, November 20, 2002.

Stroehlein, Andrew. "Land Corridor Brings Clearer Roles." *Central Europe Review* 31, April 26, 1999. http://www.ce-review.org (accessed June 13, 2005).

Taagepera, Rein. "Eesti keele ja kultuuri väljavaated Euroopa Liidu ja arvuka muu-laskonna tingimustes." Ettekande teesid Presidendi Akadeemilise Nõukogu istungiks ["The Prospects of Estonian Language and Culture in the Context of the European Union and a Large Alien Population." Theses for the meeting of the President's Academic Council]. Tallinn: Office of the President, April 23, 1998.

———. "Europa into Estonia, Estonia into Europa." *Global Estonian* (Summer 1999): 24–27.

Talbott, Strobe. *A Baltic Home-coming.* Robert C. Frasure Memorial Lecture, delivered January 24, 2000. Tallinn. Tallinn: Ministry of Foreign Affairs, 2000. http://www.vm.ee/est/kat_140/825/html (accessed September 7, 2002).

Tamm, Marek, and Mart Väljataga, eds. *Mõtteline Eesti: valik esseid Euroopa Liidust* [Imagined Estonia: A Selection of Essays on the European Union], Tallinn: Kirjastus Varrak, 2003.

Tarand, Andres. "Eesti iseseisvus ja euroliit" [Estonia's Independence and the Eurounion] *Postimees,* January 26, 2001.

Tarkmeel, Anneli. *Eesti Kohalik Poliitiline Eliit. Bakalaureusetöö* [Estonian Local Political Elite.]. Bachelor's thesis, University of Tartu, Department of Political Science, 1998.

Tarm, Michael. "Alliance Bound." *City Paper's Baltic Worldwide.* n.d. www.baltic-sww.com/alliance.htm (accessed November 13, 2002).

Tarto, Enn. Remarks to the Parliament, *Riigikogu toimetatud stenogram* [Edited Parliamentary Transcript], November 26, 1998.

Tartu University market research team. *Estonia's Experiment—The Possibilities to Integrate Non-Citizens into the Estonian Society.* Tallinn: Open Estonia Foundation, 1997.

Tiido, Harri. "Eesmärgi püsivus olude muutumisel" [Stable Objectives in the Changing Circumstances]. Eesti Päevaleht, December 4, 2001.

———. "Kosovo 'ppetunnid maailma ja Eesti jaoks" [The Lessons from Kosovo to Estonia and the World]. Eesti Päevaleht, June 12, 1999.

Taylor, Ian. "Hero of Czech Drama Bows Out of World Stage." *Guardian,* February 6, 2003.

———. "New Europe Gets Shock Lesson in Realpolitik." *Guardian,* April 28, 2003.

United Nations Development Programme (UNDP). *Integrating non-Estonians into Estonian Society: Setting the Course.* Tallinn: UNDP, 1997

———. *Eesti Inimarengu Aruanne* [Estonian Human Development Report]. Tallinn: UNDP, 1998.

U.S. Department of State. "Powell Welcomes Seven New East European Members to NATO." Press release. Washington, D.C.: Department of State, March 29, 2004. http://www.usembassy.it/file2004_03/alia/a4032901.htm (accessed September 13, 2005).

Veidemann, Rein. "Müütiline Meri" [Mythical Meri]. *Eesti Päevaleht,* March 29, 1999.

Vike-Freiberga, Vaira. "Larger Europe—a Stronger Europe." Address delivered at Leiden University, the Netherlands, January 18, 2005. http://www.am.gov.lv/en/news/speeches/2005/January/18-1/ (accessed October 15, 2005).

————. Speech delivered at the NATO summit in Prague during the meeting of the North Atlantic Council (NAC) and the seven invited countries. Brussels: NATO, November 21, 2002. http://www.nato.int/docu/speech/2002/s221122y .htm (accessed August 16, 2004).

Vitvar, Jan H. "Prague Castle Holds Up Its Heart for All to See." *Prague Post*, November 21, 2002.

Index